World Trade War

World Trade War

Jon Woronoff

PRAEGER SPECIAL STUDIES • PRAEGER SCIENTIFIC

New York • Philadelphia • Eastbourne, UK
Toronto • Hong Kong • Tokyo • Sydney

Library of Congress Cataloging in Publication Data
Woronoff, Jon.
    World trade war.
    "Published in Japanese by Kodansha Ltd. under the
title of Sekai keizai senso"—T.p. verso.
    Reprint. Originally published: Tokyo, Japan: Lotus
Press, c1983.
    Bibliography: p.
    Includes index.
    1. Japan—Foreign economic relations. 2. International
economic relations. 3. Competition, International.
I. Title.
HF1601.W67   1984   382'.3   83-23097
ISBN 0-03-071043-X

Published in 1984 by Praeger Publishers
CBS Educational and Professional Publishing
a Division of CBS Inc.
521 Fifth Avenue, New York, NY 10175 USA
©1983 by Jon Woronoff

Originally published in Japanese by Kodansha Ltd.
under the title of *Sekai Keizai Senso*

456789 052 987654321

Printed in the United States of America
on acid-free paper

Contents

Foreword

This is a book about conflicts which many authorities pretend do not exist. They are merely "misunderstandings," a "lack of communications," "temporary disturbances," or "surface phenomena." Yet, such things keep cropping up and creating nasty problems. With the years they have grown into an overall confrontation that is increasingly menacing.

They are the trade conflicts that have arisen most often between friendly and allied nations rather than traditional opponents or sworn enemies. This makes them unwelcome . . . but no less real. There has already been the textile wrangle, the ball-bearing bombardment, the television tussle, the shipbuilding clash, the flap over steel exports, and recently the small car war. There are also the perennial trade imbalances. And who knows what will come next?

Those who regard these conflicts as just temporary, a passing phase in otherwise smooth and satisfactory relations, had better look again. Most of the conflicts erupted into serious confrontations which could only be pacified after strenuous efforts which took months and sometimes years. And, even after they were supposedly "settled," they could flare up again. As more disputes emerge, and more countries get involved, it looks as if the world will have to live with a never-ending trade war.

Those who regard these conflicts as minor or insignificant, "given the overriding interests of the countries concerned" or whatever phrase is used to deflate them, might reflect on what they do mean to those concerned. To the losers, they have brought unemployment, declining living standards, and ailing industries that sometimes succumb. Even the winners are not pleased by the restrictions on their capacity to produce, and export, and the loss of sales. The conflicts have since become so numerous that they affect entire economies.

It is thus much wiser to give these conflicts their due. They are bitter, they are terribly hard to solve, no solution will ever satisfy all sides, and even the best solution will leave behind much damage and distress. Slowly but surely, they undermine the world trade system which is a fundamental pillar of the economic structure of every country. Rich or poor, every nation would fall a notch or two if this continuous battering is not ceased. And we would all be worse off.

It is therefore essential to make much stronger efforts to handle these conflicts properly, rather than hope they will pass. In the future, this should be done by resolving the fundamental differences rather than just suppressing the more striking surface manifestations. And, it would also be preferable to defuse as many as possible in an early stage and perhaps even remove their causes.

But this can only be done after acquiring more knowledge of just what is happening than has been visible in the past. Some of the material is well known, all too well known, since it appears in the newspapers and magazines regularly as each conflict arises. Only, the analysis is much too shallow and the interrelations and links are missing. Even reading a thousand such articles will not explain what the basic issues are or how they can be solved.

Other aspects have been mysteriously neglected. Loose comments are constantly made about non-tariff barriers and the difficulties of selling to Japan. The same applies to questions like dumping or aggressive trade offensives. But few are ever documented or explained. Nor is their function properly grasped. Here, much more original research and thought was necessary to fill the huge gaps.

Then, the numerous conflicts and multiple aspects of international trade relations had to be brought into a broader context before any of it would make sense. This will explain why the problems are presented from the side of the exporter and importer, the advanced and developing nations, the rising and declining economies, while considering the somewhat different situation in each industry. It is also necessary to weigh the economic, political and social ramifications.

Once you get through the rhetoric and apologetics that mask the existing business practices and economic structures, the conflicts become much more comprehensible. This does not mean that everything has been said. That is impossible in one book. Hopefully others will add to these ideas, or correct them if need be, so we can finally come to grips with what is bound to be one of the major crises of the present decade.

There are three points on which the author may, or may not, owe some explanation.

First of all, since the trade conflicts are such a poorly known and complex matter, it might have been desirable to write a more learned and complicated volume. Some econometric models, sophisticated technical jargon, or dizzying mathematical formulae might have seemed in order. But trade conflicts are not as inexplicable as all that. They arise out of differences in economic policy and the contradictory material interests that result. That is the best way of approaching them.

On occasion, it may appear that the author does not have an unshakable and unadulterated faith in free trade. That is wrong, his belief in the principle is profound. He simply doubts the ability of businessmen, politicians and trade negotiators to translate it into practice. While remaining a final goal, free trade can best be attained by successive approximation whereby something less than perfect, as long as it is a step in the right direction, is better than giving up because the ideal cannot be attained.

Finally, Japan seems to be criticized more than other countries. That is unfortunate. Perhaps this occurred because the findings of the investigation turned out that way. However, if Japan is at fault due to its action, other countries are no less to blame for reasons of omission. They failed to prevent certain abuses in the early stages when this would have been much easier. And, much more fateful, they allowed their own economies to become so weak they could not impose more balanced trade.

JON. WORONOFF

1

Facing The Facts

The postwar world has witnessed the greatest experiment in free trade ever. And it has been a tremendous success. An amazing number of barriers and impediments to trade have been dismantled in the mutual interest of the liberal economies, a move which benefits both the advanced and developing countries and has even drawn centrally-planned economies further into international trade circuits. For the first time in history, most nations have been trading with one another on a multilateral basis. Freed from the constraints of balancing books with individual partners, they proved able, in most cases, to increase trade with all of them. The past decades of growth have already expanded trade from a modest $93 billion in 1955 to a monumental $2,000 billion in 1981.

Of late, however, there has been a noticeable slowdown in this growth and a fear that perhaps free trade is running out of steam. Worse, there have been repeated signs that a reversal of direction is not impossible. Thus, from a once hopeful age of growing interdependence and prosperity, in which it seemed that everyone could gain from the others' successes, the world has slid deeper into an age of conflict. It increasingly appears as if the success of any country is at least potentially a threat to the well-being of the next. Joint efforts to hoist the whole world to a higher level of prosperity are gradually replaced by individual efforts to hold on to what one has even if that becomes a drag on the rest.

There have always been trade conflicts even during the most

promising and idealistic moments of this period of astonishing trade growth. That is not surprising. After all, some naturally did better than others and economic readjustments are rarely welcome and always hard to accomplish. But the few conflicts have since turned into many and the bitterness increases with each successive clash. Moreover, there is no longer a feeling that once a conflict has been "solved" it will really go away. Rather, it tends to fester and infect the general trade climate.

The early conflicts involved relatively "backward" sectors, although they were highly significant ones in terms of employment. Then they rose through the ranks to embitter the most technologically advanced sectors as well. By now, friction has managed to occur in just about every field in one country or another. If there are a few areas in which no serious trouble has cropped up to date that does not mean that conflicts may not arise in the future. Moreover, from individual quarrels over specific products, they have grown into broader confrontations between countries which are prospering from trade and those which feel they have been injured by it.

In a disconcertingly large share of these conflicts, one nation has figured most prominently . . . Japan. It has not always been this way. In the early postwar years, the United States had by far the most dynamic, advanced, and threatening economy. Its apparently inexhaustible productive capacity could make almost anything better and cheaper. There was fear of its domination in Europe, Latin America, and Asia, and steps were taken to meet the "American challenge."

Then Europe had a go at it. Some of the countries, more often the defeated enemies than the victors, managed to reconstruct and upgrade their economies sufficiently to defend their markets and trade widely abroad. However, due to their close links and the growing integration of Europe, a substantial share of the goods never left the continent and they upset the traditional trade patterns in a smaller way.

But far distant Japan, hastily written off after the war,

turned into a greater trading power than any of them. Taking up an ever larger share of world trade, it could not help but push against the existing structure and put the trade system under exceptional strain. So, it was Japan which has been involved in most of the major trade conflicts of recent years, conflicts pitting it against the United States and Europe, and sometimes a number of other countries as well. Since Japan's economy has managed to retain its dynamism somewhat longer, it can also be expected to appear as the culprit in future conflicts that are bound to arise.

Japan's emergence has been so striking, and destabilizing, for many reasons. First of all, its economic return was largely unexpected and yet amazingly rapid. Within a decade after a defeat which was supposed to relegate it to the status of a minor nation with a weak industrial base, it began growing at the then unprecedented rate of 10 % and more a year. It repeatedly doubled its gross national product and boosted its per capita income to European and American levels.

Although just a small group of islands, Japan has a population in excess of 115 million. This is nearly half as much as the United States or Soviet Union and more than twice that of European countries like France, Britain or Germany. When multiplied by a substantial and growing output, it easily became the second biggest economic power in the free world. Its size and potential allowed it to develop not just a few branches of industry but a relatively broad array.

Because of its ravenous hunger for raw materials, it was forced to promote its exports to bring in the necessary funds to pay for them and spur further development. This, grafted onto a highly dynamic economy, led to ever greater participation in world trade. Although it traded less proportionately than many other countries, the mere fact that its economy was growing so swiftly meant that its exports were spewing forth at an implacable speed. Japan's exports (and imports) grew much faster than world trade, taking up a larger share and also reducing the share of others.

Yet, it was a bit more than this. Certain aspects of Japan's economic system made it promote exports more aggressively, and successfully, than its competitors while remaining unusually impermeable to some types of imports. Although classified among the "liberal" or "market" economies, and fiercely capitalistic, it was nonetheless more liberal with regard to exports than imports while its market worked quite differently and its capitalism took a different turn from other countries it supposedly resembled. Few outsiders, and indeed few Japanese, realized just what the differences were or how great an impact they could have. But few even superficial observers were unaware that it was often hard to sell to Japan while the Japanese rarely had trouble disposing of their own goods unless this was done so massively it provoked a protective response.

Japan's success has in many ways led to these conflicts. The other basic cause was the failure of some of the advanced countries. Only part of this was a direct result of Japanese encroachment. Much more was due to natural maturing of the other economies, which were bound to slow down (as Japan's was also doing). When this deceleration was accompanied by other signs of decay, many of them social, such as a loss of initiative, work will, ability to save and invest, obviously the collapse was much faster. And future collisions became inevitable.

Since the basic conditions that brought forth the earlier trade conflicts have not disappeared, and often only gotten worse, it must be obvious that there will be many more conflicts in the future. Not only will there be more, they are likely to crop up more frequently and with briefer intervals between one conflict and the next. Taken together, they will cover a much broader range of contention. Finally, the conflicts will probably become more bitter and intractable.

One reason to expect more conflicts is that Japan has not

ceased being dependent on exports. Indeed, since the oil crisis it is more dependent than ever in order to pay its huge oil bill. Nor has it finished upgrading its technology and moving into new fields. Targets have already been set for the most capital and technology-intensive sectors and there is reason to believe that Japan will become competitive there as well. That means that, as Japan goes upmarket, the last few products which some European and American companies still dominate will come under attack.

This might be less painful if, at the same time, the sectors at the lower end of the range, those which were weakened earlier on, were given a chance to recover. In many cases, Japan has lost its competitiveness there. But it has since been replaced by a number of countries which are no less dynamic and export-oriented and have moved in just as Japan prepared to

Sharing up the trade pie. Who trades with whom? And how much?

(in billions of dollars)

Exports from / Exports to	Year	World	Developed market economies	Developing market economies	Of which, OPEC members	Centrally planned economies
World	70	312	220	58	10	31
	79	1,631	1,116	362	98	144
Developed market economies	70	224	172	42	8	8
	79	1,079	785	236	78	52
Developing market economies	70	55	40	11	1	3
	79	404	287	99	14	15
Of which, OPEC members	70	18	14	4	0	0
	79	207	155	48	3	4
Centrally planned economies	70	33	8	5	1	20
	79	149	44	27	6	76

Credit: *White Paper on International Trade*, 1981, MITI.

withdraw or, more likely, was simply pushed out. These already include many labor-intensive and light industrial products. And the range is already spreading to more sophisticted articles and products of heavy industry.

The most prominent of the new entrants on the trade scene are the newly industrializing countries. The NICs, as they are frequently called, are a rather select group, consisting primarily of Asian countries like Taiwan, South Korea, Hong Kong and Singapore. Some others have done reasonably well, including Brazil, Mexico, Yugoslavia and Israel. For simpler products and especially labor-intensive ones, there is a steadily growing capacity in promising countries like Malaysia or Thailand and also in less accomplished ones which can make a tremendous impact due to their size, namely the world's population giants India and China.

Fortunately for the advanced industrial countries, and Japan itself, the number of serious newcomers is relatively small. As a matter of fact, the only reason the world is not racked with more conflicts is that so few countries have built a viable economy and reached the point where they can enter world trade as active partners. Most of the so-called "developing" countries have failed to develop and some have just stagnated or rotted. But even the few successes are enough to create problems and impose painful adjustments in the creation of a new world economic order that must accomodate them . . . not the economic order proned in the talkshops of the United Nations or the ivory towers of academia but in the sweatshops and factories of the countries that have what it takes to succeed.

Yet, one wonders how and where they can be accomodated. For, the world economy is no longer expanding as rapidly as before and there is no longer the bouyancy in trade that allowed the earlier entrants to join without major disruption. There is little growth in most industrialized nations and thus little desire to find new countries clamoring to enter their markets. There is somewhat more growth in the Soviet bloc, but it remains relatively isolated from trade except among its own members. The NICs themselves are still too poor to offer a major market. The only likely outlet is the few countries which have grown rich through sales of oil or other raw materials. And they are not enough to absorb the growing industrial production from all sources.

This means that the incessant conflicts *must* continue— because Japan has more new products on the way, because it is still a bit more successful than the others, and because it is not the last of the new economies that have to be integrated. They *must* be broader because these newcomers will also compete desperately and often effectively. And they *must* be more bitter because markets have stopped growing as rapidly. For the moment, the leading protagonists will remain Japan, the first to challenge Western technological superiority, and America and Europe, the only areas that can provide a major market and feel it is necessary to do so in the interest of world peace and prosperity.

But one can expect much stronger resistance from the West than ever. Its economies are no longer in a position to reflate the world economy or impart a new dynamism. It is even uncertain to what extent they can absorb more goods. Worse, their earlier defeats are making them somewhat less active participants in world trade. None of the setbacks was decisive, neither textiles, nor steel, nor automobiles. Cumulatively, however, they have been disastrous. Once a country has been repeatedly shaken by crises in crucial industries and has reduced, or actually lost, one branch after the other, its economy as a whole tends to be less resilient. There are not many new sectors into which dynamic entrepreneurs can move and the weight of the rest of the economy is a heavy burden.

At this point, economic issues cease being strictly economic and take on a political hue. Governments can hardly stand idly by while major companies or sectors collapse and they may respond at first by subsidizing or taking over those hardest hit. That only makes them more concerned if things do not improve. With rising numbers of bankruptcies, unemployment will grow and there are not likely to be as many new jobs created. So, the anxiety spreads to broader segments of the population. This makes it increasingly expedient, and seemingly much easier, to close the economy and protect it from shocks.

This tendency, as must be obvious, would make the competition for new products and new markets even more frantic, as fewer opportunities exist and more people try to seize the remaining ones. And those who lose in the competition would find it less worthwhile to make a try and more appealing to opt out. The whole impetus for a more open trading system and greater cooperation among nations could then collapse and the direction be reversed. Protectionism by one country has always provoked more by the next and the vicious circle, once started, is hard to stop.

This is certainly not a time for complacency. For, the survival of the world trade system is at stake. There is a limit to how much battering it can take. The danger is clearly recognized in some circles and serious efforts are being made to patch things up and jolly everyone into pulling together. But the general trend is still a stubborn refusal to take a close look at the problems and see just what is wrong and what can be done or to admit the vast dimensions of the impending crisis. More often leaders have taken to running away from the problems or settling them in their own interest no matter what this does to others. Meanwhile, the optimists continue whistling in the dark.

There is little hope of improvement without a better understanding of the problems . . . and a will to tackle them. So far, many of those who set out to clarify matters have ended up doing the exact opposite. Rather than crudely point

There's no misunderstanding here. The factory
is closed and you're out of work.

Credit: United Auto Workers

out the failings on either side, they play down the differences and talk of "misunderstandings." Some conflicts are traced back to a slip of the tongue, poor interpretation or overhasty judgements. It seems that an inadequate understanding of one another's position is at the root and once people show greater maturity, speak up clearly or listen more attentively to what the other party has to say, things will be solved of their own.

Yet, it is hard to conceive how the trade conflicts we have witnessed in the past could be such petty matters or could be overcome by talking to one another a bit more. They were very real conflicts. They involved concrete interests, most palpably vast sums of money and the livelihood of many workers. They were also conflicts in which it was hard to conceive of a solution in which there were not winners and losers or at best some gains and losses on each side. That is why they dragged on for months and sometimes years.

Not only are the conflicts very real, by the time they erupt, they usually involve very high stakes. It is hard to regard the collapse of Europe's proud shipbuilding industry, the disappearance of hundreds of textile mills, or 300,000 unemployed in the American automobile industry alone as a *misunderstanding*. Nor can one speak of the threat not to buy Japanese textiles, a sharp cutback in its television exports, or a drop in its automobile sales as a mere *difference of opinion*. These are bona fide *disputes* and sometimes also *tragedies*.

Nor does it help very much to take a more lofty view of things by insisting that moral aspects must prevail over the material concerns. It is all fine and good to stress that we are all part of the same community of nations, that we all have a vested interest in increased trade, that we must think of one another in our actions. Certainly, such statements are basically true and should be made from time to time. But they will never solve any actual trade conflict. And they gloss over the embarrassing fact that sometimes one country or another is indeed breaking the rules or benefiting unfairly. Even when every country acts in good faith, this does nothing to help those which are in serious trouble.

Moreover, morality gets in the way. It is always a two-sided weapon. In past disputes, no party has ever been at a loss for perfectly noble and disinterested explanations of its own action (while seriously doubting the sincerity of its opponent). It is always possible to insist that mutual interest would be best served by the other party taking the first step or making the necessary concessions. Just as one can praise free trade for contributing to world prosperity one can speak of the need to secure jobs, to aid ailing industries or nurture infant ones, as a justification for protection. One can also insist that what is most desired is not free but fair trade.

Since little can be done to find solutions to the unending succession of trade conflicts without first seeking the basic causes, it is necessary to take a good look at some of them. The most recent one has been the major standoff over automobiles. It is reasonably typical. In addition, it is one of the most decisive given the role of this industry in the economies concerned. But other disputes should also be considered to see what parallels and similarities exist and also to review the different stages trade conflicts can pass through.

However, it is essential to dig much further. For, no trade conflict arises in a vacuum. It is the result of different approaches to economics, different attitudes regarding trade, different degrees of success in creating productive machinery and fashioning products. In fact, this background is far more crucial than any of the individual conflicts since it can explain not only why conflicts tend to occur but why it is almost impossible to avoid them and so hard to solve them once they break out.

Finding the causes is obviously not enough. It is still necessary to find solutions. These are even less likely to comply with the prevailing, and often prejudiced, views of right and wrong. While respecting certain broad principles based not on higher virtues but rather mutual interest, it is necessary to see what one party can gain in return for what it offers. This means a resort to petty haggling and crass deals. There is not even the exhilaration of a major round of trade negotiations in GATT. Now that most visible barriers have been eliminated, it is no longer a question of relatively neat and balanced reductions of tariffs but a willingness to do away with non-tariff barriers or more subtle restraints on trade whose very existence the countries concerned frequently deny. Going much further, it will require a reshaping of the world economy so that more countries can produce goods to exchange for what they need and can participate more actively in trade.

It will not be easy to find the solutions. Worse, even if they are found, they will no longer be as clear-cut and impressive as in earlier days. In fact, most of the solutions will just be poor and doubtful compromises instead of truly promising and satisfying achievements. Rather than offer the best, they will just be the least harmful way out. Some compromises may even restrict trade. But anything is better than destroying the whole system because it shows inadequacies and cannot withstand the incredible strains it has been subjected to.

2
Export-Biased Economies

Import-Process-Export Syndrome

Traditionally, foreign trade has been seen pretty much as an adjunct to the domestic economy. What could not be produced at home would be sought abroad, such as crucial raw materials, exotic products like spices or a symbol of wealth like gold. In return for this, a country would offer what it has in greater abundance. It would give something it needs less, or is cheaper, for something it wants more. But it would hardly go out of its way to purposely create products to trade and which were not an outgrowth, and usually a surplus, from the normal economic process.

Only of late, and in relatively few places, have exports been given priority over imports in the sense that they are deliberately created in large quantities, and sometimes with little or no regard to the needs of the domestic economy, in order to accelerate economic growth. It is not surprising that this should be done, since a poor and backward country has tremendous needs that it wishes to fulfill in a sharply abridged period of time. And, almost by definition, it has relatively little to give in return unless it produces something special. Yet, no matter how logical this may be, the appearance of export-oriented or export-led economies in a mass of more traditional economies for which exports are still marginal or secondary, was bound to create some difficulties.

Japan is the first, but far from the last, country to take this path. Abruptly emerging from a feudal society when it was "opened" to the outside world little more than a century ago, it was in a rush to acquire the many symbols of wealth and power it suddenly encountered. The urgency was made far greater by fears that, if it did not catch up with the more industrially advanced countries, it would fall a victim to them as happened to most other backward countries. That is why the Meiji government set upon industrialization as one of the primary concerns of the nation and successive leaders, to this very day, have done what they could to accelerate the process.

In Japan, it is not hard to understand why it was necessary to develop export products. The country is unusually bereft of raw materials and therefore has few to sell. The land is thickly populated and mountainous, making it hard and costly to produce food crops thereby blocking another alternative. All Japan has to offer is the sweat of its workers and the ingenuity of its entrepreneurs. Moreover, simply to develop some products for sale, it is forced to purchase most of the raw materials as well as many foodstuffs. Exports are doubly necessary, to obtain the wherewithall to purchase machinery and technology and to provide the inputs for a modern industry.

The Japanese sometimes claim defensively that their economy is no more dependent on trade than most others. The ratio of exports or imports to gross national product is only 12%, admittedly more than the 7% in the vast United States, but much less than about 20% in Germany, 40% in Holland, or 50% in Belgium. But there is a big difference in the nature of this dependence. Most of the trade by these other counties is with closer neighbors, often people living on different sides of a border that has become largely meaningless economically. Equally important, the trade is frequently in goods that are similar, selling one another steel, or automobiles, or foodstuffs that are only slightly different or somewhat cheaper. Much of this could cease without causing serious hardship.

In Japan, what trade there is remains vital. Its dependence on imports for crude oil is 100%, for industrial inputs like coal and iron 79% and 99%, for agricultural raw materials like wool and cotton 100%, and for foodstuffs like wheat, maize, and soybeans from 93% to 100%.[1] Without them industry would collapse and the population would starve. And this knowledge has reinforced the concept of Japan as a poor country whose people must work hard and export to survive despite its present prosperty. The "poor islands" complex constantly hovers about the older people who have gone through hard times and is taught in school to the younger generation.

This has made government and business circles lean heavily toward the promotion of exports. The first step, both in the earlier development period and after the war, was to produce as many manufactured products as possible at home. This left more money over to purchase raw materials which, due to increasing industrialization, became yet more important. But import-substitution was only a step toward export production and soon huge quantities, sometimes more than half of total output, were being sent abroad. This could hardly be regarded as just a surplus, what was left over from domestic needs, since for many companies exporting was an aim in itself. It was only by exporting that the vital inputs could be purchased and also, by increasing exports, it was possible to raise economies of scale making operations yet more efficient.

In a surprisingly large number of cases, the Japanese factories were not producing for the local market at all. They were working under contract with foreign importers, mainly from the United States at first, to sell products under the foreign brand name rather than their own. Even some of the products were designed for foreign markets and, at times, simply not available in Japan. Thus, production of black-and-white television rose due to exports and not domestic sales and, when the population could finally afford it, the manufacturers had already switched to exports of color television sets. Many of the household appliances were made exclusively for the American market, the only one then sufficiently affluent or sophisticated to absorb them, before their use became widespread in Japan. And the same thing is happening all over again for video tape recorders.

To see to it that its industries could recover and develop, the Japanese government adopted measures to protect and promote crucial industries, mainly through the Ministry of International Trade and Industry. Immediately after the war, it started constructing massive tariff walls interspersed with quotas to keep out imports that could harm its own "infant industries." Although theoretically intended to encourage import-substitution, these barriers remained in place even after the same industries became strongly oriented toward exports. The barriers did not promote exports as such. However, by sheltering them from competitors and allowing local producers to expand scale and upgrade quality, this provided a very solid foundation for launching exports.

The government often went much further by providing direct assistance to exports. Among the incentives offered were tax reductions on export earnings and low interest rates for export financing. State-related banks provided long-term export credit without which many smaller companies could not have exported due to perennial cash flow problems. Given the need for foreign exhange, exporting companies were granted higher interest rates on settlement. These various incentives made it more advantageous to sell abroad than at home, both by providing rapid access to earnings and receiving prices that ended up 10% or more above domestic prices.

Obviously, imports were just as essential to keep the economic machinery running. But not all imports. Those which were given precedence throughout have been energy and raw materials. In the earlier stage, it was also necessary to obtain capital goods and technologies. Yet, even they were restricted somewhat due to limitations on foreign exchange resources and a desire to pick only the best. Manufactured articles, especially consumer goods and luxuries, were limited much more. At first, they were subject to stingy allocations of foreign exchange and later on became less necessary as Japan produced its own domestic substitutes. The same soon applied to basic products like steel, other metals, chemicals and petrochemicals.

The path trod by Japan after the war was promptly taken by a number of other countries which have often been nicknamed the "new Japans." Most of them were its close neighbors like South Korea, Taiwan, Hong Kong and Singapore. They, too, faced the problems of a relatively small territory, very poor in raw materials, and terribly overcrowded. Indeed, they were worse off than Japan in most respects. They were also more backward at the end of the war and more eager to bring about economic development. In trying to do so, they naturally tended to rely on exports, both because they had nothing else to offer and because this strategy seemed to work for Japan. But they went much further in that direction and launched a new wave of export-led development.[2]

Much of their industry, as it grew, was harnassed directly to foreign markets. More even than Japan, they tended to work under consignment to major wholesalers and retailers in the United States or Europe. Numerous companies sold none of their produce domestically aside from some rejects. Nor did they really bother producing articles that were needed on the domestic market. There was a tendency to import cheap consumer goods, or buy used ships, while selling their most sophisticated products, including ships, to foreign countries. This tendency took an extreme form with the creation of export processing zones, first in Taiwan and Korea, and then throughout the region. Completely cut off from the domestic economy, often forbidden to sell anything there, factories were busily turning out masses of manufactured products for export. Not surprisingly, these countries showed incredible levels of exports as compared to gross national product, 30% for Korea, 50% for Taiwan and, since they were also entrepots, 90% for Hong Kong and 130% for Singapore.

Normally, one would think that exporting and importing are equally valid occupations and that the primary goal should be to maintain a balance. Alas, a large number of countries seem to think they can import whether they have the money to pay or not. And a much smaller group has developed a clear bias toward exporting. For Japan and the nearby developing countries, this is explicable because of the tremendous amount of imports they needed to develop. Year after year, they ran a trade deficit and Japan finally managed to show surpluses in the mid-1960s, slipping back into a deficit position briefly after the oil crisis. Korea, Taiwan, Singapore and Hong Kong have usually shown deficits until present. And all five have balance of payments problems.

The constant pressure to export has gradually created a conditioned reflex, not unlike that in Pavlov's dogs, where they fear they cannot export enough and continually try harder. In Japan and Korea especially, the necessity to export has been reinforced by an appeal to national sentiment and some earlier social customs which have made producing and exporting relatively noble functions, which deserve the gratitude of the nation and bestow higher prestige, while importing is regarded as base and lowly. If it is still justifiable to import essential raw materials, the same can hardly be said of consumer goods or manufactured articles that can be made at home. Once acquired, it is extremely difficult to shed such a bias. And this is particularly true since some countries have developed unique features that make them astonishingly proficient in promoting exports.

Mania For Market Share

If the Japanese companies were like their counterparts abroad, and if the management system were similar, there would still have been a strong emphasis on exports merely to keep the resource-poor country afloat. However, certain aspects of the manner of doing business which arose after the war have impelled Japan even more sharply in the direction of exports. In some ways, these characteristics merely stimulated exporting. In others, they almost forced companies to export whether they wanted to or not, whether it was entirely purposeful or not.

To understand the situation, outsiders must realize that Japanese management is quite different from what one finds in other liberal countries. It is not "inherently" Japanese in the sense of being indigenous or traditional, and it may even disappear some day. Nor is it truly "unique," since similarities can be found with many less liberal economies, in developing countries, or even among planned systems, although only Korea has perhaps unconsciously copied it. But the differences are great enough to have a strong influence on how Japanese companies function and a far greater impact when they compete with others.[3]

The most striking difference, although it has been wildly exaggerated and romanticized, is the practice of lifetime employment, namely recruiting personnel directly from school and keeping them in the company until retirement. From year to year, they will receive promotions and gradually work their way upward. Many Japanese expect to spend their whole career with the company and will therefore make greater efforts and accept greater sacrifices. This already has advantages for exporting. For, they will not hesitate to accept temporary transfers abroad and give their all on an overseas assignment which may be crucial for later promotions.[4]

But less known, and more dubious, advantages have far

greater consequences. In order for the older employees to keep rising in the hierarchy, there must obviously be a constant influx of younger staff. This is only possible through expansion, and most Japanese companies are very keen on any type of expansion, into new product lines, into new areas, and obviously also through overseas ventures. Top managers are far more interested in this than the rank-and-file, for it is through such "successes" that they show their ability and consolidate their position. Dynamic staff members are carried along, since this will provide the new posts needed to receive them later on.

While additional employees are recruited for normal expansion, or just to fill out the personnel or enhance the company's prestige, another process is continuing. The Japanese quickly learned the advantages of increasing productivity and they have shown an amazing ability to do so to the present day. To this end, they will invest heavily in new machinery and technologies. To keep up with, or get ahead of competitors, they will not even hesitate to tear down the old factories and construct new, more efficient and usually also larger ones. Naturally, this leads to an ever greater expansion in capacity and output since the productivity of what labor there is rises tremendously. Increases in capacity of 30% or 40% a year are nothing exceptional in Japan. But, since the domestic market cannot possibly keep growing at that rate, there must be a massive spillover into exports.

It is often pointed out that the system of lifetime employment broadens the horizon of the managers. Since they will be with a company for thirty or forty years, they can plan ahead and do whatever is necessary to consolidate it. This, indeed, leads them to recruit personnel which may not really be necessary for many years to come until future projects go into effect. It allows them to invest in plant and machinery which will not be amortized for many years and may not bring a substantial return for many more. This is obviously costly and risky and is only possible because of another quirk of the Japanese management system, namely the relative disconcern with profits.

Unlike American or European managers, who are judged on annual, and even quarterly, profit results or dividends, the Japanese managers are given a very loose rein. The board is packed with present or former company executives and the major shareholders are usually banks or members of the same group of companies. Financing also comes largely from banks. Not only for traditional enlightened or patriotic reasons, but in their own self-interest, they too prefer expansion to more immediate rewards. Since members of a group do business with one another, the growth of one helps the others. Banks are not really anxious to get their money back, they much prefer having interest paid over the longest possible time. Private companies cannot really behave differently, and their founders are often more hell-bent on expansion than the relatively bureaucratic companies.

While they apparently show limited interest in profits, Japanese companies tend to be obsessed by market share. This, too, has traditional roots since prestige was based more on the number of retainers or amount of land a lord had than on such a petty thing as money which only vulgar merchants might covet. Yet, that is not the only reason why today's business elite is working so hard to expand market share. Profits it must be remembered, can be obtained in two rather different ways: either by increasing the margin on a definite quantity of goods or by increasing the quantity sold even with smaller margins. In an expanding economy, it is actually the second reasoning that makes more sense. So, managers pull out the stops to increase sales even with modest profits with an eye to much bigger profits later on.

There is a second explanation of the preference for market share, and this is rooted in the distribution system. As we shall see further on, the Japanese are not counting simply on

show palpable results over some time frame rather than enjoying the pride of having a few more percent of market share. Here, it is not only the wisdom of the Japanese in seeking long-term profits but frequently also their foolishness in assuming that market share is all-important that defeats the competitors.

In a war between those seeking market share and those seeking profit, the former will win every time . . . as long as they have adequate backing. They are not necessarily behaving rationally or wisely. In fact, they may be making the most absurd mistake by losing money so long it can never be recouped and in some cases ruining the mother company for a misconceived venture that anyone in his right mind would have withdrawn from much earlier. Yet, in this game of "chicken," as long as they have more funds available than their competitors, the Japanese can destroy the other companies before they have to "chicken out."

Obviously, the Japanese system is extraordinary in a period of steady and rapid growth. But there must come a time for any economy or sector when expansion is no longer possible even by promoting exports to the utmost. That time already came for some Japanese companies by the early 1970s and the oil crisis put a damper on all of them by suddenly raising costs and making it harder to produce in large quantities. Creeping protectionism also blocked some markets. When this happened, the Japanese companies were in exceptionally difficult straits. Part of their capacity became useless while they were still saddled with heavy debts. The recession unleashed a continuing chain of bankrupticies among the smaller and weaker companies and especially those which had been overly ambitious. The companies which got by had to pull in their belt and rather than deferred profits sometimes had losses. But this did not put an end to the Japanese export threat. To the contrary, it made the danger greater than ever.

The most serious drawback to lifetime employment—at

least as far as management is concerned—is that it is difficult to dismiss staff. Since much of the personnel is hired for a whole career and relatively little can be done with them otherwise, they become pretty much of a fixed cost just like plant and equipment. As such, Japanese companies are obliged to keep on producing or waste their assets. But the recession makes it harder than ever to sell on the home market. Thus, a greater share than usual is shifted toward overseas markets. These circumstances compel the Japanese to export more aggressively than ever and make them more formidable competitors in times of recession than in times of general prosperity.

Quite different reactions in the other liberal economies only magnify the effect. Companies will find markets shrinking and rapidly cut back on production, something they can accomplish most readily by laying off personnel. In so doing, they may raise prices to maintain profits or cover the higher costs arising from reduced economies of scale or growing wage and welfare burdens. This makes them even less competitive. Meanwhile, the people who are suffering from inflation or unemployment will try to buy cheaper products. So Japanese goods first fill the vacuum left by the decrease in domestic production and then proceed to undercut the products that remain on the market.

Thus, for good reasons and bad, in good times and bad, the Japanese have been conquering export markets—and market share—and their advance has not been halted to date. Nor is there much reason to expect a reversal of the trends as long as their management system and philosophy remain the same.

Competition And Concentration

When reading some of the more fanciful books and articles on how the Japanese engage in business, one frequently has the impression that Japanese managers are the direct descendants of the former *samurai* whose every action is determined by a strict code of honor. There is constant mention of loyalty, dedication, cooperation, harmony and the like. In the greater community, everyone seems to be looking after the common interest, in the sense of Japan, Inc., as well as seeing to it that no one gets hurt while the whole nation prospers, along the lines of Ezra Vogel's "fair share."[5]

Alas, the old-style *samurai* never acted that way. Nor do modern Japanese managers. The one thing most foreign observers fail to pay sufficient attention to, but Japanese know full well, is the intense competition that exists. Business is a constant warfare for sales or new products that is far tougher than encountered nearly anywhere else. It includes tactics that would be disapproved of abroad, and are not highly praised in Japan either, but can be excused by the need to attain the only worthwhile goal . . . success. What happens to the losers is an afterthought for those who win, and even for the government, which makes the competition yet more bitter since no one can afford to lose.

This, too, is eminently typical of Japan and grows out of some of the characteristics already referred to. The mere fact that companies engage in lifetime employment means that they have to provide work for their staff come what may. There is little concern about how this is done since, if it is not, there will be such friction among the staff that the rather tenuous harmany imposed in good times will disappear in periods of recession or just slack growth. With little hope for unemployment benefits, social security, or another job, the employees must make their company a success if they are to get by themselves.

Not surprisingly, the urge for market share results in much sharper clashes than a mere interest in profit. It is possible for all companies to become more profitable by raising prices and/or lowering costs. But it is patently impossible for them all to increase market share at the same time. Market share (as opposed to an expanding market) is finite, there is never more than 100% to any market. If companies confront one another for an extra percent or so, there will be no end to the competition until the added effort for each additional percent sales really becomes prohibitive.

Yet, even when most managers have realized that the struggle for market share hurts more than it helps, they may find themselves at odds because one company or another thinks it can do better or a new company is entering the field. Or, perhaps some company has once again made a mistake about the potential growth of the market and expanded production too much. With this excess production, it may be forced to engage in a form of "dumping" at home, either because it has to cover fixed costs or simply does not know what else to do with the inventory. Since new factories are being built regularly, there is almost always some company that expands capacity at the very time when no expansion in sales can be expected except by taking part of the market away from a competitor.

As if there were not enough economic reasons for cutthroat competition, the Japanese have grafted their economy onto a social and political tradition that lays tremendous weight on ranking and prestige. In fact, the urge for market share comes almost directly from this tradition rather than any rational commercial assessment. Nowhere in Japan's history has any person or group been highly regarded for making more money. Prestige and respect, as we saw, is related to size, number of personnel, amount of assets, turnover, and especially market share. When profits are compared, it is more often in terms of total profits and not degree of profitability.

The keen interest in market share is shown by the many publications that list market share, product by product, company by company, and year by year so that there is no doubt which company ranks where and whether it is rising or falling.[6] Companies fight to be among the top five, or ten, and slipping one notch down or rising one rank is immediately noted and copiously written up in the newspapers. Meanwhile, college graduates looking for a job will automatically put companies with a higher ranking in a higher category. And, more significant, government officials will tend to be more helpful to bigger companies. Pushing this to ridiculous extremes, companies will compare themselves to competitors not only at home but abroad, as when Toyota checks whether it is selling more or less cars or trucks than Nissan in New Caledonia.

The rivalry in Japan is not only fierce between individual companies in a given field, it overflows into broader contests between whole groups of companies. Although the former *zaibatsu* were officially disbanded, most of them reformed a bit more loosely later on as *keiretsu* and similar groups were created around the leading banks. Many of the more dynamic companies also have their subsidiaries or full-fledged groups. By now, such units dominate most fields of industry and finance.[7] Rival groups keep a close watch on one another and frequently maneuver not as a function of the economic situation but simply to counter their opponents.

When they compete, it is a pitiless battle. And these battles come frequently due to the strong tendency to copy one another. Theoretically, each company could go its own way, developing its own products and specializations. Instead, when one comes up with a likely product, the others immediately jump on the bandwagon. Perhaps they trust their rival's judgement more than their own. Or, more likely, they are afraid to leave it a head start and a chance to consolidate its hold on the market. Whatever the reason, the result has been repeated dashes into a given sector, for pharmaceuticals, or cosmetics, or VTRs, or robots. In no time, rather than one or two companies, there are a dozen or even a hundred producing the same thing.

The "bandwagon effect" is reinforced by government

planning, such as it is. The government does not really choose key or growth sectors so much as it relies on industry views. But, once the industrialists agree and special incentives are offered, the move into a given sector accelerates. It is facilitated by the existence of mammoth companies and groups, which can readily shift resources or obtain financing, and quickly turn out the latest products. This has led to companies with a broad range of products and groups which offer products in a broad range of sectors. Under the "one set" policy followed by major *keiretsu* like Mitsui or Mitsubishi they manage to produce one of nearly everything from steel, to ships, to electronics, to consumer goods or sugar.

Naturally, the competition is yet fiercer when it is not simply among individual companies of a modest scale but very large ones. For, they can use any profits derived from their broader range of products to support the latest addition. And, if it spills over into groups, they can mutually support whichever member is trying to strengthen its hold on the market. This includes offering cheaper supplies or making purchases. But the crucial element is relations with the bank, which will provide the financing needed not only to develop a product quickly but to sustain periodic price wars, since price cutting is the primary weapon in fighting for market share.[8]

The encounter is quite deadly. In fact, it rarely concludes before some of the participants have been driven out of the market and perhaps gone bankrupt. After repeated bouts, there are usually only between five and ten companies making any product in large quantities and sometimes as few as two or three. It would be a bit hasty to regard them as the best, since the key to survival is not quality or service but financial backing. Still, if not always the best, they are undoubtedly the strongest.

Thus, Japan has spawned an economy based extensively on oligopolies and even monopolies, just a few large companies which basically dominate the market in numerous sectors and

Once the big companies claim their market share,
there isn't very much left for anyone else.

Market Share of Major Companies (%)

Sector	Top 1	Top 3	Top 5
Steel	30	54	72
Copper	26	65	90
Aluminum	25	65	91
Polyester	25	62	84
Data processors	20	56	73
Desk calculators	38	81	96
Copying machines	47	73	88
Passenger cars	32	72	92
Automobile tires	47	79	98
Still cameras	34	63	70
Movie cameras	24	61	86
Wrist watches	61	86	93
Refrigerators	31	64	83
Microwave ovens	29	71	89
Color television	25	61	82
Ball bearings	30	56	92
Wheat and flour	34	63	70
Cheese	53	88	98
Beer	62	93	100
Whiskey	77	96	99
Toothpaste	70	96	100
Soap	29	71	89

Source: *Market Share in Japan*, Yano Economic Research Institute, 1981, and *Oriental Economist*, Toyo Keizai Shinposha, 1981.

also join together in broader groups. Of course, once these survivors have sorted things out and accept the existing market share as their "fair share," their behavior changes markedly. From price cutting they turn to boosting prices, not only individually but in unison through formal cartels, informal agreements, or seemingly spontaneous but parallel price hikes. This promptly compensates for any earlier losses during the phases of development and competition and permits them to launch future projects.

Such concentration is obviously not limited to Japan. Other

countries have huge companies.[9] But none have anything to equal Japan's groups where the relations are stronger and more pervasive. Nor do they allow self-interested relations between companies in the same sector to proliferate. In fact, in a world where public opinion increasingly turns against big business, the Japanese are definitely out of step. They prefer bigness and even approve of something like cartels, usually forbidden aside from exceptional cases elsewhere. The government not only tolerates bigness, it actively encourages it in order to strengthen the economy, especially in export-oriented sectors. Japan does have antitrust legislation, but it has been gradually watered down. And the Fair Trade Commission, ostensibly created to prevent or at least inhibit unfair business practices, has been weakened to the point where it is more of a gadfly than a watchdog.

So, the first category of exporters consists of companies which were strong enough to survive in the economic jungle of Japan. Since it is more a case of a few large than many small that do survive, these companies have attained substantial economies of scale. They have a broad range of products of more than acceptable quality. On their own, they are quite solid financially. As members of groups, they also enjoy the support of other companies, often including a trading company. With access to the group bank, they have no trouble in getting enough financing to start and even to run at a loss for some time until they get a foothold in a new market.

However, it should not be forgotten that there is a second category of exporters, namely those which have lost out in the Japanese free-for-all. Although often quite efficient and competent in their own right, they were too weak to resist the pressure from larger or luckier companies, most often due to inadequate funds. Faced with the very unpleasant alternative of being driven to the wall in Japan or turning to exports, they naturally chose the latter. As reasonably tough companies, with an urge to survive, they were usually strong enough to succeed in more relaxed or backward markets.

Thus, when Japanese firms take to exporting, they tend to show a number of unexpected characteristics. The first is an exceptional concentration on relatively few goods. This is partly due to the bandwagon effect where, as soon as one company takes the lead with a given product, many others follow suit. It is all the easier since large companies, with bank support, can shift resources very quickly and step up production for the latest export articles. However, almost by definition, other products or sectors must be neglected. This results in many old export articles fading out while new ones appear, a phenomenon that is rarely noted because the latest products get all the publicity and attention.

Making the concentration yet more alarming, there is also often a sudden and massive rise in these exports. This can be traced back to the speed with which Japanese companies can develop and produce new articles as well as the excesses of competition. With too many companies entering a given sector at the same time, expanding capacity for economies of scale, and ultimately finding that the domestic market is not large enough for them all, the spillover will be tremendous. If, as typically happens, exports are first directed to one country (traditionally the United States), it will be faced with massive imports which only let up slowly as new markets are prospected. Each successive market, again discovered by several exporters at the same time, then receives the oft mentioned "torrential" imports.

Business abroad may be pursued no less fiercely than back home. For, the Japanese have usually brought their rivalries along with them and, in addition to the old rivals, they also have new ones. More often than not, the competition is between several Japanese firms which compete by matching products, cutting prices, and pushing sales to gain market share. Often, the intention is not even to take over a large share of the foreign market but just to block their traditional opponents. Nevertheless, the other domestic and foreign companies are seriously affected as the Japanese, amongst themselves, reach higher market shares and trample on them almost without noticing.

When the competition reaches a fevered pitch, and one would think that the Japanese companies would realize that further action would offer little profitable growth and might turn the local government and populace against them, they do just the opposite. As talk begins of the need for restraint or outright restrictions to control them, instead of relaxing their efforts, they make a final push. For, the Japanese know that if any quotas are imposed, they will be based largely on the market share already attained and it is vital to squeeze out that final sale before the flag is down. This may be the last opportunity to win market share for years to come.

Oddly enough, protectionism creates further bursts of sales and unexpected clashes. As the Japanese are limited in sales of one product, they develop others. From cotton textiles they move to wool, or synthetics, from televisions to video tape recorders. These moves are even greater since some of the resources devoted to older products are now released. Or, when they are blocked on one market, they shift to another. Once again, the export offensive can be larger since they will be selling not only the goods originally planned for that market but others that have to be rerouted. Not unsurprisingly, the new waves of exports and unprecedented surges create a mood encouraging further protectionism, a step which is much easier to take since it follows earlier moves.

Hard-To-Sell And Hard Sell

Much of Japan's success with exports can be traced to the strong points of the economic system. But a certain share also derives from what is admittedly one of its biggest failures, namely the apparent inability to modernize the distribution sector. Despite decades of effort, it is still characterized by a multi-stage network where goods pass through many hands before reaching the final consumer. There are sometimes several layers of wholesalers who receive the goods from manufacturers and pass them on to myriads of small retailers. Given the large number of outlets, the quantities of goods sold by each is relatively small and costs comparatively high. Thus, the margins at each stage have to be substantial.

More recent efforts at modernization of the sector have produced new department stores, supermarkets and chain stores. These units have large sales spaces and are ultra-modern and convenient. However, they have not really replaced the earlier outlets. Rather than have the inefficient units disappear, they coexist with the efficient ones, which in the meanwhile have turned out not to bring such great savings. So, today Japan's distribution system is actually supporting more wholesalers, retailers and employees than ten years ago.[10]

Naturally, the cost of distributing goods must be added to the final price. When this happens, even Japanese products which have gained wide acceptance abroad for their cheapness end up being rather expensive in their country of origin. With higher prices, as everyone knows, sales will be smaller. Since the Japanese producers can sell less in their own country, they are forced to sell more abroad. There, if the distribution system is more efficient, the markups will be smaller. Indeed, the whole cost of distribution can be lower by putting goods directly on ships for such markets than selling them in Japan. With lower prices, the sales will be that much greater abroad.

But it is sometimes not only a matter of finding it costly to distribute goods in Japan. The distribution network is so extensive and complex that smaller manufacturers cannot set up their own channels and must use those available. They, however, tend to be exclusive. Either the existing marketing networks were established by the major manufacturers and are reserved largely for their own needs or they consist of units which have traditionally worked with certain manufacturers and would tend not to accept products from others.

This means that smaller Japanese manufacturers would not produce enough to warrant setting up their own marketing channels and might not fit into existing ones. New companies, no matter how dynamic, would also be blocked when they try to sell. This pushes them in the only possible direction, outward toward foreign markets.[11] If they found it hard to enter those markets they might well take another crack at the Japanese market. But they usually find relatively open and efficient distribution systems abroad which will absorb their products without difficulty and give them a better return.

Although the Japanese have done an extremely poor job of rationalizing their domestic distribution system, one of their prime achievements has been to create companies for sales and purchases abroad. These are the trading companies, whether the famous general trading companies (*sogo shosha*) or the smaller specialized ones. Realizing Japan's inexperience with foreign trade, its lack of familiarity with the markets and the dearth of personnel that could speak foreign languages or deal with foreigners, they were first created a century ago in the hopes of getting a foothold abroad. Meanwhile, they have overcompensated and provide an extraordinary tool for penetration of overseas markets.

The trading companies now have offices around the world in all major countries. They are staffed with well-trained and experienced officers whose primary task is to buy and sell just about everything. They have modern means of communication and ready access to funds. When one considers the size of some of them, it is obvious that they can be exceptionally efficient by handling huge quantities of goods in both directions. This enables them to attain amazing economies of scale and arrange deals for cash or on a barter basis between two or more parties. They not only handle such trade as may already exist but, by their very presence, become aware of trade opportunities that might arise in the future or could be exploited by going out and seeking a producer rather than just looking for purchasers of existing goods.

These trading companies are often associated with the major *keiretsu* or leading companies in their field. This already assures them of a substantial volume of business. In addition, they are willing to handle products for other firms and serve as their agents as well. That is why so many smaller Japanese companies, firms with neither the personnel, funds nor expertise to engage in exporting on their own, obtain easy access to foreign markets by leaving the task to the trading companies.

The trading companies can render even greater assistance to exporting firms than they could ever obtain otherwise. For, the trading companies live from both import and export. Where they earn their money is relatively unimportant. Since exporting usually involves smaller quantities and more detailed work, while importing is frequently in bulk goods which are easy to handle and transport, there is a tendency to earn disproportionately more from them. Even if exactly the same commission is charged on an import and an export deal, the fact that importing involves less work for the money is a form of subsidy for exports.

By now, the trading companies have assumed such large dimensions and engage in so much trade that their commissions actually are quite modest. Some boast that they only take 1% or 2% on sales, others are a bit higher, and obviously the commission rises as volume falls. But the fact remains that by handling as much trade as they do it is possible to spread the huge overhead costs among many customers. Overseas operations that would be far too expensive for individual companies are easy to bear when trade rises to the extent that, say, the top nine *sogo shosha* have over 60,000 employees and more than ¥60 trillion in sales.

In order to give exports an added boost, the Japanese government established a special body called the Japan External Trade Organization. Created in 1958, JETRO has grown rapidly to comprise a staff of nearly 1,300 employees and a network of 30 local offices as well as its Tokyo headquarters and 74 offices abroad in the major cities of 56 countries. Through its local offices, it was able to inform Japanese businessmen of potential needs abroad and then, through its overseas offices, it could help them enter into contact with potential customers, suppliers and services. It also organized special exhibitions of Japanese products or encouraged businessmen to attend foreign trade shows. Although it only spread information and facilitated contacts, leaving the actual negotiations and commercial transactions to the private sector, JETRO's contribution was far from negligible.

Over the years, business has expanded so much for some successful companies that they have stopped visiting JETRO and no longer have to work through the trading companies or just use them to handle specific matters like transport, storage or insurance. Otherwise, they have reached a volume of sales that permits them to set up their own marketing arrangements abroad. This may just be a representative office or a warehouse to hold goods until they are put into the existing distribution channels. Or it can include a team of agents and salesmen. Or it can reach the scale of automobile companies which have specially designed ships to pick up cars near the factory in Japan and deliver them abroad at amazingly low transport costs and then pass them on to a nationwide network of dealers.

Japan has a final advantage in its repeated campaigns to penetrate foreign markets. This one is most unexpected, namely rather mediocre salesmen in a certain sense. Given Japan's recognized excellence in manufacturing, and its very dynamic economy, no one would expect Japanese salesmen to be poor or even average. But the fact remains that sales is the most despised calling in the business world. Traditionally, those who sell have always been looked down upon, while those who produce, farmers or craftsmen, and now manufacturers, enjoyed much greater prestige. In any company, even today, the sales division is the one shunned most by self-respecting salarymen. And new employees are almost forced

Sorry, we don't want any beef or oranges.
Japanese farmers rally against imports.

Credit: Foreign Press Center-Japan

to go through a period in the sales division before moving on to bigger and better things.

Unlike the Chinese, who will spend untold hours bargaining and enhancing the value of their wares, and managing to raise the price gently over time, the Japanese want to get over with the whole thing as quickly as they can. They engage often in a strong hard sell, in which not only one but two or more salesmen will present an excellent product. Yet, they do not haggle or press for a better price. Quite often, they will sell at lower than whatever their competitors offer without checking the merits of such a gesture. It is to poor salesmanship like this that some of Japan's export "success" is due.

The salesmen, however, are not alone to blame (or be praised, if that is one's view). Few Japanese companies have shown much ability at costing. They rarely know just what a product costs them to make and is therefore worth. Market forecasting has not been much better. Companies do not really check on demand before expanding production but rather expand production to keep up with the competitors, to attain greater economies of scale, or because the management feels optimistic. Periodically stuck with too many goods, the best solution is to sell them at whatever price, since they are worth nothing if they remain unsold. Similarly, the whole ethos of market share counts a good sold as a good sold. The fact that it could have been sold for a bit more is immaterial.

This inability to obtain the best price for their products is probably the most serious weakness of Japanese companies. Yet, it is hardly noticed since managers are too busy rejoicing about all the good news . . . for they are selling in greater volume than ever! This may be for very good reasons such as having come up with a stunning new product, excelling in quality, or offering better after-sales service. But there is almost always a price element as well, namely that the product costs less than its closest competitors. When this happens abroad, however, it can lead to serious complications if it turns out that goods are being sold too cheaply.

Periodically, there are charges of "dumping" by Japanese manufacturers. The complaints may come simply because the Japanese have whittled down costs to the point where they are genuinely cheaper or because they will accept lower margins. It may also be because they have solid support on the home market or ample financial backing and can go even further. But the only valid charges are those which fit the accepted definition of selling at "less than normal value" or "less than fair value."[12] It is often hard to know whether this is actually so given the differing structures and pricing policies. Still, there have been so many accusations it is hard to imagine some are not true. This is not just a feeling that where there is so much smoke there must be some fire. In certain cases it has been proven that goods are sold under market price, or cost, and by such large amounts that even admitting a margin of error the ruling would stand.

Of course, just because Japanese companies are pushing their products very hard and sometimes selling at "unfairly" low prices does not mean that the customers will not be delighted to take advantage of them. They couldn't care less about charges of dumping. Nor do they even notice the damage to their own economy. They might, however, bear in mind that this is not kindness on the part of the sellers. They are simply going through a stage when everything must be done to increase sales and market share. Then will come a time, as already in Japan, when it is regarded as more important to stabilize the situation and replenish funds . . . and the prices will be jacked up!

Trading Giants And Cyclops

Due both to its tremendous need to trade, and the exceptional ability it has shown, Japan has risen to become one of the world's leading trading nations. Although, back in 1950,

Japan only had some 3% of world trade, by the 1980s it boasted a good 8%. This put it on a par with much larger countries, like the United States, and more active traders, like Germany, and ahead of just about everyone else. Somewhat more modest for the moment, Korea, Taiwan, and even tiny Hong Kong and Singapore also became significant trading nations. The four Asian NICs together managed to handle more than 40% of the developing world's manufactured exports.

This has made them all trading giants accounting for much more trade than their size would normally warrant. Japan's 8% of world trade, for example, emanates from a country with a mere .3% of the world's land and 3% of its population. But their appearance has been far more startling since they are not ordinary giants, but rather cyclops with their one eye riveted on exports and that largely concentrated on manufactured products. This results from the strong export-orientation of their economic policy and an export-led growth. Thus, while Japan only controlled 8% of total trade, for manufactured goods it held 12%. Since the "new Japans" were also exporting almost exclusively manufactured goods, any extra trade they won automatically fell in that sector.

Certainly, this has been an extraordinary success for them. But it could not help being an embarrassment or annoyance to others who did less well. It is obvious that the arrival of any new industrial power within a rather restricted club is going to require adjustments. The mere fact that Japan and the NICs could grow at over 10% a year during the 1960s, and somewhat less in the 1970s, meant that the world community had to make room for them. It was already difficult to find enough raw materials to feed their growing appetites. But it was particularly hard to integrate them when exports, and especially industrial exports, expanded so rapidly.

Fortunately, during those two decades, world trade was growing at a rate of some 8%, and then 6%, providing a reasonably bouyant environment. Yet, with Japan's exports increasing at a rate of 16%, and then 12%, it was constantly taking a greater share for itself (and eating into the share of others). With an economy that now commands about 10% of the world's gross national product, the amount involved was tremendous. The Asian NICs, although working from a much smaller base, within smaller national economies, nonetheless created waves when their exports grew by 29% a year for Korea, and 30% for Taiwan, during the 1960s and early 1970s.

Despite the vast magnitude, there would have been much less trouble in accomodating the newcomers if this did not also involve a basic change in the structure of world trade. As countries with few natural resources, they were not merely exporting more, they were specifically exporting more manufactured goods. Not only that, they were specializing in certain sectors where growth was astronomical, as much as 100% a year for articles like ships and VTRs at their peak. Finally, they were not trading with everyone to the same extent but primarily the advanced countries, where exports would repeatedly bunch up.

This implied a major shift in existing trade patterns. Gradually, as Japan created its own heavy and chemical industries, it had to import these products less. It increasingly turned out more of its own machinery and even reached the point where it had to license rather few new technologies. It kept on manufacturing a broader range of consumer goods and many luxury articles. What it needed to import in the category of manufactured goods was constantly narrowing. At the same time, it had to import more raw materials to feed its own industry. When fuel prices rose, to cover the higher costs, it showed an even greater concentration on raw materials and energy than before.

However, this process involved more than just a switch in products, it also entailed a change of suppliers. Rather few of the advanced countries were able to provide the raw materials and fuel it needed, aside from the United States and Canada. And the United States still found Japan importing relatively less as its needs for capital goods and technology contracted. Europe, which could not provide raw materials, was far worse off. Even the Asian NICs were in some difficulty, for they were short of raw materials themselves, and needed Japanese capital and intermediate goods, but had little to offer in exchange.

Only the oil producing countries and others with abundant sources of raw materials, including Indonesia and Malaysia, had much to offer in return for Japanese goods. But they were not yet a sufficiently large market to absorb enough of these goods and completely restructure trade. So, Japan kept

Working its way through the ranks. Japan was already the number three trader in 1977. When will it reach number one?

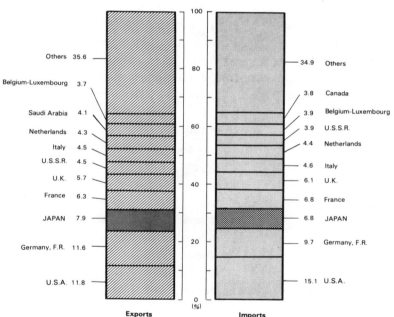

Credit: *'79 Japan*, Prime Minister's Office, p. 12.

– 51 –

running deficits with the countries which provided the crucial inputs for its economy and, quite naturally, this kept it toiling to churn out more export products. The newly industrializing countries followed the same path, yet more desperately.

The other industrialized countries were caught in the same squeeze. They had to exchange their own manufactured goods for oil and raw materials. This brought them into direct conflict with Japan and the NICs. Unfortunately for them, they lost more bouts than they won. The rising economies proved amazingly competitive for many products and they were more aggressive in pursuing trade. Gradually the advanced countries were forced back. First, Japan and the NICs drove them out of their home markets either through trade barriers or by creating competitive industries. Then they penetrated third countries where price was a primary concern. Finally, once quality had been improved, they tackled more sophisticated markets. The attack began in lower categories within the Western countries but spread as the goods improved. While Japan ultimately lost its edge on cheaper or simpler articles, this did not help the advanced countries since the "new Japans" were following right behind.

This process was more painful since it eventually combined two different trends. One was a natural reaction to the industrialization of some Asian countries as well as a few others in Europe or Latin America. But it was intensified by the oil crisis, which led to an even greater shift in resources from all industrialized and industrializing countries to the oil producers. For, in order to pay their oil bills and the mounting costs of some other raw materials, the rising economies had to push harder than ever. This drained resources from the advanced countries of Europe and America not only toward the Middle East but toward Asia as well.

The 1980s therefore ushered in an age that contrasts sharply with the encouraging era of the 1960s. Most of the world's economies have already started declining. Those which did

well slipped from over 10% toward 5% grc
did passably could expect little or no grov
becoming poorer. Only the oil produc'
future with confidence. Even those w'
some anxiety. Meanwhile, trade grov
fact, in 1980 it fell as low as 1%. And
and-take, it looks like an arrangem.
the others take. Some countries sysk
surpluses while others regularly suffer a den.

That naturally creates an unpleasant atmosphc.
growing number of countries around the world are
checking on their trade flows, just how much they import anu
how much they export. If they are not careful, they will end up
with a serious strain on their limited reserves and ultimately
have to impede some imports. They also start noticing more
clearly just who they are running imbalances with, a matter
that was once almost irrelevant. For those which are often in
the red, it begins to rankle if it is with the same countries year
after year. Eventually, they stop seeing trade as a multilateral
operation in which you win with some and lose with others,
especially if you seem to be losing too much, and start
worrying about bilateral trade relations.

At present, in the world trade roulette, aside from OPEC,
only Japan is still piling up more chips on its side of the table.
Whatever the reason, it is distinctly unpleasant for anyone to
be too fortunate. The oil producers are even more successful,
but they were just lucky to have the wells. In Japan's case, it
may also be luck, or it may be ability, or it may be cheating, its
partners tend to think. It does not take long to seek the
reasons or just imagine them. Although it resembles the other
liberal economies, Japan does show some striking differences.
That is more than enough to wonder whether it is doing so
well through sheer ability or by adopting beggar-thy-neighbor
policies.

1981 *White Paper on International Trade*, MITI.

See Joel Bergsman, *Growth and Equity in Semi-Industrialized Countries*, World Bank Staff Working Paper No. 351, August 1979.

3. See Rodney Clark, *The Japanese Company*.

4. See Jon Woronoff, *Japan: The Coming Economic Crisis* and *Japan's Wasted Workers*.

5. See Ezra Vogel, *Japan as No. 1*, p. 97 ff.

6. See *Market Share in Japan* or *The Oriental Economist*.

7. See Dodwell's *Industrial Groupings in Japan*.

8. To get IBM, the Japanese computer firms apparently did not hesitate to offer price reductions of 50% to 80%.

9. Japan boasts nearly 130 of the 500 largest foreign industrial firms and a good share of the largest banks listed by *Fortune*.

10. See Jon Woronoff, *Japan's Wasted Workers*, pp. 166–75.

11. Even major listed companies like Crown Radio, Akai Electric and Minolta export 96%, 91% and 81% of their production respectively.

12. The far from precise definitions of the GATT Anti-Dumping Code and the American International Trade Commission.

3
Doing Business In Japan

Reopening Japan

Judging by its economic structure, it is not surprising that Japan should be highly successful when it comes to exporting. On the other hand, there were bound to be difficulties with regard to the other side of trade, namely imports, which suffered from severe distortions inherent in the unbounded urge to produce export goods. For, the only articles the Japanese paid much attention to or made energetic efforts to obtain were those that fit in with the import-process-export syndrome.

If Japan had a rather unusual trade profile for its exports, it had a no less unusual one for its imports. If put together, the pieces matched perfectly, almost like a jigsaw puzzle. For the basic raw materials Japan needed to produce its exports, the share of total imports was large and tended to grow. Oil, in which the Japanese economy was solidly rooted, expanded tremendously while oil costs rose. To compensate for this, there was often a stagnation or shrinkage of just about everything else. This included most manufactured articles, whether capital or consumer goods. Not only did they have to bow to the clear priority for raw materials and oil, many of them were less necessary as Japan took up domestic production.

It is nonsense to say that you can't sell to Japan. Any country which could offer coal, or iron ore, or bauxite, or uranium, or oil found the doors wide open. There were never any complaints from the Middle East. Japan would not only buy, it would prospect, mine, and ship whatever raw materials it needed. But this fact hardly interested its principal trading partners, those which bought most from Japan, because they found it increasingly difficult to offer anything in exchange (if they didn't also have raw materials). The market for capital goods slumped as industrialization was completed, consumer goods aside from some luxury items were less sought after, and even some agricultural products were denied entry.

While Japan was still developing and had to import capital goods and technology, there was a market for the advanced countries it depended on so heavily for its own sales. The trade was usually imbalanced against it. However, during the 1960s, Japan's exports increased rapidly while its imports of capital and other manufactured goods stagnated. Then, after the oil crisis, Japan tried desperately to come out of the slump by pushing exports with a renewed zeal while inhibiting all other imports than the precious oil and some other raw materials. With this, the share of manufactured products in total imports dropped to a low of some 20–26%, much smaller than any other industrialized economy (about 45% in Europe and 55% in America).[1]

This left the advanced economies in a difficult bind. They, too, had to export in order to cover higher oil costs. But they found it terribly hard to export what they produced to Japan. At the same time, the developing countries in the region which depended on Japan for capital goods and technology, could not sell their manufactured goods either. This was rather intriguing, and doubtlessly suspicious to those concerned, since it is hard to explain how Japan could do without both high quality and costly products as well as those in the lower quality, lower price range. The bias against manufactured goods thus seemed to be systematic.

The Japanese sometimes explained that they simply did not

"need" these imports, since they made most of the products domestically as well. Indeed, they repeatedly made a clear distinction between good and bad imports, namely things we cannot do without, like raw materials and advanced technologies, and things we can handle ourselves, like manufactured products and capital goods. Just how pervasive that concept is can be shown by an attempt by Marubeni, one of Japan's biggest trading companies, to explain the reasons for the Japan-European Community trade gap. "Here lies the crux of the problem of redressing the current Japan-EC trade imbalance. What the Europeans have to offer Japan as export goods are mainly what Japan already has: high-quality manufactured goods, both capital and consumer. The EC nations cannot offer what Japan needs most—an abundant, reliable supply of raw materials."[2]

Japan's distinctive trade configuration. Not much chance of selling it manufactured goods... or of buying anything else.

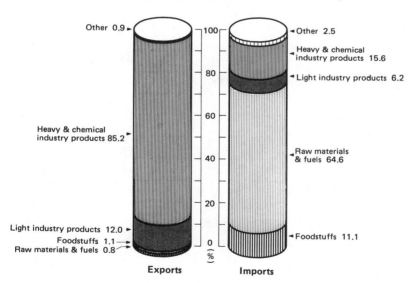

Credit: Foreign Press Center-Japan

Unfortunately, this concept neglects a number of crucial elements. One is that the argument applies just as well to Japan as the United States and Europe. Neither of them really need Japanese manufactured goods in the sense that they can survive without them and usually produce reasonably good substitutes at home. They could just as well stop buying from Japan. The results of such an argument when applied to their own nation might awaken the Japanese to how others feel. More important is that trade has nothing to do with absolutes like what a country needs and produces. As has been pointed out repeatedly, a large portion of world trade consists of manufactured goods exchanged between industrially advanced countries. Even if they make much the same thing, for reasons like price, quality, availability, style or design, etc., countries still find it better to trade than to produce everything themselves.

This latter point is quite simply the basis of all trade everywhere, comparative advantage. Once national leaders think in terms of what should and should not be imported this is a big step backward from free trade or indeed any trade. It is therefore rather frightening to see such an argument used by a leading *sogo shosha* which, aside from merely thinking about the matter, is deeply engaged in commerce. That the outdated notion of a "poor island" nation that must import raw materials and export manufactured goods is hopelessly tenacious transpires from the public and private utterances of countless politicians, government officials, and especially MITI personnel, once again people who not only think about trade but influence the way it is shaped.

Since trade patterns that prevailed elsewhere did not automatically emerge in Japan, its trading partners tended to seek deeper—more devious—explanations for the extraordinary difficulty in selling. The first cause noticed was an impressive bulwark of formal protective barriers. The Japanese had not left their development to chance. To keep out competing products, in earlier days, they simply controlled imports by rationing the foreign exchange available and requiring import licenses. Then, reaching back to prewar precedents, they built up solid walls of tariffs or constricted entry through quotas. They also prevented penetration from within by sharply limiting foreign investment.

This protection was by no means haphazard but rather carefully designed to nurture industries the government or business community regarded as promising or useful. The official justification was based on the "infant industry" argument which made it not only a right but almost a duty to protect a whole string of sectors. The result was several layers of barriers with a bias shown quite clearly by the tariff structure. It had low rates for the raw materials and capital goods Japan needed and high rates for all finished products, especially consumer goods and luxuries. Rates were much lower for crude raw materials than for processed ones. It had lower rates for such products as its businessmen did not produce nor intend to produce and much higher rates for anything that was being produced then or might be so in the future. For selected articles, namely those being given priority, unusually high rates were levied and sometimes imports were simply blocked by quotas.

These barriers had two effects, only the first of which is usually noted. Obviously, it encouraged Japanese companies to manufacture as many goods locally as possible. But it was no less fateful that it left foreign businessmen with no other way of entering the market than to form joint ventures or license production. In both cases, it was locally produced goods which replaced any shipments of goods from their home factories. Admittedly, the companies did earn royalties or modest profits and this helped the current account. But the fact that so few goods were actually moved deflated the trade balance immeasurably. Moreover, it was not long before other Japanese companies developed similar products or improved on the state of the art and just discarded the originator.

This means that during the 1950s and into the 1960s, any lack of imports was hardly a result of neglect, it was part of a carefully calculated policy of promoting Japanese industry. At the same time, it had to be admitted that Japan was also subject to considerable trade discrimination abroad. There were numerous restrictions on its light industrial products in Europe and, through the former mother countries, in the British Commonwealth and British and French colonies as well. If this continued, it would have been very hard for Japan to restore its economy. To obtain broader access to export markets, the United States sponsored Japan's accession to the General Agreement on Tariffs and Trade, where acceptance as a full contracting party was finally granted in 1955. Yet, even then, many members waived full application of the most-favored-nation treatment under Article 35 (which became known as the "Japan article") for a while and some still maintain special restrictions to the present day.

Despite the waivers and restrictions, membership in GATT brought Japan substantial advantages. It opened new markets and helped expand trade rapidly. In return, although the basic principle was theoretically *reciprocity*, as a developing country with balance of payments problems, Japan did not have to go as far. In fact, its own steps toward trade liberalization were painfully hesitant. The first spurt of tariff reductions only began in 1960 and soon petered out. While the Kennedy Round was held from 1964–67, in a major attempt to bring tariffs down worldwide, Japan kept out as much as possible and avoided making concessions. Still, it gained tremendously from the substantial reduction in tariffs and indeed moved from a trade deficit to a trade surplus. Only with much delay did the Japanese government reduce Japan's duties on manufactured goods to 12.7%, much higher than the average for advanced countries, and then in October 1972 to 8.5%, on a par with the others. This meant that Japan had enjoyed a "free ride" for some time but, having proposed the Tokyo Round, it appeared that a new age was coming. Yet, even in this round, the Japanese often dragged their feet until coming under strong enough pressure. In the end, however, Japan pledged to lower its average tariff rate on manufactured products to about 3%, below the United States' 4% and European Community's 5% target.

A similar path was taken with regard to quotas on agricultural and manufactured products. Although there was some liberalization as of 1960, there were still quantitative restrictions on nearly 500 of its 600 categories of imports. In 1963, Japan agreed to eliminate quotas but still maintained many "illegal" ones. Repeated efforts to dismantle them ended in failure, or modest concessions, and it was not until about 1972 again that Japan reached a level similar to other advanced countries. On manufactured products, it has very few quotas, although over twenty exist in agriculture.

The rationing of scarce foreign exchange, which went first to importers of raw materials and capital goods or technology, only phased out over the 1950s. In 1964, the yen was made convertable. But strong efforts to keep the yen undervalued and thereby promote exports while impeding imports continued through the 1970s and can even be sensed today.

While the Japanese government, with general support from the population, proved very reluctant to open the economy to imports, even this pales when compared to the determined efforts to avoid foreign investment in Japan. During the 1950s, despite the tremendous lack of capital and a general attitude in most developing countries to welcome investors, the Law Concerning Foreign Investment subjected all investment to licensing in which procedure "administrative guidance" and bureaucratic distrust or inefficiency served as additional barriers. For over a decade, investment was only permitted if it contributed to self-sufficiency or improved the

everywhere and also cause headaches for Japanese when they export. Others were more unique, an outgrowth of Japanese traditions or techniques. What was most striking thus became their great variety and the lively imagination in developing more refined NTBs than its competitors could conceive.

A first hurdle, not only in Japan, was the application of customs regulations as opposed to the tariff level itself. Classifications were frequently vague and, depending on which category a good fell into, the duty might be large, small or nothing. Some categories also included quantitative limits. In addition to the actual choice, it could take long to obtain any decision thereby blocking the product for some time no matter what the result might be. This was a standard problem. What was less standard was the tremendous leeway given the customs inspectors on such crucial matters and lack of a proper system of appeal. A product might be categorized differently by two different officials, at two different ports or even the same one, and nothing much could be done about it.

Was it that the Japanese customs officials were more obtuse or just meticulous? In one case, an importer couldn't get his goods through customs because of a typographical error on the airway bill, in another because one of the cases got lost in transit, and in another it was impossible to keep sample bottles because they were filled and not empty. This sort of nitpicking is not restricted to Japan, especially not among customs inspectors. But other cases were more suspicious. For example, American apple butter was first classified as a jam and then, once it found a buyer, reclassified as fruit paste puree, which is subject to a quota. Or, a type of potato chips was first classified as a processed food and then as a confectionary, rising from a 16% to a 35% duty. While fighting this case, the exporter was undercut by a Japanese manufacturer which launched similar potato chips.[3]

Product approval and testing also create numerous hurdles. The approval procedure is complicated to begin with, and must be redone if any changes (or improvements) are made in the product. More worrisome for foreign manufacturers, it must be accomplished at the request of the local importer. This means that the manufacturer would have to redo everything if he changes his import channel and, in the process, his importer becomes privy to the detailed information required for approval and which is often enough to make a competing product. Testing can be annoying since the requirements are occasionally unclear, tend to change frequently (often without forewarning) and differ from methods used abroad. Standards are set by Japanese manufacturers and sometimes designed to favor them. Worse, approval is often given not for a type but a single unit, meaning that for some while every boat or car imported to Japan had to be inspected individually at great cost in time, effort, and money.

Over the years, individual foreign businessmen had on occasion raised complaints but most were afraid to do so since this might get them in trouble with the bureaucrats or spoil their relations with local partners. Ultimately, through the American Chamber of Commerce in Japan and other chambers, some of these complaints were brought before the Japanese authorities. They were discussed very much at length in a U.S.-Japan Trade Study Group and more formally through the U.S.-Japan Trade Facilitation Committee. But pitifully little headway was made. Most items were rejected as unjustified or written off as mere misunderstandings. The official position of the Japanese government and the individual ministries, repeated ad nauseum to foreigners, was that there were no non-tariff barriers.

Nevertheless, the charges became so annoying that finally, in January 1982, two special committees reported on their findings, one consisting of Japanese businessmen involved in importing and another under the auspices of the ruling Liberal Democratic Party. The amazing result of their examination was the admission that, yes, there was a multitude of non-tariff barriers. Some 99 complaints had been studied and 67 were seen as justified while another 9 were possibile. The government thereupon decided that the various rules and regulations incriminated would be modified and, to avoid further trouble, an Office of the Trade Ombudsman was to be created at vice-ministerial level and all major ministries and agencies would also have their own machinery to handle grievances.[4]

This enlightenment came as a surprise even to most Japanese who had not realized how petty and foolish some of the barriers could be. For example, it was necessary to specify the number of pieces of fruit in canned fruit. Mineral water had to be heat-pasteurized. To collect imported drugs, pharmaceutical companies had to present the personal health certificates of all their executives. When labels indicated both centimeters and inches or kilos and pounds, the latter had to be erased. Or, for preclinical tests on animals, the actual testing had to occur

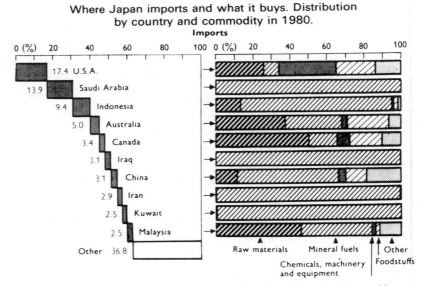

Where Japan imports and what it buys. Distribution by country and commodity in 1980.

Credit: *Statistical Handbook of Japan 1981*, Prime Minister's Office, p. 88.

in Japan, as if it made any difference whether one used foreign or Japanese mice!

Having taken this decision, however, the Japanese felt that the matter was settled and could be forgotten. That is unfortunately not the case. Given the fear of retaliation, the 99 complaints presented were hardly all that existed and the most serious, by the way, were ones that could only be raised by businessmen who had given up on Japan and left. More significantly, many of the problems arise out of basic practices that have not changed and are unlikely to change in the future. Some of this is a preference for extreme flexibility, which leads Japanese bureaucrats to give specific advice or just hints about what to do rather than laying the rules down in general codes or regulations that are accessible to all. Another is to handle things on a case-by-case basis in direct consultation with a particular party and little concern for the general situation. A final aspect, probably common to all bureaucracies, is a liking for red tape and formalities since this is what gives them work and authority.

That is why some of the problems will not go away. For example, pharmaceutical and cosmetics firms have complained that they are restricted to a small number of ingredients given on a "positive" list while most other countries have a "negative" list only indicating those which cannot be used because they are dangerous or harmful. This puts the onus on them to prove, at great cost and effort, that an ingredient generally used abroad should also be accepted in Japan. They are also annoyed that, for testing, they must repeatedly consult the ministry to find out exactly what is desired, whereas elsewhere there are general rules for this. Even such a simple matter as a code of Good Laboratory Practices was hard to impose.[5] Finally, due to the strength of personal relations, the Japanese tend to establish approved laboratories and factories rather than approved products when, in reality, it is the product that can create any hazards.

And this runs into the general issue of "administrative guidance" (*gyosei shido*). It arises from the decisive role the bureaucrats assumed during the period of postwar economic growth and which they have failed to relinquish. This permits them to ignore existing written rules, to bend them, or to create new verbal ones in what they deem the interest of the nation. These rules have often directly inconvenienced foreign companies and were most striking in the decision to promote a domestic electronics and computer industry as well as aid to agricultural interests. In the financial sector, it has been reduced somewhat for banking and securities but is still very strong in the insurance sector.[6] When it comes to actual purchasing policies of the public sector, and to the extent it influences the private sector, this has contributed strongly to a generalized "buy Japan" mentality.

In most cases, administrative guidance has been limited to advice given the Japanese companies. With increasing foreign infiltration, there is some fear that the whole machinery will break down because it becomes necessary either to ignore the operations of such establishments in Japan, which creates a double standard, or impose obedience on them as well, which might be resisted. There are relatively few recorded cases of such guidance although some were noted regarding requests to limit imports of ski boots, fuel tubing and channel boxes, and diammonium phosphate.[7] One foreign company was asked to raise the price of its soft drinks so as not to hurt local competitors. Some of this advice was taken, but other suggestions were ignored. And this added to the conviction that foreigners tend to rock the boat and are not good team players. All the more reason to keep them out!

By the way, the Ministry of International Trade and Industry is not the only source of administrative guidance. It emanates from all ministries and agencies, in the central and local governments. But MITI does have a special function that implies an import-inhibiting effect, namely the creation of anti-recession or other cartels. The Jones Report referred to "import cartels" existing for aluminum, copper, naphtha, caustic soda, and so on. This was denied by MITI, insisting that there were fewer, and more specific, import cartels. However, the broader cartels which are created to cut back on domestic production are hardly likely to allow a simultaneous increase in imports. Nor are the many more informal ones uncovered by the Fair Trade Commission likely to encourage imports. How they can regulate the flow is shown by the cases of phenols and monosodium glutamate where the major trading companies chose one to make all purchases and then distribute to the others. This made it possible to buy more cheaply and also to avoid any superfluous purchases, all the more so since the trading company chosen had interests in domestic production.

In a somewhat different form, the full force of the Japanese economy has regularly been mobilized to prevent imports and promote exports by sustaining an artificially low value of the yen. This derives from the extensive power of the Bank of Japan and Ministry of Finance to influence government policy and also action in the private sector through things like "window guidance." Admittedly, this was much easier under the fixed exchange rate system but did not completely disappear even with floating rates. Twice, in 1971 and then after 1977, the pressure was great enough to force the yen to rise in value by about 30% and then stabilize at about 20% higher than the previous level. Obviously, making the whole range of imported products a good 20% more expensive for the Japanese than they should normally have been would go far in inhibiting sales.

The question, of course, is whether these various non-tariff barriers and other forms of administrative intervention constitute discrimination or are just a manifestation of another way of doing things. To some extent, they are a result of different customs and traditions. But, in just about every case, it is possible to note that some Japanese company or industry, or the whole economy, stands to gain. This is because the bureaucrats are not working in a vacuum, as purely objective authorities, but are to the contrary very closely tied up with the various companies and trade associations and this evidently has an influence on their action. Just how close the relationship can be on occasion is shown by the fact that many high officials later retire into executive positions in private companies they once supervised.[8] And, even if their decisions were fully motivated, the mere fact that things are so much vaguer and more complicated in Japan than abroad is a bit unfair.

Alas, having gotten past these first barriers and landed his products physically in Japan, the foreign producer will find that he must still face a further series of hurdles. These are related to the Japanese distribution system which is one of the most complex and costly in the world. It consists of many stages, going through primary, secondary and even tertiary wholesalers into a maze of retailers before reaching the consumer. Due to its size, twice as many wholesalers and retailers as the United States or Britain for a comparable number of customers, and the many stages involved, prices tend to rise. Due to its complexity, many foreigners simply do not know how to get in and add to the complications—and costs—by entering through a trading company.

If things would then run smoothly, they would have little concern. However, once the merchandise gets out of their hands and into the distribution channels, they lose control over it. Depending on which trading company or wholesaler they use, and its relations with the successive links, their goods will be distributed to many, or rather few, outlets. More subtle relations will determine whether their goods are positioned well or hidden in a corner. Most seriously, the price will not only increase due to normal costs but as part of a generalized tendency to sell foreign imports as "luxury" goods or because of the higher costs of handling smaller quantities. Whatever the cause, prices on imported goods are almost always higher than for similar domestic products. The difference can be quite substantial and may even reach three or four times the price the product is sold for back home. This obviously hurts sales and gives foreign products a reputation for being expensive.

There is very little a foreign company can do to influence the marketing of its goods without raising the ante considerably by setting up its own office and perhaps distribution channels. This alternative, which will be dealt with later, was formerly hampered by the various restrictions on foreign investment. In the early stages of liberalization, it was still subject to considerable manipulation by the officials empowered to approve investments.[9] Even now, other problems can arise. One is to obtain the necessary premises, a question not only of cost but an inability to get prime locations usually held by competitors. Dow Chemicals, in an amazing case, was authorized to build a soda plant but could not buy any land. Every time a local community agreed to sell, something happened for the deal to fall through. Foreign companies will also find it difficult to bring in enough people from the home office since the immigration authorities are not overly generous in granting visas.

These various hurdles, and many others like them, are quite enough to make doing business in Japan anything but a pleasure and on occasion sheer hell. That message has been conveyed by businessmen already in Japan and others trying to enter and the multiple problems are documented in various reports, most comprehensively in the Arthur D. Little Report and the papers of the U.S.-Japan Trade Facilitation Committee. Nevertheless, progress in solving problems has been slow and painful. And it is further hampered by efforts to play down the effect of these non-tariff barriers. Thus, a leading Japanese economist Kiyoshi Kojima referred to them as "inconveniences."[10] The Arthur D. Little group went even further when it put the question: "Have 'second tier' barriers within the Japanese bureaucracy plus 'structural' barriers such as the distribution system and domestic supplier preferences combined in such a way as to maintain a trading pattern which otherwise would have allowed in a larger proportion of finished manufactured imports from the United States?" Its response was " . . . we firmly believe that the answer is no."[11]

This kind of intellectual short circuit, clearly showing the problems involved and then denying their effect, has many grounds. One of the more unfortunate, as in the case of the Arthur D. Little Report, is that it was commissioned not by an American sponsor but by a Japanese semi-governmental research institute,[12] while the Wisemen's Group was foolish enough to have its background paper on the same matter drawn up by none other than Keidanren, the association of big business. It also derives from the fact that foreign businessmen who fail just leave Japan while those who succeed, even moderately, do not want to get in trouble by complaining. The major explanation, however, seems to be the reasoning that, although the barriers are annoying, most could eventually be overcome and thus few were an absolute impediment to trade. This makes them just a contributing factor and other causes may be seen as more directly related to an inability to make sales.

But one could hardly write these things off as mere "inconveniences." One that seems quite petty, namely the excessive need for labelling things in Japanese, is not only time consuming but costly. And this is nothing compared to the need to have every single automobile brought to an inspection office and carefully checked. Some tests that are imposed, or must be repeated in another manner, take years and require copious documentation, while also costing a sheer fortune in actual expenses and loss of sales. Whether one can import as much as one wants or has to meet a quota, or whether the duty is zero, ten or twenty percent, is very significant. Finding one's products hidden in a corner rather than out front or marked up higher than the competitor's is more than just an irritant.

Moreover, all this ignores the dynamic aspects of economics and business. If entry in a given market is hard, or more pertinently, harder than elsewhere or otherwise, many companies will decide that it is not worth the effort or try other, more open markets. If they encounter one barrier, then another, and hear that there may be others, they will adopt an attitude that is hardly conducive to making yet greater efforts. If some products are made more costly, and others are kept off the market until tests are completed, they will not be able to get their operations started properly in the early stage and may well find a Japanese competitor has preempted the market. Any one barrier or "incovenience" can be a petty or minor annoyance while an unusual accumulation would in effect make for a rather uncongenial climate that would keep out considerable numbers of companies and products.

Just how much harassment would actually prevent penetration is hard to tell. But it is considerably less than the more academic observers seem to realize. Aside from very exceptional cases, trade is not based on an exclusive product that no one else has or quality that cannot be matched. The great bulk of goods that are traded consist of products that can be made elsewhere, often in the importing country, and have many competitors. All they have to commend them is a slight edge on quality, some minor novelty, or a somewhat lower price. They possess a comparative advantage—not an absolute one—and various trade barriers can readily deprive them of that. The price advantage is rarely more than 20% or so, which means that tariffs or higher markups could make them far less competitive. Their quality or novelty can be imitated quickly enough by keeping them off the market for a while. And they can be effectively sidetracked by quotas or market manipulation that keeps them out of major retailers.

If a company's products fail to catch on promptly, the cost of launching them, which is rather substantial, will grow rapidly and could in the long run become prohibitive. If it does not expand market share to a minimum level, it will merely subsist as a marginal element in the market and perhaps disappear in a slump. To succeed, the newcomer must be a real success and each bit of sales lost is harmful since everything is cumulative. The larger sales are, the more advertising can be afforded, the more it is justified to hire one's own sales staff, the cheaper it is to import larger quantities of the products or eventually the easier it is to reach a sufficient scale for local production. Far from being small, each barrier has a reinforcing effect that makes doing business in Japan purposeful or not.

Behind The Barriers

As we have seen, behind the tariff barriers were the non-tariff barriers and one might be tempted to blame most of the difficulties on them. Yet, if that were true, there would be no explanation as to why it is so much harder in practice to do business in Japan. There is nothing among the NTBs or administrative constraints that does not exist elsewhere, sometimes to a greater extent, and that could not be legislated out of existence if the Japanese were so inclined. Obviously, for historical reasons, they are not so inclined. And, for various social and cultural reasons, they tend to resist outsiders. Thus, attention has shifted to what are now largely referred to as the "cultural" barriers.

This has been explained by Mark Zimmerman, General Manager of Winthrop Laboratories and then President of the American Chamber of Commerce in Japan. "What we are now faced with is another layer of non-tariff barriers which are much more structural, much more difficult, since they are ingrained in the Japanese way of doing business and are not deliberately fashioned so as to keep foreigners out. They are just part of the Japanese way of doing business. And many Japanese businessmen themselves don't even realize that these practices are negative in so far as the internationalization of Japan is concerned. It's only when you bring it to their attention and cite examples that it makes them aware of how difficult this market can be for foreign companies."[13]

It is not only a question of some particular or striking cultural differences, such as might be encountered in Zaire, or Sri Lanka, or Saudi Arabia. In Japan, they are incorporated in a comprehensive management system that is only a shade less systematic, and different, than some of the centrally-planned economies. Although not always applied, there is a tendency toward lifetime, or at least long-term, employment, recruitment fresh from school, promotion and wages by seniority, and a willingness to stay with the company. Within the company, considerable emphasis is placed on involving staff at lower levels in discussions and decision-making, allowing some initiatives to emerge from below through the *ringi* system, and providing for relatively decentralized operations and implementation through groups rather than individuals. This does not really create a "bottom up" type management, as its promoters claim, but it contrasts substantially with the prevailing Western system of "top down" management.[14]

Even for outsiders, whose only relations with a company are relatively casual, this creates complications. If you wish to sell something to an American, or French, or other firm, it is possible to approach either the senior executive or the specific division, such as purchasing or marketing. With a more complex structure, it is hard to know just who to approach in a Japanese company, and even harder to tell exactly who is taking the decision. In fact, with group decision-making, it may be a number of people. Due to internal problems, the process may also take an inordinately long time. So, there is no question of making offers by mail or simply displaying goods and hoping to win an order. There is a need for repeated personal visits and a lot of patience. This may result in a sale. Or it may not. And it may take months to know.

Among the Japanese, there is a preference for avoiding the one shot deals and instead seeking long relationships. They want a supplier who can be counted on indefinitely in the future. This implies a very small sale first, then a larger one, and finally reasonable sized purchases. The first time around, the margin may be very tight and the effort required seemingly extravagant. It is often pointed out that this can lead to very substantial business later on. Few mention that it may just as well end with a complete breach once a Japanese firm can produce the same article. But, whatever the case, businessmen are expected to make a much bigger commitment than they would when selling in most other liberal economies.[15]

To really get anywhere, this commitment almost necessarily implies opening a local office. The kind of relations that are expected by the Japanese cannot be fulfilled by periodic trips. Purchasers or agents must be able to telephone the local office and get an answer to their queries at any time. They want to know where to get help for repairs or to complain if something goes wrong. But, since the Japanese also appreciate solidity in any company they deal with, it is not a matter of opening a tiny office with a small staff. It is essential to have a representative office with superfluous staff just in case some-one comes by. Such an operation is expensive anywhere in the world. With the high cost of real estate and rentals in Japan as well as wages which are rising rapidly, the effort can be tremendous for what, at the outset, is almost by definition a modest turnover.

Although these prerequisites may seem fair, they are clearly biased against any newcomer. No matter how much cheaper or better his goods, he will appear as an inferior until he has finally won the confidence of his clients. This means that there must be a very substantial investment up front to cover the lean days and the long period of becoming part of the scene. And the system is further biased against foreigners. For, in order to create proper relations, it is necessary to set up a permanent establishment as opposed to just writing letters or making visits which are quite sufficient elsewhere. This "presence" in Japan can be a very costly initiation fee and only represent a small share of the headaches that arise.

The first of the rather unusual problems that crops up is that

Not a maze nor a puzzle. Just Japan's distribution network for toys.

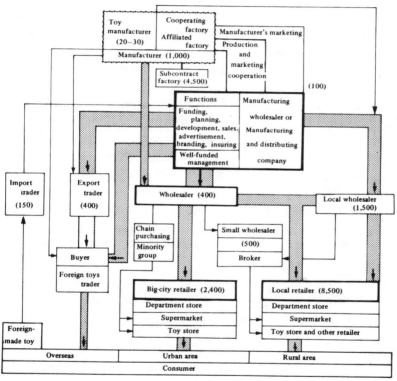

Source: *Report in 1976 by the Toys subcommittee of the Daily Necessities Committee, the Industrial Structure Council, Ministry of International Trade and Industry.*

Credit: *Tradescope*, February 1982.

it is so hard to acquire a proper staff. In just about any other liberal economy, there is a substantial labor market where all comers can obtain the personnel they need with rather little trouble. Employees are available for recruitment and offer their labor in exchange for wages on a short or long-term basis. They possess specific skills for which they are paid and fill specific jobs for which they are trained. A company just hires people to fill the slots in its manning table. If it wants more competent or experienced personnel, it simply pays a premium.

Only in Japan, due largely to the lifetime employment system, is there no real floating labor force. Since employees are recruited straight from school and kept basically until retirement, the only personnel readily available is either rather young or rather old. Moreover, this personnel does not really possess any specific skills and is merely a mass of employable persons to be used as seen fit . . . after undergoing training at the employer's expense. Thus, attempts at recruitment by placing ads in the newspapers or notices on the factory walls, or even going to commercial placement agencies or government labor exchanges, as is done regularly elsewhere, will yield few candidates.

Therefore, many foreign companies have to turn to executive search services to recruit not only managers but quite ordinary staff and secretaries. If the candidates proposed are drawn from the floating labor force, they may not be terribly suitable since it is not usually the best who are looking for a job. If they are recruited by "head hunting" practices, there is reason to doubt their loyalty, a consideration which may not be crucial abroad but immediately occurs to the mind in Japan. For, the labor market being so shallow and there always being new foreign firms in need of labor, the temptation will be great to switch jobs yet again. Whatever the result, the foreign company is likely to pay top wages without obtaining first-rate staff.

The alternative, however, is to do things the Japanese way. This means taking employees in straight from school, having the new recruits rise slowly through the ranks, year by year, until the whole hierarchy has been filled with authentic "company" people. It implies waiting something like thirty years to have a comparable team to the Japanese competitors, which is much longer than one can normally wait. Moreover, most schools do not readily refer their students to new companies and Japanese students are very selective about which company they enter. They will want one that is sufficiently prestigious to enhance their own status and solid enough to pay their wages throughout a full career and then provide a pension. Foreign companies rarely fill either criteria and many Japanese simply do not like the idea of working with foreigners. So, how can they get the best?

Foreign businessmen, who are stuffed full of talk that the Japanese employees are the most loyal, sincere and hardworking in the world often assume that once they have recruited a staff that is the end of their travail. They usually find out that this is really the beginning. For, the much vaunted virtues of the Japanese workers would seem to result not from innate characteristics but extraordinary efforts by their employers to impose strict discipline and also offer exceptional perks.[16] None of the virtues are gratuitous. Thus, foreigners are faced with headaches if they try to impose a similar, or even a much looser discipline, because they don't know how it's done. Not only that, most Japanese employees are clever enough that their managers never even know who works well or poorly. As for the perks, although small or beginning Japanese companies rarely offer much, foreign companies—like foreign products—are always put in the upper category and have to be as generous as the biggest and the best.

Nor is it easy to handle the staff. Despite all the talk of "bottom up" management, Japanese are slow to take initiatives unless pressed hard. Any Japanese manager worth his salt knows how to influence the decision-making process subtly so that the results are what he wants. Foreign managers frequently find that they are faced with projects they don't really like or that nothing is being done. They also find it impossible to impose what they regard as more effective methods of doing the same thing. It may happen that they are wrong, not knowing Japan. Sometimes they are right. But that is unimportant. If the Japanese staff decides that it disagrees with company policy, it will simply act in such a way as to prove that the foreigners were wrong. If the foreign managers stubbornly persist, they will either be ignored and circumvented or there can be an open and damaging conflict.

Dangers of this happening are increased by the contrasting business philosophies. The parent company wishes to make a good return on its investment. This may not necessarily be an obsession with short-term results, as some Japanese claim, but certainly it wants to earn as much as can be obtained elsewhere. Meanwhile, the Japanese personnel will press for market share, because that is the Japanese way, and because they gain from it in wages and status. Such divergencies can hardly be resolved and, if the returns are inadequate, the foreign company may well withdraw . . . proving that foreign businessmen cannot be trusted to behave properly in Japan and that all they want is a quick profit.

This makes the Japanese personnel and management system one of the biggest "non-tariff barriers" even in the view of those who have really tried to do as the Japanese. It takes an incredible amount of time, it is terribly expensive, and it demands the utmost tact of people from outside with little idea of what is required of them. A minor slip, such as firing someone or just yelling at an employee, is enough to destroy years of painstaking effort. The Japanese system can, indeed, offer superior results. But only in the hands of sufficiently knowing Japanese (not all of them by far). For foreigners, it is full of traps and unpleasant surprises. And it ends up taking more of their time and effort than desired while keeping them from more crucial tasks like production and sales.

Given these unusual difficulties of doing business in Japan and the extraordinary costs involved, many foreign companies find that the easiest and apparently wisest thing to do is to seek a partner. Thus, if they simply wish to sell, they may turn to a trading company or a major wholesaler and let it take charge of getting them into the distribution system. If a greater presence is sought and especially if a company wishes to manufacture locally, a joint venture would be established. In this, the foreign company will provide the product, the technical knowhow, the brand name or speciality, and leave the actual distribution to the Japanese partner which would also usually provide the premises and recruit the staff.

Yet, even this sort of halfway house can have serious drawbacks. The basic problem here is that a company often finds itself faced with a choice of partners between a competitor in the same field which has its own factories and distribution channels it will offer for a price and another firm with no vested interest in the field, but also with limited experience and capability. The former may not be too trustworthy, the latter may not be too efficient. Moreover, a joint venture leaves the foreign company with only part of the ownership and part of the control, until recently the smaller part. It also leaves it virtually dependent on its partner since the foreign company will usually just appoint a few executives while the mass of personnel is recruited through, or just borrowed from, the Japanese partner. All too often, they turn out to be a mixture of elderly managers and young recruits the mother company didn't really need too badly. There may be differences of views over pricing, marketing, advertising, and so on. Whatever the situation, it obviously cannot run the show itself yet has to put up huge sums of money over an extended period of time.

If things proceed smoothly, working through a trading

company, a wholesaler, or a joint venture can pay off. If there is trouble, it is almost always the foreign company that loses most. For, during this period, its partner will have found out enough about the products to replicate or replace them and will control both the markets and the personnel. If the foreign company drops out, it can continue quite nicely. If it gets annoyed with the foreign company, it may chuck it out and do about as well as before. Nevertheless, the situation is clearly such that even companies which operate freely and success-fully on markets around the world just cannot get started in Japan without somebody's help and advice.

But, what can be said about "cultural" barriers? After all, each nation has its own customs and traditions. Are the Japanese superior because they are faithful to long-time suppliers and clients, because they go to greater trouble to serve the customer (even if this adds to price) or remain loyal to a company they cannot really afford to leave? Are the foreigners superior because they accept new things if the price is right, work for whoever pays the most, promote their own interests by changing jobs? Both sides have virtues and vices and it is sometimes hard to tell just which is which. The only thing that seems clear, and creates problems, is that the Japanese vices (or virtues) are blocking foreign trade and investment while American or European virtues (or vices) are facilitating Japanese penetration!

The Japanese Connection

After peeling off layer after layer of impediments to trade and investment, one would think that there could hardly be any more. Alas, that is not the case. Behind the annoying tariffs, the irritating non-tariff barriers, the frustrating cultural differences, there is one final element which may well be at the core of the whole system. But it is carefully concealed by the other barriers and is still kept out of view as much as possible since it is hard to describe as either a virtue or an unpleasant but excusable national custom. It consists of the very close relations between Japanese companies arising out of far more palpable interests.

Although this does not figure in the many books about how to do business in Japan, perhaps the single most important factor is connections (koné). It is not simply a question of developing long-term relations with customers, meeting their every wish, trying to prove that one's products are good and one's delivery reliable. One must develop closer contacts even than this. For, once one has a solid connection, there is rarely any trouble in selling thereafter. This will apply even when the products are not quite as good, the delivery not quite as rapid, and the price not quite as low. Indeed, the situation is such that once a proper koné has been established, it is hard for an outsider to slip in under any conditions.

There is much talk of the need to go and visit the wholesalers or retailers, to give them gifts during the gift-giving season, and perhaps help them out in times of hardship. But this is only the face presented to society. Far more significant is the fact that most of the selling is done on credit. Most small retailers, and to a lesser extent wholesalers, have a very tight cash flow and cannot obtain enough credit from the bank. Thus, the manufacturer basically has to finance them and accept its payments at a later date. This may be unpleasant for the manufacturer. But it thereby gets a stranglehold on the marketing channels. Some manufacturers make the links even closer by buying stock in the wholesalers or retailers or setting up their own. This results in many rather closed and frequently exclusive outlets as opposed to independent agents which can sell whatever they want.

Something similar occurs between the wholesalers and retailers while a more refined system prevails between the trading companies and the sales outlets as well as the smaller manufacturers. The sogo shosha are much larger and more solid bodies than any of their lesser suppliers or customers. They are also closely related to the leading banks. Although, in most other countries, even a small company could approach a bank for a loan, in Japan banks frequently do not wish to deal with small borrowers. They are only interested in big loans to the big companies they know. So, trading companies sometimes take out huge loans and then lend small portions to the companies they deal with. Obviously, they charge a higher interest rate and make money on the operation. However, more significant is that these companies become more dependent on them than ever, not only for sales or purchases but also for credit.

Banks will do much the same thing for their own group. Obviously, their primary interest is to lend money at remunerative rates and they would not refuse to make a loan even to a company from another group. With the smaller borrowers, however, banks may go further than just lending money. They will not hesitate to give advice to the solvent ones and impose strict conditions on those in trouble. With such leverage, it is not difficult to steer the borrowers to their own clients, to the mutual benefit of the clients and the bank which hopes to increase its business. It may also help acquire or control companies which fill a gap within the group framework.

Somewhat different methods are used within the subcontracting network of major manufacturers. Since they are burdened with credit to the distributors, they tend to work the same practice in reverse with their own suppliers which are already dependent on them for sales. They pay with a reasonable delay in good times and a longer one in times of credit tightness. In return, they may well offer to guarantee or make a loan to the very same subordinate bodies they are squeezing. In addition, they frequently sell their subcontractors used machinery or offer technical assistance and advice.

But the relations tend to be much tighter than this on occasion. Many of the suppliers or subcontractors are not even independent companies. They were sometimes set up purposely by the parent company to produce a specific range of products or to supply specific parts and components. Even if not wholly owned, the parent company may have well over fifty percent. And, where the figure is lower, it may still be the major shareholder which, combined with being the major purchaser, gives it quite adequate control. Other companies, once independent, have in hard times had to sell some of their stock to the major company they work for. This makes any relationship a very real and effective one.

Moreover, for all the above cases, in addition to the financial arrangements, there are often human links. The

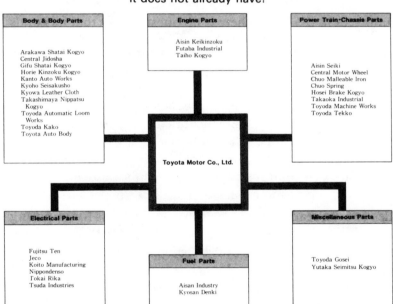

Selling to Japan: What can you offer this company that it does not already have?

Body & Body Parts	Engine Parts	Power Train-Chassis Parts
Arakawa Shatai Kogyo Central Jidosha Gifu Shatai Kogyo Horie Kinzoku Kogyo Kanto Auto Works Kyoho Seisakusho Kyowa Leather Cloth Takashimaya Nippatsu Kogyo Toyoda Automatic Loom Works Toyoda Kako Toyota Auto Body	Aisin Keikinzoku Futaba Industrial Taiho Kogyo	Aisin Seiki Central Motor Wheel Chuo Malleable Iron Chuo Spring Hosei Brake Kogyo Takaoka Industrial Toyoda Machine Works Toyoda Tekko

Toyota Motor Co., Ltd.

Electrical Parts	Fuel Parts	Miscellaneous Parts
Fujitsu Ten Jeco Koito Manufacturing Nippondenso Tokai Rika Tsuda Industries	Aisan Industry Kyosan Denki	Toyoda Gosei Yutaka Seimitsu Kogyo

Credit: *Industrial Groupings in Japan*, Dodwell Marketing Consultants, 1981, p. 128.

larger groups will have interlocking directorates. The industrial combines will appoint directors to the boards of their subsidiaries and related companies. The banks will also appoint board members where the relations are close enough. But this introduction of people to observe, supervise or advise goes much further. The dominant company will frequently impose some of its own staff in key positions 'within management, including even the president. Banks often provide the auditor. And government bureaucracies tend to foist some of their superannuated personnel on companies they do business with.

Looser, but quite beneficial links often exist between producers and distributors. Many manufacturers send their young recruits to retail outlets for a bit of training and to see what consumer trends are like. The small retailers, who often cannot afford enough staff, are delighted to have this free personnel. The manufacturer is assured that with its own employees in the stores there is no question but that its goods will be strongly promoted. For certain sectors, such as cosmetics and fashion goods, it is usual for the manufacturers to simply rent space in a large department store and handle their own sales activities.

In such circumstances, it becomes clear that a foreign company will find it extremely difficult to get into the market. Its original investment is quite enough without having to advance massive credit to the retailers. If it does not want to be dominated by another company, it cannot enter the group. And, if it stays on the outside, it will not benefit from group sales or even ready access to Japanese banks. As for imposing its personnel on any other company, it is hard pressed enough to find personnel for its own needs. Moreover, some of the practices necessary to play the game are likely to be unacceptable to the head office, unfamiliar to the manager on the spot, and perhaps even forbidden back home.

How then does one tackle the market? For consumer

goods, no matter how fine your products, they still have to reach the retail outlets or no one will know they exist and no one can buy them. It is obviously impossible to get into the exclusive shops which prevail for certain products, especially household appliances. And the independent ones are much fewer. Moreover, many are only independent in name since they will tend to give better treatment to the companies with which they have the closest connections or biggest debts. Opening one's own retail outlets is extremely expensive and it would take years to have as many as more established competitors. Even advertising aggressively on television, a "must" in the eyes of the marketing experts, is a complete waste if the products are not sold widely enough for the consumers to find them readily.

Things become even more difficult for capital and intermediate goods, since they must be sold to companies that are almost always part of one group or another. In the major *keiretsu*, like Mitsubishi or Mitsui, there is a rather complete set of companies covering the broadest range of activities. This is what makes them different from the hodge-podge Western conglomerates. One member or another will produce steel, light metals, textiles, chemicals, electronics, paper, glass, cement, oil, even sugar. What can you sell to them? Moreover, since they also have banks, insurance companies, a shipping line and real estate, you cannot even provide services.[17]

Taking each individual line, things are no more promising. Each major electronics or household appliance maker already has its own suppliers for most components and parts and also for specific products. Each major automobile manufacturer has a whole network of suppliers for carburetors, brakes, spark plugs, axles, wheel caps, you name it. What can you produce that they do not already have?

Of course, it can be claimed that the mere fact of making a competing product should not keep one out of the market if the price is right. This basic rule does apply in most countries

Selling to Japan: What products do you think a group like this needs from you?

Mitsubishi Group

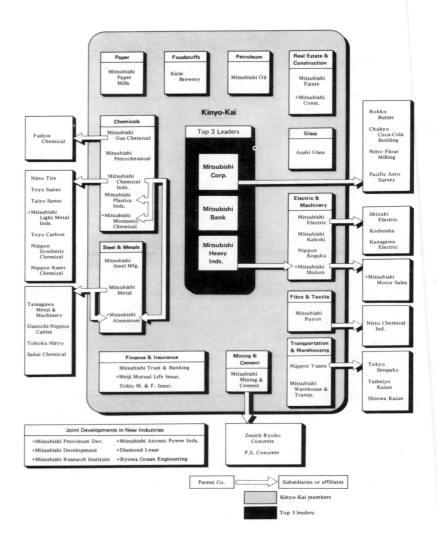

Credit: *Industrial Groupings in Japan*, Dodwell Marketing Consultants, 1981, p. 69.

which are primarily concerned about price. But in Japan, we have seen, there is more interest in reliability, very h quality standards, tight deadlines, and long-standing lations. The clincher, however, is none of these. A Japanese manufacturer simply would not want to buy from someone else because it has a vested interest in the success of its subcontractors. It holds stock, has given loans and retires its personnel there. It cannot forsake them for some outsider. Nor can the distributors forsake their regular suppliers as long as they are in debt.

Moreover, if more refined methods do not suffice, Japanese companies would not hesitate to use other tactics. For example, to keep a foreign company with a unique product from getting a foot in the market, they would willingly lower their prices on similar products or quickly produce the same thing. A good price war usually does the trick. Otherwise, they might try to convince the distributors that it is unwise to carry such a product and, if they persist, that they might no longer receive the major company's much broader range of goods. A household appliance dealer would not risk its whole stock of brand name articles just to sell the latest in hair dryers. Or, a steel manufacturer might refuse to sell its whole range of products to a company that toyed with the idea of importing a particularly attractive variety. This "refusal to sell" is a crushing blow against any company that cannot mount a powerful offensive all along the line.

The foreign companies are obviously not the only ones that face such obstacles or are hurt by these tricks. They apply to the Japanese companies as well, especially the newcomers. The main difference, however, is that most Japanese companies belong to one group or another and have relations with one bank or another. They can thus start by dealing with the related firms, which represent a relatively protected market and where sales are easy. Only later will they approach companies outside the group. And they will never sell much to rival groups that have a member producing the same thing. A foreign company, on the other hand, has no protected market and is discriminated against when it tries to penetrate anyone else's preserve.

This explains why most foreign companies have ended up in a joint venture or working through a trading company, which allows them to plug into a group. It also explains why they were not always as successful as they hoped. For, the Japanese partner does not have access to the whole market either. And plugging into one group means giving up on the rest. Moreover, a foreign company that produces a product that competes with another member of the group, or their own partner, or another client of the trading company, cannot really expect much support. This makes the trading companies and the joint ventures both a very useful door to those with truly unique products or technologies and almost a non-tariff barrier for all others.

These business practices, many of which are forbidden by antitrust legislation in other countries, remain an essential part of doing business in Japan. The Fair Trade Commission is hardly in a position to suppress them, any more than it has been particularly effective in keeping Japanese oligopolies from jacking up their prices when they want to. And, as long as these practices exist, they will remain the most forbidding barrier to entry. Oligopoly and connections, domination of the market and marketing channels, unfair business practices and discrimination are not quite as pretty an explanation as loyalty and friendly relations. But they express the reality behind most of the closed doors.

Let's Make A Deal

It is not surprising that, once foreign businessmen found it so hard to sell to Japan, they should have reacted in anger. Although some simply left for better, more open markets, other companies tried to fight individual cases. This led to a series of complaints lodged with the U.S.-Japan Trade Facilitation Committee.[18] Where enough complaints showed that a specific field was more impenetrable than others, subcommittees worked out a broader approach, as for automobiles and electronics. Given widespread annoyance, these issues and some others also became part of the regular trade negotiations within GATT. Particular concern was expressed regarding items where Japan claimed its industries still needed protection while, in fact, they were already solid and capable of exporting, such as photographic films, computers, and integrated circuits.

One field which proved unusually difficult to handle revolves around all government procurement, a very important sector since the government's own budget represents about a tenth of national expenditures. It also has about 140 agencies under its wing making purchases half as extensive, including some that procure huge quantities of goods for railroads, housing, construction, or telecommunications. Although, simply to obtain the best prices and avoid corruption, it might be thought that the government would centralize purchases and use open competitive bidding, it rarely did so. Rather, most purchases were made through designated suppliers on the basis of negotiated bids and this was often carried out in a highly decentralized manner, sometimes at the local level. This made it extremely hard for foreign companies to bid or even know what possibilities existed.

A prime example was the Nippon Telegraph & Telephone Public Corporation. Although run under rather loose state supervision, it theoretically worked on commerical principles and should have accepted equipment from any supplier. Instead, it adopted the traditional Japanese system of not dealing with just *any* supplier but establishing close relations with a tight "family" of suppliers. This had the advantage of permitting close collaboration on new equipment and a feeling for what NTT wanted. But it also excluded all outside suppliers, both foreign and domestic (including giants like Toshiba and Matsushita). This prevailed to such an extent that, in 1980, only about 4% of some $3.3 billion in communications equipment was procured through open bidding, and foreign companies only obtained a minute 0.5% of the total.

When Washington first raised the problem, it was pointed out that many other telephone administrations were relatively closed. But the United States was even then receiving huge imports of communications equipment from Japan and wanted more reciprocity. NTT's stubborness, due not only to rational grounds but the close relations with its suppliers (including retirement jobs for its own top personnel), made things drag on. And the comment by its former president that all he could buy from abroad were "mops and buckets" rankled strongly. Companies like IBM or Western Electric in America and others in Europe were perfectly able to provide first class equipment . . . if given a chance. Only after three years of haggling did NTT agree to give them a chance, and then only for about half its purchases, much less than originally asked.

Different problems arose with the Japan Tobacco Corporation, a government monopoly which purchased leaf tobacco abroad and produced cigarettes in its own factories. To avoid any undue competition, it resorted to other traditional Japanese methods. Aside from a massive duty of 90%, it would impose markups two to three times higher than for its own brands. This made foreign cigarettes far more expensive than at home and also more costly than competing brands of the tobacco monopoly. A final trick was simply to allow sales only in a very limited share of the retail outlets, meaning that even if the Japanese wanted to buy foreign cigarettes they were hard to find. After some more haggling, the tobacco monopoly finally agreed to lower the duty and increase the number of sales points. But it would take some time for imported cigarettes to gain much more than the absurdly small share of 1% of an $8 billion market.

Although these two items received special attention, they were only part of the broader problem since this sort of practice occurred throughout the government and agencies. It involved purchases by the Agriculture, Education or Health Ministries. For the latter, there was also the question of equal treatment for foreign pharmaceuticals under the national health insurance. Of course, negotiated contracts were the rule in Defense. Even the Japanese National Railways, related to the Transport Ministry, refused to buy rolling stock from abroad although this was currently done elsewhere. In one case, it would not import railroad wheels and axles although they were half the price of locally made ones.[19]

Until such practices cease, it is unlikely that the degree of penetration will change much. This sheds a rather strange light on the broader negotiations. For, although the Japanese fought bitterly to withhold concessions on government procurement, none of them were granted out of kindness but in return for like concessions by other countries. The final results of some fifteen years of negotiations, completed early in 1981, was that the United States would open an estimated $17.5 billion worth of contracts to foreign bidders, the European Community would offer $10.5 billion worth, and Japan $8 billion. Whether by limiting concessions or by using less visible tactics to hold on to their own market, it seemed likely that Japanese manufacturers would gain far more than they lost.

A second major group of complaints revolved around agricultural imports. Here, despite considerable pressure, Japan has maintained over twenty quantitative restrictions which are theoretically "illegal" under GATT. They cover imports of beef, dairy products, marine products, oranges, pineapples and other fruits and juices as well as leather. Restraint is also imposed by import cartels on items like Thai maize, Australian sugar and Taiwanese onions. This naturally restricts imports but is often only a first step. The importers then take advantage of their monopolies to boost prices and thereby decrease demand (while earning handsome windfall profits). In order to protect local producers, the government also charges special levies including major ones on beef and pork. The government monopoly on wheat resells imported wheat for about twice the price. Some of the government monies are then channeled to domestic producers to help raise productivity, but the result is again to artificially decrease sales of imported goods.

Japan is already the world's biggest agricultural market and, if these restrictions or methods were eliminated, it could become more so. It has therefore been subject to considerable pressure to raise its quotas and dismantle other barriers. Yet, other countries are in a poor position to demand too much since the United States and European countries also protect their agriculture. The Japanese government cannot do too much since it faces a very strong farm lobby, one that is particularly potent since farm communities elect a disproportionately large number of Diet members and are the mainstay of the ruling Liberal Democratic Party. Thus, any concessions have been extremely modest and were sometimes reversed. This, Australian farmers discovered after raising Kobe-type beef especially for Japan and then not being able to sell it.

However, Japan could doubtlessly change some of the methods for others that protected the domestic producers without increasing prices of imported goods as much. And it could at least reduce the hassle of formalities in seeking importers with open quotas or the need for special grading as well as stricter, and sometimes fictitious, bans on "harmful" pesticides or additives. More crucial is for Japan to realize that it will remain dependent on foreign foodstuffs and not make conditions yet more difficult by pursuing a policy of agricultural self-sufficiency such as promoted by the Agriculture Ministry. Fear of insufficient supplies or sudden cut-offs, as occurred once for soybeans (the soybean "shock"), should not push it toward ever more expensive and futile efforts to grow what it needs. It would do much better by improving relations with exporting nations.

Taken individually and seen superficially, these cases are all relatively straightforward and could be solved with a modicum of good will. The fact that they were so hard fought by Japan, even when its concessions were returned and sometimes multiplied by other trading partners, shows that further down there is an unwillingness to accept certain basic rules of the game. Trade must be based on a mutual exchange. There must be gains for both parties. If one takes, but resists

Let's shake on it, partner! Mike Mansfield and Saburo Okita agree to open telecommunications procurement.

Credit: Foreign Press Center-Japan

giving or uses other methods to evade its commitments, there is bound to be trouble. The basis for exchange should, in theory at least, be comparative advantage. The fact that Japan can, or does, produce a given article is no reason why it cannot also import the same article if the price is lower or the quality better. If it is going to specialize in manufactured products, this should not preclude imports of similar products. And it should most definitely include a willingness to buy what other countries manifestly produce better and cheaper, such as agricultural produce.

We Try Harder

Why don't the American companies sell more to Japan? The answer the Japanese have adopted, on the whole, is that the Americans don't try hard enough. When asked why the Europeans don't sell more, the answer is the same: they also don't try hard enough. And the Taiwanese, and the Koreans, and the Australians, and the Israelis don't try hard enough either. No one, apparently, tries hard enough to sell to Japan . . . aside from the Arab oil sheiks.

This explanation is presented by politicians, bureaucrats, and businessmen. It is served up in various forms by MITI, JETRO or Keidanren. Prime Minister Suzuki took great pains to spell it out to an American journalist. "Japanese business has been very energetic and hardworking in developing overseas markets. It may be impertinent to say it, but I don't think the European Community and, with all due respect, your country have been as energetic as Japan. I feel our market in Japan is as open as American or European Community markets."[20]

Obviously, the prime minister is expected to defend his country. But he doesn't know more about selling to Japan than President Reagen does about supply-side economics. So, it is always more impressive when similar comments come from top businessmen who continuously harp on the same line: how hard they had to work to get into foreign markets and how little effort foreign companies make to get into Japan. A leading exponent of this view is Sony's Chairman, Akio Morita, who tells his audiences things like this:

"Many companies which are trying to enter Japan at present complain about Japan's non-tariff barriers. However, in order to sell our products in countries around the world, we ourselves had to overcome many non-tariff barriers. In order to overcome these barriers, we had to make considerable investments. . . . When I look at foreign companies that have entered the Japanese market, I cannot but feel they are busily thinking in terms of doing business in a very short period of time. . . . I believe that the Japanese market is very easy for foreign countries to enter. I cannot understand why this wonderful market is being left untouched. I believe that foreign industry should become more serious and make a real effort to sell in Japan."[21]

This "explanation" has been heard so often that it is increasingly accepted as plausible. It appeals to something deep down in the Western soul at present, an urge to admit past failure and prod oneself on to greater efforts. Certainly, most of the foreign journalists agree with the conclusion although they know dreadfully little about doing business in Japan. Ambassador Mike Mansfield repeatedly chides the American business community. Some academics have made a career of criticizing their own businessmen . . . and the public loves it. Meanwhile, more and more business consulting firms spring up to show foreign companies just how easy it can be (for a price). But, if it is so easy, why all these business consultants, executive search services, seminars and courses, to say nothing of the quasi-experts of that pseudoscience called Japanology?

Strangely enough, there is one last group which holds the view that foreigners haven't tried hard enough. These are the eager young businessmen who periodically arrive in Japan and boast that, even if no one else can, they most definitely will break into the Japanese market. It is delightful speaking to them during their first few months here, full of plans and ambitions to turn things around, and happily heaping abuse on those who have been in Japan longer and did not succeed. Of course, the pleasure is somewhat dampened when one meets them again one or two years later, pained and crestfallen, and regarding as a victory a fraction more of the market than their predecessor had.

True, many foreign businessmen do not try very hard. They come in, display their samples, and expect to get orders just like that. They go to a trade show, make a few contacts, then return home and wait for the orders to pour in. It sometimes happens that the products they offered were attractive, but not quite adapted to the market, or that they could not provide the necessary after-service. Perhaps, if they had come more often, or extended their visit, or actually set up an office, they would have done considerably better. In this sense, they are lazy. On the other hand, they can object that similar efforts in other countries were quite adequate to do plenty of business. Or they may point to other companies that made far greater efforts and had little to show for it.

Claiming that foreign companies are not willing to make a commitment is a bit unfair without admitting just how much is expected of them. Foreigners know that Japan is a good—and a tough—market and, if they decide to try, they do not do so lightly. They are willing to put up a fair amount of capital and accept the need to wait for business to build up. Most executives stationed in Japan are senior people with ample experience elsewhere. They are also coached by experts and consultants if need be. Since the effort is a bit much for smaller firms, those represented in Japan tend to be major companies with fine products and a good reputation. Some should perhaps never have come to begin with. But, on the whole, they are a reasonably good lot. If they fail, it is not because they refuse to make a commitment but because it takes more than usual efforts to succeed.

Success is possible . . . but terribly elusive. That is best shown by the many articles that are churned out about the "success stories" among foreign ventures. What is most striking about them is that it is always the same ones which appear time and again, and they are not hundreds but a few dozen at most. Moreover, they are frequently in sectors where the foreign company has an exclusive product (Coca Cola, Dior or Nestle), very advanced technologies (IBM, Polaroid or Texas Instruments), or has made a major effort at finance and staffing (Olivetti, Johnson & Johnson, or Max Factor). A look at the figures, however, will show that even those successes are not always doing too well. Some only succeeded at first and later found themselves with a shrinking market share while profits did not always justify the effort. And a fair number of companies, including very large multinationals, have actually withdrawn despite their tremendous investments.

But the most important point is that many foreign companies only succeeded because they found the right partner or went through the right middleman and not because they showed their own ability. This applies to many big names visitors readily notice and regard as a visible sign that foreigners can indeed do business in Japan. Take McDonalds and Colonel Sanders'. Just because the name sounds better than Fujita's hamburgers or Mitsubishi fried chicken doesn't mean that one can forget the local partner entirely. Nor would it make any sense to ignore the role of the Japanese member in dozens of other teams such as General Foods and Ajinomoto, Bristol-Myers and Lion, Colgate and Kao, Spalding and Bridgestone, Schick and K. Hattori, Caterpillar and Mitsubishi, Xerox and Fuji or all of the foreign automakers and their respective agents. Without this backing, any success might well have been harder to attain or remained just out of reach.

Before criticizing the foreign companies for any failings, however, one should take a look at how well the Japanese companies perform on their own turf. In Japan, as we saw, there is just a small circle of really successful companies, a few percent at best, which have managed to expand rapidly and take over the markets. This is shown by the fact that in most sectors only a handful of companies control the bulk of sales. Their competitors, the vast number of companies in the small and medium category, have fared poorly under the Japanese system. They have limited access to credit, trouble hiring first rate personnel no matter what they pay, and difficulties with marketing. It is easier for them to sell abroad than at home. In fact, many of these companies have taken to exporting simply to survive.

So, penetrating the market has been a big problem for Japanese companies as well, not only the masses of smaller subcontractors or suppliers but also some pretty big firms. They may be those just beneath the major companies that share the market and sometimes regulate it. They also include names that are now well known but once had trouble taking root in Japan. One is Sony. When Sony first got started, most of the outlets were controlled by older companies, so it had to try America, where it made good. Only then could it really tackle the Japanese market by slowly creating its own distribution channels.[22] (It might therefore be more helpful for Morita to tell foreign audiences about his own problems in selling to Japan.) Honda and the smaller automobile companies had like experiences. And there are thousands more that remain relatively anonymous. If it is so hard for Japanese companies to succeed in Japan, it cannot be very easy for outsiders.

But, dealing with the Japanese context alone does not really explain the situation, since trade and investment go both ways. It is much more enlightening to compare what the foreigners face in Japan with what the Japanese face—as foreigners—when they venture abroad. A close look will show that it was not easy. However, it was not as hard as many of the Japanese executives claim. And, more pertinently, it was nowhere near as hard as getting started in Japan.

The United States does maintain tariffs and it has quotas. In fact, it has more of both than Japan and it has earned a very nasty reputation for clamping down with new barriers each time a sector is hurt. But these barriers are usually introduced at a rather late date, *after* the sector has been flooded with imports. Before that, it has one of the freest markets in the world. Europe is more restrictive on the whole. However, since the existence of the EEC and EFTA, it is only necessary to get into one of the more open countries to penetrate the wider markets. And there have always been a few highly receptive places to start. Developing countries are a mixed batch. But they have usually been a pushover for Japanese exporters.

More pertinently, there is ordinarily not much hidden behind the formal barriers although there are still numerous problems. Of course, American and European customs officers are painfully meticulous. Valuation and "uplifting" are annoying. Safety regulations are even worse. But there are usually channels for recourse and at least the codes are reasonably straightforward. Administrative guidance does not exist as a practice and, in many cases, would be impossible. As for testing, Underwriters Laboratory has an office in Tokyo and the Japanese can have their products tested locally while Americans have to send them to Japan first. There has been a worldwide trend toward a unification of technical standards, something the Japanese benefit from immensely, even if they do not always cooperate fully. This does not mean that no one plays dirty tricks on the Japanese. But it rarely keeps their goods out for long.

As for the marketing system, it is quite open. There is a much simpler path from wholesaler to retailer and no need to seek entry via a trading company. The number of outlets is usually smaller to reach a larger market and sales don't have to be subsidized as much. Moreover, there is no need to pass through one distribution channel, several can be used at the same time. And, rather than the distributor getting in the way, it is often possible to eliminate the middleman and go straight to the retailers. Shopkeepers will take on Japanese products as readily as domestic ones and the customers will buy whatever is good and/or cheap with little concern as to who produced it. Price and quality are also crucial in selling to manufacturers, not how long you have known them or how good your relations are.

It is not only a question of just getting into the existing distribution channels but how your goods are treated. Since most of the outlets are non-exclusive, even for electronics or automobiles, there is little problem. Japanese goods, far from being marked up are frequently marked down to sell larger quantities. And, if you give the dealer a bigger margin, you will get better treatment. The next step is also readily accessible if a Japanese company wants to have its own distribution network. It is just a matter of hiring a few staff and renting some premises. Neither of these is terribly difficult or unusually expensive. But that may not even be necessary. If you make a good enough offer, you can take over your competitors' outlets. There is no shortage of Toyota and Nissan dealers who once sold Ford or GM.

To give an idea of how "hard" things can be, why not summarize one of the articles run by the *Marubeni Business Bulletin* to show just how diligent and enterprising its employees are. This particular chap, Shiro Yamamoto by name, was sent off to the United States at the tender age of 29 to sell Kubota tractors. The boss "must be kidding," he thought, realizing how much competition there was. Sure enough, the first effort failed. Their American agent couldn't sell the tractors at the recommended price and almost gave them away. Then, miracle of miracles, the farmers who got the tractors started calling Yamamoto for spare parts. Thus encouraged, he decided to set up his own distribution network. But, as a Japanese, he needed an American manager. Who else could he think of than the marketing director of his former agent? The guy accepted the job (no loyalty in America, you know) and they began looking for dealers. When they put an ad in a trade journal, they got so many replies they could choose, and signed up 47 dealers in one year. Ten years later, they had a staff of 180 as well as 940 distributors across the country. Sales grew, and how! For some reason, rather than the excessive price charged by the first agent, Kubota managed to bring the price down low enough to knock out the competition. Thinking back on his experiences in America, Yamamoto, now a happy manager in the Tokyo head office, could reflect: "I learned an important lesson—that if you try very hard, a lot of things become possible."[23]

No doubt about it, a lot of things are very possible in America. Are they equally possible in Japan? It is hard to think of any companies that did as well in Japan on the basis of a young salaryman and a minor investment. In fact, there are plenty of stories of companies sending in top men from the home office, offering excellent wages for Japanese employees, investing all the time and money necessary, and even then not getting off the ground. Finding dealers through a magazine ad is out of the question. And stealing the marketing director from your agent just isn't done. When in Japan, do as the Japanese. But don't assume it will get you anywhere fast!

Foreigners have to make a tremendous commitment when they enter the Japanese market. What about the Japanese going abroad? Often, no great commitment is needed. Indeed, some penetrate the American or European markets without ever leaving Japan. They deal with the local office of a foreign mail-order house or department store or they produce for foreign companies selling their goods under private brand. The trading companies can also take over the basic chore of picking up their goods at the factory and getting them into the overseas distribution networks. Even when they wager a-broad, it is possible to send off some young staff, open an office with one month's rent down, hire employees through news-paper ads and have a real presence in no time at all. If they want to manufacture, they can rent a complete factory at an industrial estate or buy someone out. If things don't work, they can pull out with only modest losses. But usually things do work and at any rate it does not take long to know.

Some foreigners regard obtaining proper Japanese per-sonnel as the biggest non-tariff barrier of them all. Judging by the way Japanese managers grumble about the poor quality of labor they find abroad, this must also be their principal headache. The problem is usually that they cannot find a dedicated staff that will remain with them and are upset by the constant job hopping. Although white-collar workers are usually acceptable, they have serious complaints about the training, discipline and work will of the blue-collar labor. And they cannot get adjusted to employees who insist on doing a nine-to-five job, want to enjoy their holidays, and organize aggressive unions. Still, there is no problem in recruiting personnel as such and, if they are willing to pay a bit higher wages or show more consideration, they can get a team as good or better than anyone else. And that, basically, is all they have a right to, equal treatment with the domestic companies.

If the Japanese want to run things in their own way, and this means that they must bring in large numbers of people from back home, this is usually not terribly difficult. Most invest-ment codes provide for this and many immigration services have been quite lenient. As a matter of fact, a burgeoning Japanese community is a standard counterpart of Japanese business. And this includes not only top managers or technical personnel but even secretaries and waiters, as well as the wife and kiddies. This might be compared to the hassle a foreign businessman goes through to get a visa to Japan, only to find out he may have to wait another six months for his family to come in. So there was soon an amazing discrepancy with about twice as many Japanese in America as American businessmen in Japan for roughly the same amount of work. When the Americans decided to screen the Japanese more strictly, this suddenly became a non-tariff barrier in Japanese eyes.

As can be seen, it is not all that difficult for the Japanese to sell their goods abroad. If they wish to invest abroad, the contrast is even sharper. Not only is it not difficult, they will immediately be courted by potential sites for investment. Hardly a month goes by without foreign dignitaries, from ministers down to mayors, making a special trip to Japan to urge firms to invest in their particular area. This happens not only for America, or Australia, or the many developing countries, but also more open parts of Europe like Britain, Ireland or Belgium. And this is more than just a polite invitation since many places offer generous incentives, facilitate the necessary adjustments, and even help finance the operation.

If this process is too slow, a Japanese company can simply buy up a going concern in many foreign countries. And it can get them at bargain basement rates if they are in a depressed industry or region. This way, the company will start with its own premises (often including the factory), a trained and experienced staff, marketing channels, a local brand name and a reputation in the trade. By pumping in a bit of money or introducing superior technology, it can usually do well. In some cases, this forms an ideal entry and more. For, the overseas operation can help with importing and production. Or it can entice personnel from the competitors and discover their plans or profit from their research efforts.

It is not really hard to do business in America, or Europe for that matter. This has been proven by literally hundreds, and perhaps thousands, of success stories and rather few cases of patent failure. Those which did well include not only big names like Sony, or Toyota, or Nikon, or YKK. In certain fields, all of the major companies have been successful, as for automobiles, electronics and steel. In a mass of others, even rather small and insignificant companies managed to sell, as for textiles, garments, toys, and optical goods. The general advance is clearly marked by the presence of most major trading companies, banks, insurance firms and even such minor operations as restaurants and flower arrangement schools.

Given this situation, every effort must be made to distinguish between two very different concepts that are frequently confused. It is often pointed out that the barriers in Japan are part of the Japanese way of doing things and that all companies face exactly the same difficulties. In theory, this may be true; in practice, as we saw, the foreign companies usually face additional hurdles. Yet, even if it were true one hundred percent, this would only show that there is no *discrimination*. The essential problem is not that but whether foreign companies are treated as well in Japan as Japanese companies are treated abroad. That is the question of *reciprocity* which would be the fairest basis of trade relations. And it is perfectly clear that foreign companies usually have much more trouble penetrating the Japanese market than the Japanese encounter when doing business abroad.

NOTES

1. See *Japan's Manufactured Imports*, JETRO, 1981.
2. *Marubeni Business Bulletin*, No. 96, June 1981, p. 10.
3. Frank Weil and Norman Glick, *Japan—Is the Market Open?*, pp. 863–5.

4. *Japan Times*, February 2, 1982.
5. See Jon Woronoff, *Inside Japan, Inc.*, pp. 152–65.
6. *Asian Business*, August 1982, pp. 68–70.
7. Weil, op. cit., pp. 890–3.
8. See Jon Woronoff, *Japan: The Coming Social Crisis*, pp. 189–235.
9. See Dan Fenno Henderson, *Foreign Enterprise in Japan.*
10. Kiyoshi Kojima, *Japan and a New World Economic Order*, p. 28.
11. Arthur D. Little, Inc., *The Japanese Non-Tariff Trade Barrier Issue*, p. V-13.
12. The National Institute for Research Advancement.
13. Foreign Correspondents Club Press Briefing, July 7, 1981.
14. See Woronoff, *Japan's Wasted Workers*, pp. 24–65.
15. Many seasoned foreign businessmen feel it takes at least five years to get established and ten years to get a modest market share.
16. See Woronoff, op. cit., pp. 66–110.
17. See Dodwell's *Industrial Groupings in Japan.*
18. See *United States-Japan Trade Study Group* and *United States-Japan Trade.*
19. Weil, op. cit., p. 888.
20. *Los Angeles Times*, October 19, 1980.
21. *Japan-EC-US Editors Symposium*, October 10–12, 1977, Tokyo, Nihon Shinbun Kyokai, pp. 19–21.
22. Sony still only has about 1,000 outlets to Matsushita's 21,000. And this affects sales.
23. *Marubeni Business Bulletin*, Documentary Series XVII.

4

From Conflict To Conflict

Turmoil Over Textiles

The textile industry usually has the dubious honor of being the first to cause serious trade disruptions and come under the threat of protectionism. This is largely because textiles is the first sector that most developing countries have traditionally entered. In earlier days especially, it involved relatively simple technologies that could be easily mastered, machinery that was for sale at accessible prices (if not new, then secondhand), and raw materials that were widely available. A competitive edge could be obtained since it required large quantities of the one local resource that was usually cheap, namely labor. This meant that dynamic businessmen, or determined govern-ments, could readily make the necessary investments and get started. In time, the sector was bound to expand as newcomers were attracted and more plants went up.

Thus, during its early stage of industrialization, Japan developed textile manufacturing to the almost grotesque point where, by the 1920s, it represented nearly 45% of industrial output and 53% of the industrial labor force. Moroever, since the country was still relatively backward and had few other industries, this exaggerated the share of textiles in exports, amounting to no less than two-thirds of the total. After the war, somewhat more balanced growth was attained, although textiles were again regarded as the easiest place to get started and production of cotton textiles grew by leaps and bounds. Still the primary product in a country starved for capital, exports were soon growing faster even than production. The primary destination was the United States, just about the only affluent market in the 1950s.

The Japanese manufacturers had no trouble getting into the American market. In fact, the American government was concerned about Japan's rehabilitation and regarded trade as vital. Local importers were even keener, and many of them traveled to Japan to buy fabrics or order garments made to their own specifications. The rise in imports was thus nearly explosive. Sales of cotton cloth shot up from about 10 million square yards in 1950 to 140 million in 1955. While no women's blouses were imported in 1950, about 48 million arrived in 1955. Although textile imports equalled a mere 2% of domestic production, in some categories the quantities were alarming (blouse imports, for example, suddenly took over 25% of the market).

It was not surprising to find the American textile industry seriously aggrieved by this intrusion. It came at a time when sales were relatively stagnant and squeezed the existing producers somewhat more. And it was complicated by the fact that about 300,000 workers had already been laid off over the past decade, mainly due to increased mechanization. This obviously made Japanese goods, no matter how many, most unwelcome. Soon imports were being fought by a coalition of manufacturers, unions and politicians from depressed areas who lobbied for protection. Still, since the situation was not too serious for the moment and Japan's recovery and the maintenance of good relations were more in the national interest, the Eisenhower administration resisted the pressure for legislation. Instead, it urged the Japanese to adopt "voluntary" restrictions.

In December 1955, the Japanese government accepted this method. In January 1957, a more formal bilateral agreement was adopted to impose limitations on cotton cloth, garments and knitwear for a period of five years. This temporarily brought Japanese imports under control. But it had no effect on other developing countries, especially in the Far East, which got their textile industries into gear. Hong Kong was amazingly successful, boosting its sales from close to nothing in 1955 to over $63 million in 1960, not far behind Japan.[1] Thus, the Kennedy administration had GATT negotiate a broader multilateral agreement called the Long-Term Arrangement Regarding International Trade in Cotton Textiles (LTA), which came into force in October 1962.

But the LTA was not the end of the road. Blocked in the direction of cotton manufactures by the various restrictions and also increasingly unable to compete with new producers in Hong Kong, Taiwan, Korea, India and elsewhere, the Japanese tried to enter new product lines. One of them was wool. A more significant switch was to manmade fibers. Although the Americans had an early monopoly due to their technological head start, they agreed to license Japanese companies which were soon also producing synthetic yarn and fabrics. Gradually reaching a more advanced level, in fact, the Japanese found this an ideal sector since it required less cheap labor and too much capital or knowhow for most developing nations. At the same time, the Japanese improved on the borrowed technologies and created some of their own. Thus, the 1960s saw a sharp increase in their sales of manmade fabrics, although due to surges in specific branches it often appeared much more than it really was.

As the Japanese entered new areas and American producers were hurt or just worried, further bilateral agreements were negotiated to provide additional "voluntary" restraint. This happened in 1962, 1963 and 1965. When pressured to adopt similar restraint for wool exports in the latter year, the Japanese balked for the first time. The American textile industry was not willing to give in either and repeatedly called for more protection, although its case was often not very convincing. It, too, had benefited tremendously from the revolution brought about by synthetic fibers and imports, even if unpleasant and occasionally harmful, still represented less than 4% of production.

All this while, any American president was bound to come under strong pressure from the industry and states concerned to continue this gradual process of expanding restrictions. But Richard Nixon's campaign pledge to aid the textile industry by negotiating international quota agreements on wool, manmade fibers and blends precipitated matters. Shortly after taking office, in February 1969, he stated a preference for doing this on a "volunteer basis" and sent Secretary of Commerce Maurice Stans to Europe and then Asia to look into the possibility of negotiating an agreement like the LTA. In Europe, the reception was cool; in Asia and especially Japan, icy. This time the Japanese industry decided to stand pat and mobilized all the support it could within the ruling Liberal Democratic Party and especially the Ministry of International Trade and Industry.[2]

Nixon's hopes for a quick solution were dissipated in fact-finding and talks that led nowhere. He therefore decided to hasten matters by linking this textile accord, rather important for him personally, with the negotiations for the reversion of Okinawa, crucial for Prime Minister Eisaku Sato and a national cause in Japan. It was assumed that an understanding had been reached when the two men met in Washington that December. But nothing came of it. To win the impending elections, Sato had to deny any "secret deal" on textiles. Then his attempts to obtain concessions from the textile manufacturers were rebuffed and he could not even bring MITI into line. Both refused to budge until the American industry could adequately prove serious injury due to imports.

Finding it impossible to make headway through repeated, and usually futile discussions, the Nixon administration announced that it "reluctantly" backed the legislation being brought before Congress. This would involve highly restrictive general quotas that could seriously hurt Japan and put America back on the path to protectionism. Such a possibility alarmed the Japanese Foreign Ministry and prime minister, but they were unable to persuade MITI, let alone the textile manufacturers. American free traders were also worried. But for the moment this was simply used as a threat to convince the Japanese that an amicable settlement would be preferable. When Prime Minister Sato arrived for his second summit in October 1970, he was put under renewed pressure by Nixon and Henry Kissinger, and again he agreed basically to what Nixon wanted.

In Japan, however, no amount of prompting could get the manufacturers to back down. Their biggest concessions were far from America's minimum demands. As for legislation that might impose restrictions, they refused to take the threat seriously and seemed revindicated when the trade bill including textile quotas failed in the Senate. Intransigence by the American manufacturers was no less destructive. It torpedoed an agreement being worked out between presidential assistant Peter Flanigan and Ambassador Nobuhiko Ushiba. And President Nixon rejected a plan supported by the Japanese Textile Federation to unilaterally restrain exports, both because it was insufficient and because it was sponsored by Democratic Congressman Wilbur Mills without the blessings of the Republican President. Then came the turn of Ambassador-at-Large David Kennedy to seek a stronger agreement. Three missions later he had accomplished nothing, although MITI under its new minister Kakuei Tanaka was finally making an effort to help.

In the meanwhile, the Japanese had obtained the reversion of Okinawa pretty much on the terms they desired while Nixon had nothing to show for his efforts. The Japanese in general did not admit the need for any quid pro quo and the textile manufacturers were in no rush to compromise. None of them seemed to reckon with the reactions of President Nixon. Not a particularly patient man, he felt cheated by the repeated failures at reaching a still elusive solution. There was also a growing sentiment in his administration, as well as more widely throughout the nation, that Japan had since become strong enough not to require special consideration while it was surprisingly ungenerous in meeting American requests. This involved not only the failure to find a positive solution to the textile issue but more so its general tendency to delay liberalizing imports and investment and to keep the yen artificially undervalued.

Although it was taking an inordinate amount of time and effort, textile imports were only one aspect of America's economic problems at the time. Its overall trade balance had severely weakened and it was running deficits. To correct this situation, on August 15, 1971, President Nixon took drastic action to restore the economy. This included the imposition of a temporary import surcharge of 10% and the floating of the dollar. Without being directed specifically against Japan, what came to be known as the "Nixon shock" undoubtedly had its greatest impact there. And it was followed by the threat that the United States would impose textile quotas unilaterally if no agreement were reached by October 15. Only then could concessions be imposed on the Japanese textile lobby by Tanaka, who barely managed to negotiate the framework of an agreement with Kennedy by the final day. (And it took another three months, until January 3, 1972, for Kennedy and Ambassador Ushiba to adopt the detailed arrangements.)

After some three years of wrangling, the apparently simple matter of reaching a further textile agreement was accomplished. But it left no one particularly happy. This issue had embittered relations between Japan and America at a time when they should have been at their best, with the reversion of Okinawa and no serious difficulties elsewhere, and despite the avowed intentions of both Nixon and Sato of preserving harmonious relations. They angered the American and Japanese textile industries, and alarmed supporters of free trade on both sides, as the situation continued to degrade. For these reasons alone the exercise had been foolish and dangerous. But it soon turned out that it was rather purposeless as well.

The Japanese textile industry was bound to be a loser from the outset, since it would have to accept some cutback in exports. Althouth its primary concern was the exact level imposed it kept talking in terms of principle and this made it harder to negotiate concessions. But the few years of relatively unhampered trade, while it delayed action, were paid for by having to accept an agreement under duress rather than negotiate amicably. It ended up with about half what it wanted, a quota of about 1,000,000,000 yards a year as of 1971. Yet, soon it could not even fill this quota. By 1974, exports had fallen to 690,000,000 yards and somewhat later they barely reached 15% of the ceiling for cotton, 15% for wool, and 50% for manmade fibers.

What had happened during these years apparently went unnoticed by both the Japanese and Americans. Other developing countries, especially those in Asia, managed to break into the same sectors and produce more cheaply than Japan again, quickly taking up its share. In Japan itself, there was an unexpected reversal in 1973, when for the first time there were more imports than exports of made-up goods and imports of all textiles grew while exports tended to stagnate or decrease. This resulted from the normal evolution of the industry and was hastened by the appreciation of the yen, initiated by the Nixon shock. And it was bound to continue.

By 1977, the United States could safely relax the hard fought textile agreement since the overall ceiling was about twice the actual level of imports. But the textile issue per se had hardly disappeared. Rather, it spread to include new exporters in the developing world and more importers among the advanced nations, about fifty in all, which negotiated a broader Multi-Fiber Arrangement in GATT. The MFA, which first went into force in 1974 and was renewed in 1978 and 1982, was theoretically designed to promote an orderly expansion of textile trade. But the developing countries' interest in growth, limited to 6% a year, was gradually overshadowed by the advanced countries' fear of import surges and further loss of domestic production.

By the early 1980s, the American industry was clinging tenaciously to 90% of the domestic market while the EC countries only held on to 65% of theirs. But the cost to the consumers was substantial and the benefits to the producers modest. There had been scant progress in restructuring the industry except in Germany and the United States, which suddenly expanded its own exports of certain categories. Although Japan's efforts were more systematic, it could not produce as cheaply as its neighbors whenever labor was a major input. Some developing countries, like Hong Kong, Korea and Taiwan, managed to do amazingly well in boosting their production despite the poor economic climate and a growing number of bilateral restraints. Their success was due to upgrading quality and price and moving into more sophisticated items while newcomers entered the lower categories. But none of them felt assured about the future of an increasingly competitive and restricted sector.

Television Turnabout

Even while the textile conflict was raging, another trade conflict was building up although it remained quiescent for a long while. As early as 1968, the U.S. Electronic Industries Association brought dumping charges against the Japanese television industry. In 1971, the Treasury ruled that in fact Japanese television sets were being dumped and ordered certain makers to pay countervailing duties. In that same year, the Tariff Commission concluded that American producers were being damaged by the sale of Japanese receivers at less than fair value and added that Japanese pricing had "contributed substantially to declining prices of domestically produced television receivers."

However, not much was done about this. Roughly $1 million in duties were assessed for the period up to 1971, and some of this was collected. Meanwhile, the Customs Service was looking into the matter and its officials ultimately held that Japanese-made televisions were being sold for as little as half the sales price in Japan and therefore recommended that bonds be required to cover the "dumping margin." In its own investigations, the Treasury found that there might have been considerably more dumping than originally suspected and raised the value of bonds from 9% to 20% of the cost of a set in April 1977. But it failed to assess, or collect, an estimated $400 million in duties for the 1972–77 period. This made the threat to the Japanese makers somewhat unreal and any protection afforded the American makers rather fictitious.

Obviously, it is extremely difficult to determine the existence of dumping. Normally, this is defined by sale of a product abroad for less than the price at home. No matter how clear that may be in theory, it is hard to work out the exact figures in practice for many reasons. Among other things, it is necessary to know what the wholesale prices charged by makers are since dealer margins can vary considerably. And getting these prices is considerably more complicated if the makers and retailers, in an effort to conceal the true price engage in rebates and even falsification of documents (double invoicing, etc.) as alleged. Then there is the fact that the Japanese government offered a tax rebate on exports of 15% to 20%. Just to get some handle on the problem, the Treasury adopted the Commodity Tax Formula which took the "base price" used by the Japanese government in levying commodity taxes as the domestic price. This formula was rejected by the Japanese makers and thus a final determination remained in limbo.

Despite any uncertainty on details, it seemed relatively clear that at best the Japanese were cutting it very thin and selling their television sets with little concern as to the return and, at worst, they were engaging in outrageous dumping. Whatever the case, their American competitors could not afford to wait until more sophisticated formulas were devised. Thus, in 1974, Zenith (then the top maker) filed a suit against all the major Japanese manufacturers accusing them of rebates, subsidies, cartels and like attempts to restrain trade. And, in 1976, GTE Sylvania and others followed up with a complaint to the International Trade Commission (successor of the Tariff Commission) that several major Japanese makers engaged in "predatory pricing" and were selling their color receivers at "less than fair value" in order to dominate the American market.

Nevertheless, almost a decade after the first complaint and some five years after a Treasury ruling of dumping, nothing much had been done. Zenith referred to this as a "saga of deceit and delay." But it was not supported by the retailers which continued importing Japanese sets and the consumers who bought them or was it even backed by RCA, the second biggest maker, which refused to participate in any suit and whose vice-president could boast: "We have taken the position of being very much free trade oriented. There's no denying the acceleration of imports. There are many American manufacturers who have been pressed. . . . But it's the good old American way."[3]

While the Americans kept losing ground, the Japanese were advancing by applying the good old Japanese way of doing business. They had been producing black-and-white sets as early as the 1950s and then went over to color television. Much of the early technology came from the United States and most makers adopted the Admiral color picture tube, although Sony went its own way with Trinitron. But they managed to improve on the technologies they licensed or bought and were ultimately making products of a better quality than the Americans. Equally decisive, they expanded production scale immensely and raised productivity enough to be highly competitive. More and more the price margin was genuine, although the Japanese apparently felt that cutting profits thinner (or even absorbing temporary losses) would help penetrate markets faster.

By the mid-1970s, the Japanese manufacturers were producing as much as the Americans and they had pretty well saturated the home market (where the Americans had already been ousted). As sales stagnated in Japan, they began seeking further growth through exports and engaged in serious efforts to sell more in the United States. By and large, they found it easy enough to get a foothold by introducing their receivers under the private label of major retailers including Sears Roebuck, J.C. Penney, and Montgomery Ward. Then they began selling more under their own name, if necessary engaging in partial assembly locally. Both ways they were price competitive, since the local assembly used mainly imported parts which were cheaper than the parts made in America and used by their competitors.

Briefly, after the oil crisis, exports stagnated. Then the Japanese makers mounted an exceptional push. The share of color television imports rose from less than 15% in the first half of 1975 to over 40% in the second half of 1976. The increase in imported color televisions, which shot up from a mere 1,200,000 in 1975 to 2,950,000 in 1976, was devastating. It raised havoc in the American industry whose makers had already been decimated with 17 of the 28 producers leaving the field in less than ten years while 5 of the remaining 11 were no longer independent (2 of them had been absorbed by the Japanese). To survive, American makers like RCA, Sylvania, Admiral, GE and ultimately Zenith, had to intensify offshore assembly and production. This combined to leave some 60,000 workers unemployed by 1976.

At this point, it was no longer possible for the Americans to ignore the plight of their own industry. Better late than never, the ITC ruled in March 1977 that the American industry was indeed being hurt by imports. It held that Japanese sets were being sold about 20% cheaper and recommended to President Jimmy Carter that the import duty on color television receivers be increased sharply from 5% to 25%. In the Senate, Democratic Leader Robert Byrd among others called for a reduction in imports to prevent the "destruction" of the American industry. The Japanese also realized that something had to be done and Prime Minister Takeo Fukuda admitted that the recent surge in imports represented "a torrential downpour." With Japanese cooperation, Special Trade Representative Robert Strauss was able to negotiate a curb on color television exports. The only remaining question was the level, ultimtely set at 1,750,000 units a year for three years as of July 1977.

This did not make the Japanese happy. The quota was a good 40% less than the level attained in 1976. But at least it left them a big chunk of the market and the level was substantially higher than before the latest export offensive (itself intensified due to fear of impending restrictions). In the United States, there was now some hope that the domestic makers would recover. But this had to be counterbalanced by higher costs for the consumers and a bit more inflation. Moreover, the question of dumping could be quietly neglected as well as the unpaid duties. President Carter was able to reject the idea of tariffs which were a greater cost burden on the consumer and also aroused dangers of retaliation since they would have to be levied on all imports, not only Japanese.

Despite any dissatisfaction, both sides had to admit that this action was a lesser evil. And in some ways it was actually a rather neat solution. It allowed the Carter administration to get off the hook while the Japanese obtained a better deal than if legislation were adopted by Congress. By making this a "unilateral" and "voluntary" decision, it saved appearances all around and made it look more as if the trade system remained intact. But it is uncertain how far one could agree with Robert Strauss' claim: "This is not a protectionist move; it is a balanced move."[4]

Yet, this was not quite the end of the matter. The arrangement did restrict the Japanese considerably as America's share in its television exports fell from 51% in 1976 to 12% in 1980. But it did not stop other countries from exporting to the United States. Only one year after the agreement with Japan, Taiwan's exports nearly doubled to 625,000 sets while South Korea's quadrupled to about 415,000 sets. This made nonsense of the orderly marketing agreement as far as the American makers were concerned. And this time the Japanese backed them, with Kenji Tamiya, head of Sony's American operations complaining of "inequities" in American import policy and adding, "I think those countries have been taking advantage of the OMA."[5] Thus, similar agreements were reached with Taiwan and Korea to voluntarily restrain their exports.

However, it soon appeared that other aspects of the arrangement were working out very differently from expected. The restrictions on imports did permit domestic production to rise substantially. But much of this increase came not from the American makers but the Japanese who rushed to get around the barriers by engaging in local production. As of 1971, following in Sony's footsteps, Mitsubishi, Toshiba, Sharp and Hitachi put up assembly plants. Matsushita took over Motorola's television division and Sanyo obtained a controlling interest in Warwick. Together their output grew at an amazing pace, from about 1 million sets in 1977 to 2, 3 and 4 million in the succeeding years. While the Japanese kept on increasing their market shares, the American manufacturers were rolled back in their own country.

An even more surprising result was that soon the Japanese were not really hurt by the restrictions at all. As production in America rose, exports slumped so seriously that by 1979 only about 510,000 sets arrived, less than a third of what was allowed. Those who were seriously blocked were the Koreans, Taiwanese and others who could have more than filled their limited quotas and were held back by the orderly marketing agreement. Less advanced technologically and weaker financially, their companies could not so readily set up assembly plants abroad. In this way, the quotas ended up helping the Japanese and hurting their competitors.

By the time the agreement was drawing to a close, the situation was rather anomalous. Japan did less poorly than feared. Its home production actually rose and other markets

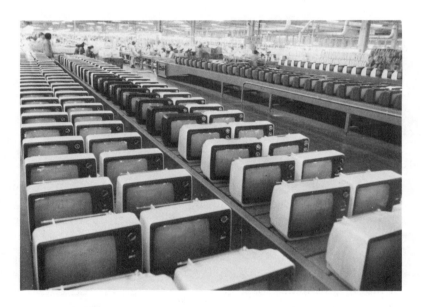

Korean television sets massed to drive out Japanese exports.

Credit: KOTRA

were conquered, especially in Europe and the Middle East, to replace the United States. Its makers were earning profits from their American plants (as well as on substantial sales of components). The United States also gained in certain ways. American workers found jobs and taxes were paid locally. Meanwhile, the American manufacturers had not really modernized and rationalized enough to keep up with the Japanese and were still hurting. So, in the end, the Japanese had probably gained more from the agreement than anyone else. But they did not even have to fight to maintain it. This was done by a coalition of companies and labor organizations called the Committee to Preserve American Color Television (COMPACT) which urged a three-year extension of the restrictions.

Steeling Markets

In many ways, Japan was fortunate to have had to reconstruct its industries after the war. Nowhere was this more evident than for iron and steel. Most of its major steel mills were built after the introduction of the BOF method and were thus far more efficient than any earlier mills. In addition, the Japanese have systematically introduced the best technology, at first licensed from abroad, then developed internally, so that they show the highest rates of continuous sintering and casting. Their steel mills, among the largest in the world, achieve very strong economies of scale and have lent themselves better to automation and computerization. The one serious drawback, namely a lack of domestic sources of coal, iron and other raw materials, could be compensated for by locating the steel mills along the coast where delivery by huge ships and then shipment of finished products by sea often proved cheaper than obtaining local sources by rail in other countries.

Japan's success with steel, however, is only partly due to its own accomplishments. As much can be traced to the repeated failures of others. While the Japanese constantly renovated plant, introduced improved technologies, and adapted production to market needs, the steel industry in many other countries failed to renew or update. The gap between the efficiency of their mills and the Japanese mills continued growing to the extent that Japanese goods could readily be sold more cheaply in most countries than domestic supplies despite any transport costs. In fact, since the Americans did not have the sense to build new mills on the West Coast, where most recent growth occurred, the Japanese could even enjoy some advantage on transport costs.

While steel output increased rapidly, the Japanese began scouting markets in the United States, and somewhat later, Europe. By 1960, steel already accounted for a third of total exports. In the early stages, most of this consisted of simple bulk products that were competitive on price rather than quality. Yet, to make any price edge greater, the Japanese may once again have been paring their margins to the bone (or even cutting into the bone for a while). It did not take long for cries of dumping to arise in the American industry.

As indicated, dumping is not easy to prove. But there are good reasons for imputing it on occasion. One is that the Japanese expanded the steel industry with no great concern for domestic or world demand, assuming that their steel could always be sold on quality and, if not, then on price. Periodically, they found themselves with tremendous overcapacity. This occurred first when domestic sales stabilized while plant kept growing. It occurred again, more sharply, after the oil crisis and recession when sales at home and abroad were stricken. With little housing and factory construction, and a serious slump in shipbuilding, they had more excess capacity than ever and had to stop many of their furnaces. Yet, even then, they could not afford to cut back too much and also had to pay the hefty bills for earlier massive investments.

One of the few documented cases was raised in connection

with carbon steel allegedly dumped by Japanese producers in 1977. Rather than compare domestic and export prices, as is usual, the Treasury calculated the cost of production, added 10% for overhead and 8% for profit, and used this "constructed value" for comparison. On that basis, it found that the firms were selling at 32% below cost. In a later calculation based on an extensive study of Japanese steel costs, it found that five Japanese makers were selling at 5.4% to 18.5% "less than fair value." Even if the Treasury's figures were not flawless they do indicate a willingness to sell at whatever price is necessary to get into a market. In a more general study, the Council on Wage and Price Stability showed that the Japanese could indeed export profitably to the United States. Due to greater productivity, even after absorbing transport costs and duties, they could undercut the American steelmakers on their home market by about 5%. Yet, at that time they were offering discounts of 10% to 20% which it regarded as "aggressive price competition."[6]

Nevertheless, the conclusion of this report and the general opinion has been that the steel industry's biggest enemies were within. Despite repeated warnings, and increasing modernization in other countries, the American makers failed to update their facilities. The combination of structural weaknesses and obsolescence made them woefully uncompetitive. To top things off, they had an unfortunate tendency to boost prices whenever they could thereby making it easier for outside producers to undercut them. The other problems were tagged to the labor force. The first big opening for the Japanese came in 1959, when a protracted strike made the consuming industries boost their foreign supplies. The threat of a similar strike in 1968 had the same effect. And, the wage settlements, combined with larger profits, kept costs well above the Japanese level.

Up until this time, Japanese imports had not been particularly worrisome. However, a major surge of 60% in 1968, which raised imports to 17% of consumption, brought a sharp reaction from the steel industry and unions. After remaining on the sidelines initially, realizing that much of the steel industry's troubles were of its own making, the government intervened to negotiate export limits with Japan and Europe in the form of a Voluntary Restraint Arrangement. This informal agreement was basically monitored by the American industry, which tried to keep imports to a level of about 10% of domestic consumption, while the Japanese makers sought to provide about half the total imports. It seemed to work without a serious hitch until 1974, when the consumers brought a successful suit against the arrangement on the basis of the antitrust laws, insisting this was an act in restraint of trade that unduly raised prices.

The situation changed little under other forms of self-restraint and remaining tariffs until the recession sharpened competition at a time of a general slump in consumption. Then the solution quickly unravelled as foreign imports shot up and reached a level of nearly 20%. This annoyed the unions and led the steelmakers to bring the charge of dumping. The findings of the Treasury and assessment of a "dumping duty" of 32%, showed that the dispute could become unpleasant. But President Carter refused to be pushed by the steel lobby. Pleading the need "to maintain the competitive nature of the free enterprise process," he refused to limit steel imports. And Special Trade Representative Robert Strauss added that protectionist measures were not the solution to the problems brought on by dumping. This message did not please the industry, then suffering from serious losses and closing down plants, or labor, faced with new layoffs. One of their backers, Senator John Heinz, went so far as to claim: "I very strongly feel Carter is going to preside over the demise of the steel industry."[7]

Quite unlike their counterparts in textiles and television, the Japanese steelmakers were more willing to listen to reason.

After hasty threats to appeal to GATT, they admitted the seriousness of the situation. Yoshihiro Inayama, chairman of Nippon Steel and head of the Japan Iron and Steel Institute, proposed that the Japanese steelmakers voluntarily restrict their exports to the United States. And Nippon Steel's president, Eishiro Saito, recalling the close relations with America and the fact that its coking coal was vital for Japan, stated: "We must avoid anything that could cause trouble or distress to the U.S. steel industry—our big brother."[8] But it was still a big step from kindly sentiments to concrete action, since the cutback offered by Japan was far less than desired by the American makers.

Meanwhile, a very different solution was being sought, and it was hammered out in record time (already going into effect on February 21, 1978). This was to establish a reference price for steel imports. The price would be based largely on Japanese costs and would in principle be decided unilaterally by the American government, although in practice it would be reached after consultation with Japan and the European Community. Any foreign steel imported at prices below what was called the "trigger price" would be subject to a prompt antidumping probe by the Treasury Department and, if so ruled, antidumping duties would be levied. Much depended on how the mechanism was adjusted. If the reference price were set too high, this would block imports; if too low, too much might be imported. The basic goal was to decrease the level of imports from 20% of consumption to about 14%. Unlike the earlier voluntary arrangements, this settlement was deemed an "orderly marketing agreement" and thus not in opposition to the antitrust laws.

This mechanism tended to be less inflationary than tariffs and more flexible than quotas. It left the share of the market won by imports to whichever maker could provide the best steel at acceptable prices. Admittedly, there were restraints on the Japanese. But it helped them in two ways. First, they were no longer tempted to cut prices too low and could reap higher profits. Secondly, they were protected from even more outrageous dumping by European producers which had grabbed some of their market share. As long as they could continue making better steel cheaper they expected to do well. But they again failed to realize how quickly new producers like Korea and Taiwan could enter the market.

As for the American steelmakers, this mechanism certainly protected them from excessive price competition. But it was still up to them to keep their prices low enough to regain any lost opportunities. Coming after an earlier period of price control, this also seemed to keep their profits unduly low and deprive them of the wherewithall to modernize. The easy way out was to push for increases in the trigger price, which they repeatedly did, albeit with rather mixed results. And thus imports still represented 16% of domestic demand as late as 1980. Fortunately, by then the industry finally seemed to be thinking seriously of launching projects for rationalization or expansion despite an estimated cost of nearly $7 billion a year.

But a new crisis broke out in the steel industry in 1982. Due to the worldwide recession, there was substantial overcapacity in most producing countries and many steelmakers were desperately trying to increase sales, not to enhance profits so much as to cut losses and avoid collapse. Despite subsidies and talk of rationalization, the situation was worst in Europe and the most attractive market remained the United States. Sudden surges of imports brought the market share of foreign steel to 25% by mid-year, before settling near 20%. This caused the American steelmakers to complain of dumping and illegal subsidizing of exports.

Complaining that the trigger price mechanism was not working right, seven steelmakers led by United States Steel filed suits against competitors in eleven countries: Belgium, France, Germany, Great Britain, Italy, Luxembourg, Netherlands and Spain as well as Brazil, Romania and South

Africa . . . but not Japan. Attempts by Washington to negotiate a compromise with the European Community were painfully slow and in the meanwhile the trigger price mechanism was discontinued. When the American steelmakers pressed the matter, Industrial Affairs Commissioner Etienne Davignon responded that the Community would fight the suits and win. But the governments did not want an open conflict and eventually it was agreed that exports of 11 European steel products should be reduced to 5.75% of the market. This was rejected by U.S. Steel's chairman David Roderick, who complained that the settlement was "neither fair nor equitable." But a trade war could be averted.

Much Ado About Sundries

Although the textile, television and steel conflicts were the most serious, they were not the only ones. There were periodic surges of other imports and the industries involved quickly called for protection, a move often backed by local Congressmen. Among the articles incriminated were footwear, microwave ovens, scales, valves and even nuts and bolts from Japan. There were also charges of dumping from Europe. This was reflected by a rather steep increase in complaints, investigations and rulings by the Treasury and International Trade Commission and many issues were also passed on to Congress or the White House. But amazingly few met with concrete results. The ITC found serious injury in the shoe industry and President Carter, rather than impose duties, preferred negotiating an orderly marketing agreement with Taiwan and South Korea in 1977. Most others simply faded away even when dumping was noted.

This left the United States with a somewhat blemished, but far from systematically negative, record on trade. Despite some very striking cases of trade restrictions, there were also notable advances. Indeed, even while textile and television imports were curtailed, Washington was preparing a renovated Trade Act and remained the major promoter of world efforts to expand trade. The United States, rather than Japan, took the lead in the Tokyo Round as it had done for the Kennedy Round of GATT negotiations. No matter how much pressure they came under from segments of the public seeking relief, American Presidents and their key advisors opposed protectionism and even the Congressmen were only openly protectionist on issues that seriously affected their home state or district. The path still consisted of one step forward after each step back, as when President Carter allowed the television quota on Japan to elapse and President Reagan dropped the OMA on shoe imports and the curbs on television imports from Korea and Taiwan.

The most nagging worry was not yet the depth as much as the breadth of the phenomenon. For, what happened in the United States was soon also occurring in Europe. This was not just because Washington had set a bad example. Some cases in Europe predated any American action and most would have arisen anyway. The root of the problem was that the same causes were having the same effects. Japan, and then the newly industrialized countries, simply began trading with the United States at a much earlier date. This was a vast market and also a proving ground. Once they could penetrate it, all the while improving quality and boosting efficiency, they were ready for other markets and Europe provided some of the best.

Since events do repeat themselves more often than desired, there is no reason not to remark that after a spurt of rapid growth many European economies had slowed down and industries became relatively inefficient. Some were soon ailing as much or more than America's. In fact, Great Britain never seemed to recover from the war and its once glorious textile industry was unable to face the competition. Successive British Prime Ministers listened to growing complaints from Lancashire and other depressed areas. As early as 1958, with little more regret than Nixon, they introduced "voluntary" restraint for a string of developing countries, including the Crown Colony of Hong Kong. Despite an originally cool reception to Nixon's proposals for a multilateral agreement, European countries quickly joined the MFA and some became very strong supporters of even stricter restraints.

Still, relations between Europe and Japan did not become very close until the 1970s. While the Japanese were exporting massively to the United States, most European markets, a bit less promising and more remote, remained largely secondary. Once the American market was approaching saturation and serious conflicts broke out, however, the Japanese found it wise to diversify. With this, trade grew rapidly . . . and so did the problems.

Another reason Japan got off to a late start in penetrating the European markets is that there was far more protectionism there. For a long time, many European countries discriminated against Japan. Even after it joined GATT, they refused to grant most-favored-nation treatment for a while and excluded it from many concessions. Nevertheless, slowly but surely, it was accepted and most of the tariffs and quotas were withdrawn. Yet, even by 1980, when Japan had largely dismantled its formal barriers, European Community members still had 56 quantitative restrictions in force and a higher tariff level than Japan. Nevertheless, it must be admitted that the countries varied greatly. West Germany, Belgium, Netherlands and parts of Scandinavia were quite open, Britain was moderately so, while France, Italy, Greece and Spain were more closed. Also, some of the restrictions had since lost any meaning such as those on Japanese silk, meat or honey.

That is why Japan has long protested that it faced relatively impervious European markets and had great trouble in entering. But the entry was not as difficult as all that when one considers that it simply had to start where the doors were wide open, such as Benelux and Germany and also Britain for traditional reasons, Once inside, they found that the Community had definite advantages. For, it was no longer necessary to knock at each door separately but rather put the goods into circulation and have them flow into other parts of the common market. For example, although Japanese television exports were severely restricted in France, it recently absorbed a quarter of all sets imported in the EC via other member states.

The best evidence that Europe could not be terribly closed, despite any formal barriers, is that the Japanese were able to boost exports at a terrific pace once they set themselves to the task. The rise was in fact much faster than in the United States at the same time. For the European Community, it marked a good 25% or more growth annually throughout the 1970s. (This was also about three times as fast as trade was growing in the opposite direction.) Still, by 1980, Japan's exports only claimed about 2% of the EC market.

This figure is often presented by Japanese spokesmen in a bemused attempt to ask: what's all the fuss about? Indeed, such a low level of imports would be insignificant . . . if not for the incredible concentrations. First of all, most of the Japanese exports went to a few countries, West Germany taking about 35%, Great Britain 23%, Netherlands 13%, and France 12%. Secondly, the exports were lumped in a rather narrow range, with machinery and equipment representing some 60% to 70% of the total. And half of this was taken up by five items: televisions, radios, tape recorders, automobiles, and ships. Finally, the entry into a given market was often packed into a strong push that created unheard-of surges. This included an increase in automobile exports to Britain of 402% in 1972, or television exports to France of 158% in 1974, or video tape recorder exports to Germany of 207% in 1981.[9]

No individual country could resist such sudden influxes and they were also a problem for the European Community as a whole in its attempts to forge a common trade policy.

Moreover, they came at just the worst time. Much of America's absorption of Japanese goods occured in a bouyant economy during a period of expanding world trade. In Europe, it came after the oil crisis and in the midst of a worldwide recession and serious difficulties in certain industries. It is thus not surprising that ad hoc attempts were quickly made to solve any problems. But the attempts were not always successful and there were soon conflicts as serious as those that arose in the United States.

Shipbuilding had been a major industry in many European countries, such as Britain, Norway, Germany or France, not only for decades but centuries. It became a leading industry in Japan during the 1960s, when capacity was expanded to an incredible extent of something like 1,000%. Smaller shipbuilding companies grew and steel or heavy industry giants joined them. The competition between them was intense and usually too much for foreign companies to take. On the basis of low wages (in the 1960s at least) and good quality, but especially through the introduction of mass production and assembly line techniques, the Japanese shipyards won a large share of the orders worldwide. Even in 1972, when experts warned of a coming glut, some yards continued increasing capacity. Then the oil crisis struck, aggravating a normal slowdown, and orders dropped precipitously. This left the Japanese in deep trouble. They were forced grudgingly to cut back on staff and production while sharply lowering prices and accepting to work at cost (and sometimes less).[10] The once prosperous industry rapidly piled up massive losses.

During the earlier period, the European shipyards had done poorly enough, losing many of their customers to Japan. In better times, they could just get by. After the recession, many only kept afloat thanks to huge subsidies. They, too, admitted the need to reduce capacity and sought to do so in a balanced manner. An OECD working party of 14 nations ultimately agreed on a uniform scaling down by 35%. To avoid excessive competition, Japan, which had reached as much production as the 13 European countries, was to accept only half the new orders. However, when the situation improved as of 1979, its shipyards grabbed as many orders as they could get on any terms. Soon they had the lion's share of export orders and were working close to capacity while the European shipyards remained in the doldrums. Efforts to hold Japan to the earlier pledge failed. Meanwhile, new threats arose from countries entering the sector aggressively, such as Brazil, Korea, Taiwan, Yugoslavia and then China.

Not long after the United States introduced the trigger price mechanism, a number of European countries prevailed on the Japanese steelmakers to accept minimum prices as well as restraints on quantity. For, Europe's steel industry was in even greater difficulty than America's. Too many steel mills were old and obsolete, some were too small, and on the whole productivity was low (with the exception of Germany). Labor was often inefficient, unruly, or both. Nationalization of the steel industry, as in Britain, had not helped. Yet, given their smaller domestic markets, the steel companies depended heavily on exports and encountered stiff competition from Japan wherever they turned. Over the years, production slumped in most countries and unemployment was high, creating some seriously depressed regions. A voluntary cartel to reduce capacity helped somewhat, until the steelmakers withdrew and engaged in mutually destructive price-cutting and dumping. By late 1980, a state of "manifest crisis" had to be declared by the EC Commission and an official cartel established to decrease capacity, stabilize prices, and hopefully restore the industry. All this while, the Japanese steelmakers had little choice but to exercise caution and exports usually fell below the authorized levels.

These two cases were particularly crucial due to their role in the economy of most countries. But there were many others which cropped up, sometimes affecting only a few countries, on occasion many. Television imports seriously worried the weaker producers and in France Japanese imports were temporarily banned. Imports of household electric appliances aroused complaints and antidumping procedures were brought against sealed compressors for refrigerating equipment. For bearings, the hearings resulted in a finding of dumping and levying of antidumping duties and/or an increase in prices. Numerically-controlled machine tools seemed likely to create similar problems so the Japanese makers formed a cartel to regulate exports. Most of the action was taken by the governments or the EC Commission but other channels were also used. The British automobile industry worked out an informal quota with its Japanese counterpart. When a French attempt along the same lines failed, the government imposed a much lower quota on its own.

Other products were, or could be expected to become, the subject of complaints, actions or penalties. Other countries were also drawn into those involved. The most prominent were the newly industrializing countries of Asia. South Korea was charged with dumping black-and-white televisions and faced a temporary ban on imports thereof, as well as of umbrellas, measuring instruments, and toys. Hong Kong had trouble regarding umbrellas and toys. Taiwan was included for measuring instruments and televisions and also subject to a British inter-industry quota on footwear (which might eventually become Community-wide). China faced a ban on footwear, gloves and crockery. A second group, for rather varied products, were the Soviet Union and East European countries. Periodically accused of dumping, it was sometimes hard to tell whether this was done purposely, to obtain foreign exchange at any cost, or because they were simply unaware of the true value of their goods.

This has left Europe, and also the European Community, a more notable stronghold of protectionism than the United

States. The tendency toward trade liberalization was more hesitant and therefore easier to arrest once specific sectors that were already in difficulty became the target of Japanese trade offensives. The pace of imports was fast enough to keep at least one conflict boiling throughout the past decade. And those countries which were most embittered gradually convinced the others to join them, as could be seen especially for steel and later automobiles. But this did not mean that the whole blame could be placed on France and Italy, which the Japanese regarded as their worst enemies, since even Germany could not withstand the onslaught. The real problems were the lopsided trade patterns and the sharp surges of certain imports.

Entering the 1980s, the European Community still retained some old tariffs and residual quantitative restrictions. It had the new restrictions worked out on a governmental basis, either bilaterally or through the Commission. There were also the inter-industry agreements. And there were various forms of non-tariff barriers or just non-cooperation by aggrieved countries. These matters eventually affected the inner workings of the common market, since one country could not afford to become the brunt of a Japanese export campaign or suffer a secondary effect of the same goods entering in free circulation. Thus, with the Commission's authorization, individual members could ban the entry of goods being freely imported into the others. And they could even block entry of goods imported indirectly through other member countries.

Early in 1981, the Commission adopted a surveillance system regarding crucial Japanese imports which seemed to be increasing too rapidly or might harm local industries. They included sensitive items such as passenger cars, color televisions, picture tubes, and numerically-controlled machine tools. The list might well be lengthened in the future with the addition of other items like machine presses, integrated circuits, light trucks and vans, motorcycles, video tape recorders, electronic watches, transceivers, magnetic tapes and sound film. Admittedly, the system was only supposed to monitor the level of imports and see that they did not rise too abruptly or too steeply. However, if they did, the Japanese feared the Community would take action. So this was seen as another alarming step in the direction of protectionism.

Cooperation Or Confrontation?

These various conflicts were all serious taken individually. Fortunately for the trade system, they occurred pretty much in isolation and one could be solved before the next flared up. However, as time passed, there were more and more sensitive areas in which brush fires could readily start. The impact of one sector on the others as well as the more general problem of unemployment increased the linkages. Thus, conflicts could spread more widely. At the same time, they tended to be deeper. For, the whole process of decline had advanced further in the West while Japan's industries were often in their prime and export campaigns more vigorous than ever. In addition, the 1970s was a period of growing recession where gains by one more often implied losses by others.

The oil crisis proved to be the watershed with the earlier period of general economic bouyancy and rapidly expanding international trade. Higher prices for oil suddenly threatened the solvency, and sometimes the survival, of crucial sectors in all industrialized countries while making life in the developing ones yet more tenuous. It stultified trade of anything that used large quantities of petroleum, either as a component or just to run the machinery, while spurring efforts to export more to cover the swiftly growing cost of oil imports. There was bound to be a shift in resources from the oil consuming to the oil producing countries. But, through a quirk of fate, the strongest impact for a while was to create friction between the oil consumers.

Well before the oil crisis, the Western economies had begun slowing down, with a few exceptions like Germany, while more had entered an advanced stage of decay like Britain and Italy. Growth rates were falling steadily, industrial production tended to stagnate, consumption was not as strong as before, and there was growing unemployment. Many factories had already closed as markets dried up and Japanese imports gave others the death blow. So it was nothing unusual to continue the same process of laying off workers, cutting production, and if necessary going out of business. This, after all, was the normal reaction in capitalist countries and attempts to hold back, through subsidies or outright nationalization, often only meant throwing good money in after the bad.

Even for industries which might have survived, the situation was very difficult. The oil crisis fed inflation and, to keep things from getting out of hand, most governments tried to control monetary expansion and imposed high interest rates. This made it hard to borrow, hard to invest, and hard to sell products on credit. The other source of funds for business, the stock exchange, was relatively depressed. In an attempt to solve what was regarded as problem number one, namely inflation, many countries encouraged cheap imports. This was a time when tariff reductions that could not be obtained by force previously were often granted freely. Cheaper imports would help the people get by a bit longer and take some pressure off the government.

In Japan, the situation was quite different. First of all, it had been passing through a period of extremely rapid growth, somewhere in the realm of 10%. It had begun to flag recently, but this was hardly noticed. Many companies were still intent on increasing capacity and boosting production. The oil crisis did not stop them. In fact, most Japanese did not realize how great the impact would be until much later. Even after 1973, major projects were launched to establish new shipyards, to expand steelworks, to build additional electronics factories and automobile plants. This was possible because Japanese companies depended on bank loans and they were still available to choice customers. Actually, since the average citizen felt the pinch first, and tended to save more, funds were relatively abundant.

This urge to continue expanding was compounded by government policy. Either the government's economic advisors did not read the situation correctly or the politicians were afraid to admit it. They had remained in power due to Japan's growing prosperity and were doubtlessly worried about how the people would react to economic adversity. Thus, a strong expansionary policy was launched and stimulative measures adopted. Subsidies were provided both for companies in difficulty and those which could move into new growth sectors. There were also special tax write-offs for investments, preferably for energy-conservation and rationalization purposes, but this was usually absorbed in an overall process that increased efficiency and often capacity. In general, massive spending was undertaken to reflate the economy although this had to be done through no less massive deficit financing. Inflation was a serious problem in Japan, too, but the government did not regard it as problem number one or wish to lower trade barriers and encourage imports . . . that would hurt the local producers too much!

In addition to the different historical background and basic attitudes which led to radically different reactions, there were also strong influences from Japan's rather unique capitalist system. And they were perhaps most decisive a bit later on when even the Japanese realized that the oil crisis had changed things fundamentally and went so far as to dub it the oil "shock." Like other companies, Japanese companies had trouble using existing capacity on occasion. But, due to lifetime employment, they could not so readily lay off staff and thus they were forced to keep output high or waste their overhead. They also had to pay back huge loans to the banks. Thus, no matter what happened, they were forced to produce and sell. Since they could hardly sell enough domestically, the only solution remained to boost exports.

The tendency in the West to see the oil crisis as an awesome challenge that could only be overcome by tightening one's belt contrasted with the tendency in Japan to see it as an equally great challenge that could best be met by increasing productivity, cutting costs, and going out to fight harder than ever. It was frequently regarded as one more opportunity to prevail over others. And this view was relatively widespread among dynamic entrepreneurs in more successful developing countries like Korea, Taiwan, Hong Kong and Singapore, which actually showed greater growth during this period than Japan. It is hard to say which group was right. Certainly the latter, if one judges by economic or trade statistics. But the outcome was bound to be an unprecedented trade conflict that might leave them worse off than before.

A look at Japan's trade figures throughout the 1970s will show not an attenuation but an aggravation and even an exaggeration of the earlier trends. While Western exports to Japan rose slowly, and sometimes stagnated, Japanese exports to America and Europe expanded rapidly, sometimes showing incredible spurts. This arose out of continuing exports of some leading products, which gained strength since Japanese companies now had solid bases abroad, and was supplemented by new products that had meanwhile become competitive. Back in Japan, lacking much of a foundation to begin with, few foreign products showed any remarkable growth and some were squeezed out by further successes at import substitution.

In the United States, the bilateral trade gap had narrowed from 1973 to 1975, only to expand again and reach $3.8 billion in 1976. This was a record figure, that is, until the next year, when it hit $7.3 billion, then $10.1 billion for 1978, and an unheard of $13.3 billion for 1981. Europe was doing no better. The European Community had a joint trade deficit of $5.0 billion in 1978, which jumped to $8.8 billion in 1980, and hit $10.3 billion in 1981. This was already painful enough. But the imbalance with Japan was only part of a much larger overall imbalance, due to the huge oil import bill. Japan also had an imbalance much of the time with the oil producers, but this did not console them.[11]

As the trade figures worsened, a more generalized negative reaction set in which has not softened to date. Tension has risen and fallen. At its peak, the situation was likened to a "trade war." Even during a lull it was regarded as preoccupying. It has kept Japan's trading partners pressing for a slowdown or reversal of the trends which made them unhappy. Japan has been little better off since it had to exercise considerable restraint yet could not escape the problems either. Each economic summit conference, called to coordinate policy among the leading industrialized nations, has revived the embarrassing quarrel with Japan for doing so well while its partners suffer.

In May 1977, Prime Minister Takeo Fukuda promised to reduce Japan's trade surplus at the London summit. He had no specific measures in mind, but hinted that the government's efforts at stimulating the economy would eventually lead to an increase in imports. This did not materialize and the American deficit grew sharply. The strongest reaction came from the trade unions, with AFL-CIO president George Meany complaining about damage to American industry from "cutthroat and often illegal foreign competition." Foreign trade is "a guerilla warfare of economics" in which, according to him, the United States "is being ambushed." The convention therefore moved to promote extensive protectionist legislation. Labor's calls found an increasing response in Congress. Even the Carter administration had to admit that. In September, Secretary of Commerce Juanita Kreps warned Japan: "Such protectionist feeling is not part of the U.S. administration's thinking at this time. However, whether we'd be able to continue given the sentiments of many people in our country is a moot point."[12]

Realizing that some gestures had to be made quickly to defuse the situation, the Japanese started putting together a package. But the Fukuda government encountered strong domestic opposition to trade liberalization from industrial and farm circles. And the proposals that Japan's new Minister for External Economic Affairs, Nobuhiko Ushiba, presented in December were far less than desired by Washington. They were promptly rejected by Special Trade Representative Robert Strauss as "insufficient" and "short of what I felt were minimum goals."[13] Nevertheless, a similar package, with some slight improvements, was accepted on January 13, 1978. It consisted of the removal of quota controls on 12 products, increased purchases of beef and citrus fruits and advanced tariff reductions on 124 items (moved up from normal application under the Tokyo Round.)[14]

Two other aspects were entailed. One was to promote sales of American products in Japan. Thus, there was a mutual wish to simplify inspection and remove non-tariff barriers as well as to encourage American imports. To be certain that something did materialize, and quick, the Japanese sent a major "import promotion mission" to the United States to make emergency purchases. This resulted in about $1.9 billion in sales, including food, raw materials, and helicopters. Other suggestions for restoring the balance, whether meant seriously or just to make America happy, were to purchase and then lease American planes or buy large quantities of oil and other raw materials and stockpile them. Few were ever implemented. More promising was that, in October, Commerce Secretary Krebs led a high-powered export promotion mission to Japan "to learn how to sell and what to sell."

The second approach, much heralded in the press, was to

hold the Japanese government to its original promise of seeking 7% growth for fiscal 1978. New measures were adopted to stimulate the economy although the prospects did not look terribly good.

This doubtlessly comforted the United States for a while, since the Japanese were clearly making an effort. But it annoyed the Europeans bitterly since a similar effort was not made for them. In fact, Japan tended to give Europe rather second-rate treatment (perhaps in reciprocity for what it had received) at a time when the European trade imbalance was becoming equally serious. Still, the Japanese realized that if their exports were to grow, it was more likely to be in Europe at this stage. While they may not have cared otherwise, they could no longer neglect the continent or allow grievances to fester.

The strong views in Europe, a mixture of resentment and fear, came as a complete surprise to the Japanese when they first surfaced in October 1976, during the visit of a Keidanren mission led by Toshiwo Doko. The complaints were directed both at surges of Japanese imports and the impenetrability of the Japanese market to European products. Not satisfied with the initial responses from Tokyo, each country and the Community as a whole initiated a diplomatic campaign that was gradually stepped up. A European Parliament resolution asked the Commission to study the difficulties of selling to Japan. EC President Roy Jenkins obtained an agreement to establish a group of experts to study the trade and payments balance. On reaching its arrangement with the United States, Japan promised to take the Community's interests into consideration.

In the end, no similar package of measures was offered to Europe although it enjoyed the general advantages of the American arrangement. Even if there was little interest in the special steps for beef or citrus fruits, the tariff reductions applied to all. As a sop, the Japanese also promised special

Don't worry, we'll take care of Europe, too, Chairman Doko consoles EC Commission President Roy Jenkins.

Credit: European Community

purchasing missions and ultimately Toa Domestic Airline ordered nine Airbus 300 worth $315 million. The Community also seemed to feel that if Japan did stimulate its economy it could become a "locomotive" to help pull the other countries out of the recession.

It did not take long for the various hopes to dissipate. Only a few of the measures could have any short-term effects, such as the special purchases. The tariff reductions would only be felt over many years if they really made it easier to export. Japan did not reach 7% growth, although it did considerably better than the other industrialized nations. Not even the normal trade mechanisms seemed to be functioning any more. Much to the annoyance of Japan, where Prime Minister Fukuda criticized American Treasury Secretary Blumenthal for making comments about an undervaluation of the yen, the yen began rising quite sharply. At one point, it was actually revalued by 30%, showing how far out of line it had been with other currencies. The normal reaction should have been a strong stimulus to imports and an equally strong inhibition of exports. Yet, Japan's trade surpluses kept growing.

This unleashed a new round of complaints. Charles A. Vanik, Chairman of the Trade Subcommittee of the House Ways and Means Committee, formally requested President Carter to impose a 15% surcharge on Japanese goods and his group began an ongoing study of the trade situation. The Europeans were even more irate and there was no end to the warnings by leaders, from heads of state on down, that something must be done. This was echoed by their ambassadors in Tokyo. Such comments included a broad hint from German Economics Minister, Count Lambsdorff, that "trade should not be a one-way street" and a more explicit one from Simone Weil, President of the European Parliament, that the Europeans could not sit idly by "in the face of a one-way strategy created in the name of free trade which is likely to destroy their own economies sector by sector."[15] During his trip to Japan, French President Mitterand intimated that Europe could adopt restrictions if the market were not opened further. British Prime Minister Margaret Thatcher was more outspoken, warning the Japanese that imbalanced trade had persisted long enough and "cannot continue without threatening the breakdown of the free trading system." And the Council of Ministers of the European Community took the unprecedented step of filing a formal complaint in GATT regarding impediments to trade.[16]

But the basic situation never varied. Even when it ran an overall trade deficit (largely with the oil producers) Japan maintained a massive surplus with Europe and the United States. As the surplus rose, tempers mounted among its trading partners and the new Reagan administration suddenly adopted a more aggressive stance. Special Trade Representative Bill Brock became a frequent visitor to Tokyo, repeatedly insisting that the barriers to American products be eliminated. More generally, Commerce Secretary Malcolm Baldrige called for stronger efforts to balance trade. Tired of vague and lofty promises, Washington increasingly demanded the liberalization of specific imports and even the establishment of "import goals" that Japan would commit itself to achieve. In Europe, the situation was even more explosive, a fact discovered by Yoshihiro Inayama when he led a major Keidanren mission there. Echoing the European complaints, he urged the Japanese government to ease the growing trade friction by curbing exports and raising imports.

Under pressure not only from its foreign partners but even, in theory at least, from the local business community, Prime Minister Suzuki gave the trade issue top priority again. The new ministers appointed in a cabinet reshuffle late in 1981 were specifically entrusted with restoring good relations and during 1982 various seemingly spectacular measures were taken. Japan agreed to advance its tariff reductions on 1,653 articles by two years bringing the average tariff rate close to

4%, well below foreign levels. MITI tried to do away with the most visible and annoying non-tariff barriers. Further steps were taken to make emergency imports of strategic metals to be stockpiled. And new projects were mooted for purchasing aircraft and leasing them to airlines in developing countries. No sooner had Yasuhiro Nakasone replaced Suzuki than he promised more "market-opening" measures and, in January 1983, another package of tariff reductions was adopted. Nevertheless, the surpluses kept on accumulating.

Thus, the same scenario was repeated time and again. Gross trade imbalances led to complaints. When they built up sufficiently, the Japanese made concessions. But they were never enough to change things dramatically and a further round of complaints, warnings and gestures was initiated. The persistent failures should have led to renewed efforts to understand why the problems remained so intractable. Instead, while the frustration grew and accusations were traded—Japan for not playing fair, Europe and America for not trying hard enough—the same old measures were tried another time in the hope that some day they might work. When they failed yet again, the threat of protectionism was invoked.

NOTES

1. See Jon Woronoff, *Hong Kong: Capitalist Paradise.*
2. See I. M. Destler, *The Textile Wrangle.*
3. *Japan Times*, April 12, 1977.
4. *Yomiuri*, May 22, 1977.
5. *Asian Wall Street Journal*, January 11, 1979.
6. *Japan Times*, October 8, 1977.
7. *Yomiuri*, October 29, 1977.
8. *Asahi Evening News*, September 20 & November 1, 1977.
9. See Masamichi Hanabusa, *Trade Problems between Japan and Western Europe.*
10. It is an open secret that most shipyards did not hesitate to accept orders as much as 20% under cost during the recession.

11. Figures of the Japanese Ministry of Finance. They differ somewhat from the MITI figures and more so from the American and European Community figures.
12. *Yomiuri*, December 10, 1977 and *Asahi Evening News*, September 28, 1977.
13. *Japan Times*, December 14, 1977.
14. See article on the 1977 crisis in William Barnds, *Japan and the United States: Challenges & Opportunities*, pp. 190–230.
15. *Japan Times*, April 29, 1981 & September 22, 1982.
16. See the decision of March 22, 1982 and the note of April 7, 1982.

5
The Great Automobile Conflict

They'll Never Make Cars

The automobile industry in Japan has a slightly different background from other sectors, for it was not originally chosen as a growth field to be strongly promoted. The planners, and especially he Bank of Japan, did not want to squander Japan's precious and then very scant foreign exchange and other resources on making automobiles. This could never be done as efficiently as in America, they argued. The Ministry of International Trade and Industry tended to disagree, but it had other things to worry about and could not offer much support in the early years. So, the automakers had to go ahead on their own, despite contrary views and mild disapproval of higher political and bureaucratic spheres.

Those first years were certainly difficult ones. Some of the companies that had made automobiles and trucks (as well as tanks and armored cars) during the war were quickly revived and converted to the peacetime economy. Toyota was back in business already by 1946 and, unlike the others, tried to go pretty much its own way with a bit of technical advice from Ford. Nissan went into a tie-up with Austin, Hino with Renault, and Isuzu with Rootes. Slowly but surely they increased production and improved their technology.

Although they had not been picked among the first batch of industries to be promoted, they were eventually supported by the standard machinery. They also found it relatively easy to obtain bank credit. By 1955, MITI decided the time had come to launch a "people's car" concept that would bring prices down to accessible levels and, as they actually did fall, production rose tremendously. By 1962, the industry was churning out nearly one million cars, trucks and buses a year. By 1970, the figure hit five million.

Even if promotion by the authorities was relatively moderate, partly because the automakers seemed to be doing quite nicely on their own, one could hardly say the same thing about protection. The automobile industry was regarded as a crucial sector that had to be defended from foreign takeovers or direct competition. Before the war, Ford and GM assembly operations represented more than 80% of domestic sales. But the nationalist regime squeezed them out. And, after the war, it was hard to invest. Until just recently, there remained severe limits on investment in the sector or purchase of shares in Japanese companies. Most tie-ups were only for technology. Only a few went further, with smaller or newer firms. Chrysler acquired 15% ownership of Mitsubishi Motors, Ford 25% of Toyo Kogyo, and GM a larger 34% share of Isuzu. But, this never really served as a foothold in the Japanese market and the partners tended to become suppliers.

The industry was also protected from imports. During the 1950s, they were strictly forbidden. Not until 1960 was it possible to import trucks and, in 1965, passenger cars. Yet, even then there were substantial tariffs which were only lowered slowly and grudgingly (much later than in Europe). Tariffs were 40% for small passenger cars and 28% for large passenger cars until 1968, then dropping a few percent at a time until they reached 6.8% in 1978. Finally, subject to considerable pressure in that year, it was decided to eliminate tariffs altogether.

Thus, by the early 1980s, Japan could boast—and did so quite loudly—that it had no automobile and truck tariffs while other nations did. For, the level was still 2.9% for passenger cars and 25% (4% if incompletely assembled) for trucks in the United States and 10.8% for passenger cars and 11% and 22% for small and large trucks in Europe. It did not take the Japanese long to forget the very tenacious tradition of protectionism which had allowed their industry to grow from infant to adult behind nearly impregnable walls. Indeed, quotas were only eliminated when Japan's production had almost caught up with Germany's and by the time the tariff was dropped Japan was not far behind the United States.

Meanwhile, behind the formal barriers that came down, a maze of non-tariff barriers had sprung up and become increasingly visible. One was a commodity tax of 17.5% and 22.5% (formerly 30% and 40%), depending on size, with the latter figure covering the larger foreign makes. It was levied on all cars, but applied to Japanese cars on the basis of ex-factory prices and foreign cars CIF, i.e. after adding the transport and insurance costs entailed in getting them to Japan. There was also an annual road tax, which was far from petty ($366 on Mercedes 450 and $613 on Pontiac Firebird against $125 on Toyota Corolla). Larger cars were obviously taxed more, substantially more, and alas most foreign imports were large.

There was also considerable trouble with tests of one sort or another. Not only were they extremely stringent, but even those that had already been passed in the home country had to be repeated in Japan since for some time the government refused to accept the results or send inspectors abroad. Sometimes, specific parts were rejected for rather unconvincing reasons and had to be replaced in order to sell the car. Japan's emission standards, the strictest in the world, almost became an absolute barrier to entry by most cars until the government graciously exempted imports temporarily. But the biggest headache arose from the tendency to grant only type notification to most foreign models which made it necessary to carry out an individual examination of every single car in special inspection centers.[1]

As if these handicaps were not enough, there was a series of other problems that added to price further. Various modifications had to be made in many models, then certain extras had to be added since they had become almost standard options, and obviously the transport and handling costs were higher due to the small numbers shipped. But this was nothing compared to the costs deriving from limited sales. Sales are very labor intensive in Japan, usually involving door-to-door salesmen, and since fewer foreign cars were sold by each salesman or each dealership, the margins had to be substantially larger. What with one thing and another, foreign cars always ended up in the higher price categories. Even the modest Volkswagen Golf sold for 40% more while a flashy American sedan was easily 100% or more above what it sold for back home.

And it was still necessary to sell them. Having arrived very late on the scene and selling small numbers, most foreign manufacturers found the cost of setting up their own distribution network prohibitive. The cost of obtaining land in the metropolitan areas where most sales were made was incredible, if good spots could be found at all. The actual sales operation often had to be financed directly by them. There were no floating dealers or non-exclusive outlets to speak of. So most worked through one agent or another, sometimes even another Japanese maker. Or they went to Yanase Motors, which handled many of the imports including Volkswagen, Mercedes and General Motors. Only Ford set up its own operations.

But this left them in a very weak position in Japan's market. Over the years, most customers had already purchased a car and tended to show some loyalty, to say nothing of the fact that the salesman kept up relations. So, most replacement sales went to the Japanese companies as well. They also had the biggest networks of dealers, Toyota and Nissan possessing nearly 4,000 distribution points each while even a smaller firm like Honda had 700. Then came the backup of authorized service stations throughout the country. Compared to this, Yanase only had some 180 sales outlets, Ford Japan about 40, and the others yet less.

To say that the foreign makers did not try would be a bit much. Admittedly, the American gas-guzzlers were hardly adapted to Japan's roads, which did not keep them from being bought as a status symbol by those who could afford it. That the foreign makers did not build cars to meet the demand can be explained by the small sales turnover. And this in turn by the exorbitant prices, for part of which they had no responsibility. The result was a vicious circle that was hard to break. But, even when a car was perfectly suited to Japan's needs, highly popular among the younger generation, and reasonably priced in the country of origin—such as the Volkswagen or smaller British cars—they still could not get into the market.

Thus, after considerable efforts and tremendous amounts spent on distribution and publicity, foreign cars never really got moving. In fact, the market share for all foreign cars put together never rose above 2%, and this for about twenty different makers. Nor was there any trend to indicate a potential rise in the future. Rather, when the Japanese market became saturated, the sales of foreign cars dipped yet further, registering only some 38,000 in 1981, far below the peak of 60,000 in 1979 and a mere 1% of the total.

Whether it was a lack of effort or hidden barriers, the stituation was deplorable and increasingly attracted the ire of both the foreign automakers and their respective governments. They felt that either no breakthrough would be possible, or it was too costly to attempt, and they were not happy about it. If, after small cars are introduced in the United States and other models become relatively competitive, the situation does not change, then a fresh and perhaps nastier bout of complaints about being kept out is bound to occur.

This nearly complete failure to penetrate the Japanese market not only exasperated the foreign producers, it put them at a terrible disadvantage. For this left the Japanese with an ample market on which they could grow, testing successive models until they acquired the skill to produce cars that could sell anywhere while building ever bigger, more modern facilities to attain incredible economies of scale. Since they had also begun exporting and were cutting into the sales of their competitors, this shifted the balance yet further and deprived the foreign makers of their own economies of scale.

Japan's export growth was both steady and rapid. The Japanese did not encounter many serious impediments to launching their sales abroad. Of course, they had the usual problems of meeting basic standards, going through the formalities, and obtaining a favorable reputation for their products. In the early years, Japanese cars were not of very good quality, but they were cheap and this made the difference. It was also necessary to get acquainted with a broad range of markets and master the customs and languages of each. On occasion, they also had to surmount tariff barriers or limit sales due to quotas. But this did not really stop them.

With the whole world to choose from, the Japanese naturally began with the easiest markets. These were often third countries with no automobile industry to protect and, if developing countries, quite pleased to obtain cars at a reasonable price. The major market was, of course, the United States. Then they became interested in various European markets. Although they all had tariffs, they were quite minimal, having fallen to a mere 6% in the United States and 11% in the European Community already by the late 1960s. Behind the visible barriers there were rather few non-tariff barriers in the advanced world. In developing countries, however, it was often necessary to undertake assembly locally.

When it came to business customs and cultural practices,

the Japanese were certainly well ahead. There was no trouble obtaining dealers even in the early years and more recently the Japanese have been flooded with offers from dealers who wanted to drop their former franchise. By 1980, Toyota and Nissan alone had over 1,100 dealerships each while all imported car companies had over 135,000 employees or dealers and distributors in the United States alone. It could hardly be said that there were many hang-ups with the customers about buying local products only. Whether the Japanese cars sold on price, as in the early days, or on quality, later on, there were always buyers.

This expansion and penetration was hardly left to chance. The Japanese head office usually kept a very close watch on sales progress and the sales division drew up neat charts

Even the Japanese had to admit that their first automobile exports were nothing to rave about.

Credit: Toyota

showing sales broken down by country, even local market, and by type or model. Then they would compare their share with that of Japanese competitors and other foreign makers. If they won as much as one percent, they were jubilant. If they lost as little as one percent, especially to another Japanese maker, they were furious and would launch vigorous campaigns to catch up, warning the local representatives and dealers in so doing that the fate of the company (and perhaps their own as well) was at stake. With this will, and using standard tactics, they managed to increase sales and market share.

Over the years, export sales kept on rising at a terrific pace. As early as the 1950s, the Japanese had begun exporting vehicles. By the late 1960s, annual exports approached the one million mark and, by the late 1970s, it passed four million. And they looked forward to doing much better during the 1980s. By then, more than half the total vehicle production was exported in assembled or knocked-down form. While exports represented about 55% of sales for Toyota and Nissan, it reached 60% for Toyo Kogyo and nearly 70% for Honda. All in all, automobile exports amounted to some 20% of Japan's total exports.

Moreover, the export network spread to cover the globe with sales on every continent and even in the Soviet bloc and China. North America remained the foundation, the United States alone having 40% of the total, but sales in Europe represented a good 20%, and even Africa came in for 5%. What was more impressive was that these sales were often very much in depth as Japanese makers managed to snap up ever greater market shares. . . as we shall see.

Much of this growth was well-deserved. The Japanese had done their best to solve the quality problems that dogged them at first. In fact, by introducing strict inspections and then quality control work among the personnel as well, they developed an exceptional mastery of quality as the results showed. They also improved their styling over the years. More decisive was the rise in productivity. Part of this came from efforts to use their personnel better and more intelligently. But the bulk came from introducing new machinery and techniques and, most recently, by replacing people with robots. The policy of building new plants and assembly lines contributed to raising efficiency. The increasing size of their units at the same time also added to economies of scale and price competitiveness.

But they were probably aided as much or more by the decline noted among some of their foreign competitors, less the Germans or Swedes than the British, Italians and Americans. There was inadequate concern with quality and a general sloppiness in procedures. Growing antagonism between management and labor resulted in the sort of atmosphere that encouraged workers to do a particularly poor job. . . just to get back. Workers were frequently less trained, and sometimes even poorly educated, while management failed to make up for this by encouraging improvement on the job. Yet, labor costs abroad remained higher than in Japan throughout most of the period and, even as Japan caught up, American or European autoworkers stayed ahead due to demands for higher wages and fringe benefits that were sometimes well above the national average. When strikes and other friction were added to this, it was not hard for Japan to be competitive.

Placing the whole blame on labor, however, is patently unfair. Management was as much at fault for not keeping up with the competitors. Funds were siphoned off not only for high salaries but sky-high bonuses for top management, which was not always the wisest or most purposeful. Profits were made regularly, keeping the stockholders and board happppy, and fat dividends were paid out even in lean years. But not enough funds were channeled back into the company to buy new machinery or renovate plants. Such improvements were made unlikelier by the general economic situation which was hardly bouyant, and thus less congenial for major investments that would not realize their full potential for a long time. More often than not, the automakers were cutting back on production and closing plants, thereby decreasing any economies of scale and hastening their own decline.

Despite this, many of the automobile companies could have gotten by and perhaps rebounded by making the necessary changes on time. There were periodic reshuffles of management and sometimes a good man came out on top. Some trade unions admitted the need for discipline and went into reasonably stable arrangements that at least avoided strikes, even if they did not put a lid on excessive wage hikes. A number of excellent and very successful models were introduced. But there was no overall plan to meet the Japanese head-on and fight to defend what markets one had, let alone to launch sales seriously in the Japanese market and weaken its home base. This was partly because the Japanese market was first closed, then too tough, but more so because there were such attractive and open markets nearer at hand, in Europe, America or some developing countries.

The troubles were only compounded where complacency arose. The American Big Three, General Motors, Ford and Chrysler, were still formidable companies and they could have moved back into the forefront of progress with ease. . . if they tried. Instead, they continued producing the same old models, large, comfortable, and costly ones they had become famous for. This brought in much more money for much less work. But it left an edge for foreign makers, Japanese and Europeans, to begin selling smaller, cheaper and more fuel-efficient cars. Even after the first oil crisis, they did not realize that this last aspect was crucial and it was not until the second oil crisis, in 1979, that they admitted that fuel-efficiency had to be a significant feature of any car.

In all fairness to them, this mistake was not only the fault of the automakers, it was shared by the consumers and the government. American cars, big, heavy, and gas guzzlers that they were, still made sense in a country with plenty of room, vast and well-developed highway networks, and cheap oil. That is why the public bought them year in and year out— until the oil prices skyrocketed and people actually had to wait in line. Once the American public realized its mistake, this became a foolish decision for the American makers as well. As for Japan, much of the merit of making small cars goes not to the ingeniousness of its managers but the simple fact that roads are narrow, few houses have much room for parking, and gas has always been much more expensive. Still, smart or not, this gave the Japanese a tremendous edge over the Americans.

However, there is one further explanation to Japan's success with automobile exports, one that is somewhat less flattering. For, although they were extremely good at pushing sales, they were quite poor at forecasting demand on their various markets. When it came to determining next year's production or deciding on even more vital matters like when to construct a new plant, they tended to let their optimism get out of control. They would use earlier growth figures as an indication of future sales and make highly ambitious projections. They tended to forget, for example, that like every other market the automobile market also matures as more people own a car and replacement purchases are slower. Thus, they were amazed to find that domestic sales remained stagnant while production capacity rose. The obvious solution was to sell more abroad.

The only hitch was that foreign markets were even more congested, since they were older and the recession had struck them yet harder. In addition, any advance by Japanese makers would imply a retreat by foreign makers, something they would resist very strongly. Yet, the Japanese never thought of holding down or cutting back on production as an alternative.

With their fine modern plants and nearly permanent labor force, they simply had to sell whatever they produced. So, they launched more aggressive sales campaigns, using high pressure salesmanship and offering exceptional prices to the customers and incentives to the dealers. They were willing to accept the tightest profit margin. . . and sometimes less. This made the Japanese more dangerous competitors in bad times than in good and that was when they tended to boost market share most.

Small Car War

Japanese imported cars had been entering the United States ever since the late 1950s. At first they were laughed off as small, uncomfortable or poorly made. But quality improved while price only went up moderately and they carved out a growing share of the market. Yet, by the early 1970s, they had failed to reach 10% of total sales and actually turned down slightly during the decade. In fact, in 1979, there were thousands of unsold Japanese cars sitting at the docks. That may explain why the American automakers regarded them as annoying, bothersome, but not a vital threat. Then, after the "second" oil crisis, the oil price shot up again and fuel-efficiency made a monumental difference. Sales of Japanese cars boomed.

This was enough to cause more than just annoyance and was bound to bring about serious friction. However, looking at the situation from the United States, there was no reason to expect a really bitter conflict. Surveying the situation in Japan, on the other hand, it was obvious that something was afoot. And it was not an export campaign like any other. The Japanese automakers clearly realized that 1980 would be a decisive year. It was the very last chance they would have to sell small cars in America in competition against big cars, a competition they could win hands down. In the future, every newspaper told them, the American manufacturers would be turning out small cars as well, perhaps not as good or cheap (although, who knows?), but certainly more of a match.

That it was more than just business as usual should have been obvious from the feverish preparations of the Japanese automakers, gearing up production and setting higher sales targets than ever. In addition, there was much talk of a "small car war" in the press. The main source of such rumblings was Toyota. At a mammoth convention of American dealers, specially flown over to Tokyo, Toyota's top management stressed that the coming year would be crucial. Either the company must advance resolutely. . . or be forced back. Dealers were told to go out and fight for market share and, to encourage them, prices were kept down while commissions were kept up. Nissan, well aware of what Toyota was doing, harangued its dealers, too. And the lesser makers, Isuzu, Honda and Toyo Kogyo, tried to take advantage of the situation by pushing their yet smaller small cars.

If there was to be a war (although an undeclared one as yet), the automakers were going to fight it according to the finest traditions of Japanese warfare. First, they began moving the holdovers on the docks at the best possible price. Then they started shipping in the new models, pushing hard on the publicity and even offering discounts. As sales picked up, the flow of imports rose apace. The Japanese, so poor at cutting back, had no trouble increasing production in short order. They simply ran their plants more hours a day and more days a week, adding an extra shift and making workers put in more overtime. The workers could hardly say no, since they were wed to the company. And they had gone into overtime so often that it was almost second nature. As their spirits came back, the managers again thought of opening more plants to really expand operations.

Taking advantage of an exceptional market situation, namely the tremendous urge for more fuel-efficient cars as quickly as possible, the Japanese makers did well. Despite a recession, or perhaps because of it, they found the American public eager to buy. It did not take long for the level of exports to rise sharply over the previous year and reach what was termed "torrential" amounts. The Japanese market share in 1979 had been nearly 17%, by mid-1980 it peaked at about 24%, and for the whole year it managed to show over 21%.

The American manufacturers did not quite know what to make of this incredible surge in imports. It was not only because they were stunned by the onslaught. They simply could not understand why the Japanese were making such frantic efforts to sell more if this did not bring some palpable gain. For, the Japanese cars were being sold at low prices, on very tight profit margins, and these were only increased reluctantly and almost grudgingly due to an appreciation of the yen. The Japanese could have made much bigger profits by boosting prices and selling less cars. But they were clearly intent on conquering market share.

Although their American competitors did not fully grasp the advantages of winning market share, it soon became crystal clear what the disadvantages of losing market share could be, especially on a market that was shrinking. For, while Japanese sales rose substantially and other exporters made lesser gains, the Americans were obviously forced back. Their sales were hurt (down 35% by mid-year) and profits were off due to the smaller number of sales. They were also squeezed because it was particularly difficult for them to raise prices at a time when Japanese cars were so popular and still selling for much less. From expectations of reasonable profits, the automakers began fearing serious losses.

This could be disastrous for the American makers since the industry was already in difficult straits. The smaller companies had been weakened most and American Motors had to be bailed out by further investment from Renault. Chrysler was threatened with collapse and could only be rescued at the last minute. Even then, it was far from certain whether it would recover and survive. Only Ford and General Motors were relatively healthy and could be expected to get back on their feet as soon as they began producing their own compact cars. It was generally felt that they would reverse the situation once GM's J-car, Ford's world cars, and Chrysler's K-car came out.

At this point, the other aspect of the export campaign began to register in some minds, although still very few. It was obvious to the Japanese automakers that they could not really take on Ford or General Motors in a broad and protracted struggle. During a war of attrition, the American giants had vast resources to fall back on. The best thing was to get in there quick and sell what they could, taking over market share and hoping to hold on to it later as the people got to know their cars. It was uncertain just how much loyalty could be expected of American customers, but at least any sales were to the good.

But that was only a short-term gain. What would help most in the long run was knocking out American car sales at a crucial time, just when the American makers were preparing to retool. For, they could only retool and fight back if they had enough profits to finance the operation. Loss of sales, loss of profits, meant that the American counter-offensive would be slowed down leaving the Japanese more time to prepare for a second round, one which they hoped to win by increasing quality and productivity with yet higher degrees of automation and robotization.

Whether or not this strategy was grasped, the American automobile industry soon realized it was in deep trouble. As sales fell, the automakers had to cut back on production and close down some of their plants. More workers were laid off with little hope of return. Early in the year, the United Auto Workers gave a figure of 200,000 unemployed in the sector, and by year's end it grew to 300,000 or about 40% of the industry's work force. The crisis in the automobile industry naturally had an impact on other sectors, including a slump in the steel industry, sales of tires and thus rubber, troubles for the various suppliers and also quite ordinary service firms and just plain grocery stores that lived off the workers.

Although the industry was in bad shape, there was extreme reluctance among the majors to speak up at first. After all, Ford did much of its business abroad and Chrysler sold Mitsubishi models under its own name while GM was supplied by Isuzu. Aside from the issue of free trade, they did not want to admit that they were hurting enough to call for Japanese restraint. The Carter administration stuck to high principles and meek requests for understanding. So, the only ones to take a stand at first were the unions. In a highly unprecedented gesture, UAW President Doug Fraser took their case to Japan. He was indeed a strange apparition there, since it was not very usual for a mere trade unionist to speak frankly to industry and government officials. And what he told them was unpalatable: either slow down exports to the United States or invest in production there, and preferably do both.

Whilst the Japanese did not pay much attention to Fraser when he visited them, they certainly perked up their ears after he got back home and started expanding the campaign. He made it known to Congressmen in depressed areas that they might be in trouble if they did not take action to defend the workers. Such warnings were particularly effective in an election year and many candidates declared their support for some sort of restrictions on Japanese imports. Even President Carter came out of his corner with token support. And his opponent, Ronald Reagan, although hardly a friend of the unions, indicated that it would be proper for the government to "convince the Japanese that. . . for their own best interest, the deluge of their cars into the United States must be slowed while our industry gets back on its feet."[2]

By fall, the political situation was becoming nasty and the Japanese automakers, which had not expected this sort of a reaction, were a bit worried. Moreover, the American market itself had grown rather sluggish and it was uncertain how much more could be sold. Thus, with tremendous production efforts going on back home, the Japanese began prospecting for new markets where they could expand exports. This quest was given greater urgency by the fact that domestic sales had slumped seriously. Part of the loss was made up for by sales to Canada, Australia, and the Middle East. But the only major markets in sight were in Europe.

So, while exports continued to flow all around, there were sudden and rather sharp surges in some European countries. Not in all, of course. In Italy, the Japanese had for the longest time been limited to minimal sales, a mere 2,200 units per year. In France, there was an informal but very strict rule imposed through the dealers that sales should not exceed 3%. In Britain, a gentleman's agreement set the ceiling at 10%. Nevertheless, exports there gradually approached the 12% mark. And a strong offensive was launched against certain countries that were relatively open. Belgium, without a major company of its own, soon saw the Japanese share rise above 25%. In Denmark and Ireland, it was 30%. Germany, which had hitherto resisted penetration through the efforts of its own makers, was amazed to find the Japanese market share had nearly doubled.

Thus, within the year, the Japanese had boosted their sales abroad tremendously (by no less than 30%). They had increased market share in just about every country in the world. And they had raised the level of exports to 6 million cars and trucks. This represented over half of total production, which itself had risen to an unprecedented 11 million. Since production had fallen in most other countries, this was an amazing accomplishment which finally hoisted Japan to the top in terms of the number of vehicles produced. At the

Ten million exports later, Toyota's Seisi Kato and
Eiji Toyoda have reasons to celebrate.

Credit: Toyota

same time, Toyota climbed into second position among the world's makers, just behind General Motors, and Nissan was in third position, ahead of Ford.

This made 1980 a high point in the rise of Japan's automobile industry. But it was also the year in which its automakers had wrecked havoc among the American and European competitors and thereby created serious economic friction and growing anger in political circles. It antagonized important segments of public opinion and created a mood that was most unfortunate. So the year will also go down in history as the one in which the Japanese almost knowingly triggered one of the biggest trade conflicts the world had seen thus far.

Forcing A Settlment

By late 1980, and more acutely 1981, it was impossible to deny the existence of a major trade conflict. Moreover, from a purely commercial matter it had quickly become a political issue that aroused strong emotions and could hardly be dealt with coolly or rationally. Nevertheless, there was still tremendous uncertainty about how to act. The uncertainty was revealed not only by the sharply contrasting positions of the various countries but also major divergencies within each.

The biggest confusion appeared in the United States, which bore the brunt of the export offensive yet failed to react with any determination or speed. This was due to rather sharp differences of opinion. There was no doubt that the United Auto Workers and related unions were in favor of restricting imports. Back in February 1980, Fraser had warned the Japanese that calls for legislation limiting imports of their cars "could snowball very rapidly." To avoid this, he suggested that the Japanese automakers voluntarily curb their exports to the 1977–78 level of 1.5 million units and that the two governments conclude an orderly marketing agreement.[3]

But the Japanese showed no haste, and thus Fraser pushed the campaign further. He urged the Congressmen most concerned to move legislation and asked the House Ways and Means Trade Subcommittee to "send the Japanese an unambiguous message—that a protectionist tide is growing in this country." The Subcommittee looked into the matter seriously and dispatched its own mission to Japan to confer with the government and automakers. Its Chairman, Charles A. Vanik of Ohio, joined Fraser in calling on Japanese automakers to restrict exports and build more plants in the United States. "No nation allows vital industries to be destroyed by temporary surges of imports," he insisted. "I suggest in the strongest terms possible that the Japanese not overwhelm our industry, but rather show restraint."[4] In June, the Senate adopted a resolution by 90 to 4 asking the Carter administration to review its import policies as a "signal" to Japan.

But these arguments did not ride with all Americans, perhaps not even with a majority of them. Many Congressmen were not from affected states, and were thus under no pressure. In some cases, they were from states that lived off exports or had long been champions of free trade. They saw any formal breach of this policy as a fateful step toward protectionism, not only in America but worldwide, and they had no trouble in evoking the perils the world had faced in the earlier depression. Both Presidents, Carter and later Reagan, pledged to maintain free trade and were very concerned about potential retaliation.

The official views on automobile imports were expressed by their Special Trade Representatives in similar terms. "We do not feel it would be in the interest of the American consumer to limit the availability of a product they want," according to Reubin Askew, and "I don't think it would be helpful at all to pass laws restricting imports in this particular area," according to William Brock.[5]

The most active opponents, however, were the numerous consumer movements that praised the superior performance of Japanese cars or supported imports to keep prices down and environmentalist groups which stressed the improved antipollution devices. At first, not too many listened. Then, as the oil prices rose, even affluent Americans were increasingly eager to buy fuel-efficient cars and some were in too much of a rush to wait for American producers to make them. Although they thought primarily of saving money, they also raised this to the level of principles, claiming it was their duty to buy quality cars. Meanwhile, they took great pleasure in knocking the automobile companies and the autoworkers for bringing them to such a pass.

The press also played a prominent role in blocking any protectionist moves. This it did largely to defend the principle of free trade and look after the consumers' interests. On occasion, it also showed a preference not only for Japanese cars but also Japanese management and labor, for having shown Americans what cooperation and discipline mean. The attitude toward American business and labor was the reverse—since the foolish mistakes and inefficiency were their fault, they did not deserve any assistance. Thus, a leading newspaper like *The New York Times* could proudly recite platitudes like "The catch in any kind of restriction. . . is that the industry's gain would be the consumer's loss." And *The Wall Street Journal*, without thinking of what this would mean in practice, could argue: "Breathing room is just what the U.S. auto companies don't need if they're to compete successfully in the markets of the future." They must learn to compete, as the Japanese had done, and "to deny GM, Ford and Chrysler a similar trial by fire is to limit their competitive opportunities."[6]

To this were added many academics, economists and liberals of one complexion or another. With the "people," they formed a loose coalition for the consumer and against

American big business, big labor and big government. In so doing, they supported Japanese products that resulted from the closest collusion between big business, big labor and big government in the world. But this didn't really disturb them, if they actually knew enough about Japan or economics to realize, for the enemy was still within rather than without.

Since no legislation could be adopted quickly, and the President would not act, the only way of clearing up the matter was to petition the International Trade Commission for redress. If the ITC should determine that imports of a particular product, automobiles in this case, had increased significantly and, in so doing, caused serious damage to the same industry in America, it could take measures to restrict imports such as the tariffs and quotas proposed by the UAW and Ford. That there had been lasting and significant increases in imports was obvious. So the question it had to decide was whether this was a "substantial cause" of injury to the American automobile industry.

The United Auto Workers, pleading the loss of some 300,000 jobs, asked for assistance. Ford and Chrysler also laid bare the difficulties of the industry. But General Motors failed to join them and added that imports were not the major cause of damage. For their part, the Japanese makers stressed that far more damage had been caused by structural changes in the industry, namely the switch to small, fuel-efficient cars and the general recession which made it harder to sell cars. There was also much emphasis on the cost of fuel needed if less fuel-efficient cars were purchased instead of imports. The Federal Trade Commission itself took a stand against import controls insisting that tariffs would raise the cost of imported cars, costing the consumer considerable sums, without restoring more than 32,000 jobs.

In November, the ITC ruled, by a 3 to 2 vote, that there was no case for recommending import relief. Although admitting that the American auto industry was suffering serious injury, it did not feel that foreign imports were the primary cause. This was due far more, in its view, to the public's shift from larger to small, fuel-efficient cars and the fact that fewer cars were being sold. That position was strongly rejected by the UAW and Ford as well as by their backers in Congress, who promised to present strong legislation for restrictions. This they promptly did and, after Reagan's election, various bills were brought before Congress. The most significant was the Danforth-Bentsen Bill urging that imports be held down to 1.5 million cars for three years. Other Congressmen spoke of reducing the level to 1.2 million and having relief last as much as five years.

The Japanese were considerably more united. Basically, just about everybody agreed with the automakers that they were producing a better product, cheaper, and that the Americans and others wanted to buy it. This was no reason to penalize them or Japan. The message was propagated by the automakers themselves, by Diet members and other politicians, by the unions and workers, and in the press. There was much talk of making Japan a "scapegoat" for the failures of its competitors. Yet, even assuming this argumentation was entirely true, it did not really solve the problem that arose. For, it was no longer a question of whether Japan made better cars but how to react to the growing protectionist sentiment in its major markets.

On this point, there was considerably more divergence. The automakers stubbornly insisted that there be no restrictions whatsoever and periodically promised to show restraint. However, since they never did, the conflict got worse. This became a constant source of embarrassment and concern for the Japanese government which realized just how dependent it was on continued good relations with America. In an interview with the *Los Angeles Times*, Prime Minister Suzuki conceded that, "Looking at it from a long-range point of view, Japan must avoid having its auto exports to the United States occur like a torrential deluge that would cause damage and have a bad effect upon American automobile workers and workers in related industries. Japan, I feel, must improve this situation as promptly as possible." And, he hastened to add, "The Japanese auto industry also, from a long-range perspective, realized that this must be done."[7]

These comments were not made solely to calm mounting criticism in the United States. There were many government leaders working actively for a solution. Foremost was the Special Trade Negotiator Saburo Okita. The Foreign Ministry was also plugging for an early end to the matter. Although MITI may have been on the automakers' side in principle, it realized that if the conflict continued it could also spread to other sectors and affect all of Japan's trade. So, MITI also joined those trying to find some compromise. Even top representatives of business, including Keidanren's past and present presidents, Toshiwo Doko and Yoshihiro Inayama, urged the automakers to grant concessions.

Foreigners thoroughly versed in the pseudoscience of Japanology assumed that business and government would promptly close ranks and seek a mutually beneficial settlement. Alas, that was not so easy. As early as Fraser's visit, MITI began talking of asking for "voluntary restraint" and none other than Eiji Toyoda promised that his company would hold down auto exports to the previous year's level.[8] A few months later, nothing had been done, and MITI spoke of the need to export cars in a "strictly orderly manner" and promised to call for "disciplined behavior" by the automakers, if need be by imposing administrative guidance. MITI Vice Minister for International Affairs, Naohiro Amaya, the man most directly involved in settling the conflict, warned that "politically inflammable gas" was building up in the United States and took the automakers to task for being inconsiderate by exporting their cars "like torrential rains."[9]

None of this seemed to faze the automakers. They increased

exports at will, vying with one another (and the Americans as well) in boosting sales, although occasionally saying that exports would slow down or they would exercise restraint. When a firm commitment was demanded, they found more than enough reasons to put one off. First, they insisted it would be unwise to restrain exports while the ITC was examining the case, since this might be construed as an admission that they were exporting too much. Then they objected that even voluntary restraint would be a violation of the American antitrust laws. Later on, they pleaded that exports would slow down naturally as the market became saturated and that American sales would rise quickly once the new compact cars were introduced. Time would settle everything and hasty action would be most unwise.

The automakers not only managed to put off a decision throughout the year, they were still arguing for patience in the spring of 1981. At that late date, Nissan's President Takashi Ishihara pleaded that this was no time to show voluntary restraint and that it was best to adopt a wait-and-see attitude until next September. When the American government issued a rehabilitation plan for the automobile industry, Toyota's Eiji Toyoda deemed it inadequate and indicated that the Japanese should not be expected to curb exports before the United States took definite steps to solve its own problems. He criticized the Japanese government for "jumping the gun." "All this talk about doing this and that about the automobile issue by such-and-such a date is like arguing that we must extinguish a fire when the fire hasn't even started yet."[10] Yet, by then Congress was busily debating whether imports should not be severely restricted. On that particular, the automakers finally gave an opinion. Restrictions were "out of the question" and under no conditions would they accept to cut exports below 1.8 million, just slightly under the 1980 level.

This action seemed to surprise the American government and dismay the Japanese government, but it now appeared quite natural to Doug Fraser. "Every time there is discussion in this country relative to trade. . . they will make noises as if they are going to agree to voluntary restraints." And he was skeptical that they would actually limit exports "unless this government holds their feet to the fire." But the American government did not seem ready to go quite that far. According to Labor Secretary Donovan, "I can say categorically no, the Reagan administration will not put import restrictions on autos." Of course, he did add that the Japanese "should, in their long-term interest, do just that and I believe they will." As for the specific level, the best Commerce Secretary Baldrige could do was mumble, "If it is truly voluntary, we would accept any number they proposed."[11]

Thus, the conflict could well have ended in the worst possible way, namely by adoption of legislation imposing sharp and strict limits which the president might have trouble rejecting. This would severely weaken America's free trade stance, undermine Japan's trade position and, be it noted in passing, cut down Japan's automobile exports to the point that the automakers would be in serious trouble. But the tug-of-war within Japan, Inc., and between the allies, was finally concluded due to an almost fortuitous event. Zenko Suzuki was scheduled to visit Washington in mid-May and his government did not want the trade issue to cloud the occasion. The automakers were also worried that while there, and under American pressure, the prime minister might accept bigger concessions than they were willing to make.

In a last minute effort to solve the dispute, the American STR Bill Brock flew to Tokyo and negotiated tightly with MITI Minister Rokusuke Tanaka and Vice Minister Amaya. And they in turn haggled over the exact figures with the automakers. The first compromise proved unacceptable and the negotiations continued. Finally, on May 1, Japan agreed to restrict its automobile exports "voluntarily." The level was set at 1.68 million units for fiscal 1981, down 7.7% from the year before. This figure was then extended for a second year and, since the American automobile market did not recover, a third. There was even talk of imposing a fourth year of restraint, but the Japanese automakers seemed unlikely to accept it. Since the action was being taken through voluntary measures, imposed by Japanese administrative guidance, the American antitrust regulations would not apply.[12]

This agreement, however, only aggravated a series of other trade conflicts the Japanese had preferred to regard as nonexistent. As was mentioned, the export campaign had spread and a number of other countries were also struck by sudden influxes of Japanese cars. This included Canada, Australia, and even places like Argentina. But the major problems were in Europe, among countries like Belgium and Germany which bore the brunt of the offensive. If the Americans were to benefit from restraint, there was every reason to fear that other countries would, in exchange, be subject to more pressure than ever.

Such views had long been expressed by the countries concerned, often reacting more rapidly and forcefully than the United States. The European countries on the whole did not face the same consumer interests nor, in fact, exactly the same economic situation. Consumers were concerned about quality and fuel-efficiency and they did like Japanese cars. But they had a broad enough array of European cars which attained roughly the same performance and, if given no choice, they could still fall back on national products.

Facing this was a much stronger coalition of government and labor. This occurred not only in countries run by a socialist government which depended on the unions, as in Germany or Scandinava. Even in Mrs. Thatcher's Britain and Giscard's France, the government had taken a strong interest in the automotive sector, part of which was actually national-ized, and it could not afford to allow the automakers to be battered any worse than they already were. Moreover, many of these countries had long since begun protecting industries and were no strangers to tariffs, and quotas, or even more refined non-tariff barriers and "administrative guidance."

In some cases, the government or industry quickly took matters into their own hands. France, which had a tight control over imports, simply refused to process the necessary papers and left the Japanese cars waiting in the harbor. The British automakers met with their Japanese counterparts and warned them that the ceiling had been exceeded, receiving a pledge that this would be corrected. Other European countries were in more of a quandry due to their own interests or free trade principles. However, when Renault warned Belgium that it would have to close the assembly plant there in the event of further imports, it also agreed restrictions might be

Small cars assembling by the thousands.
The export offensive gets underway.

Credit: Foreign Press Center-Japan

necessary. Even Germany admitted the need in the face of an incredibly steep rise in Japanese imports, over 70%.

Individually, and through the European Community, the various countries began negotiating with Japan for voluntary restraint in mid-1980. By the end of the year, it almost looked as if this would be accepted. . . until Japan was warned by the American ambassador that his country would insist on similar concessions to those granted Europe. In that case, the rivalry between importers played into Japan's hands. However, as soon as the Americans had obtained their "voluntary restraint," the Europeans, Canadians, and various others brought the matter up again and pressed harder than ever.

The Japanese did not like adding new limitations, and they felt that what had been granted the United States, their closest ally, should not necessarily be given freely to others of less importance or with less clout. Prime Minister Suzuki explained that the United States was being aided because it had worked out a plan to rehabilitate the industry. The Europeans and Canadians, on the other hand, "have no such plans, nor do they make efforts to penetrate the Japanese market, which is far more open than their home markets."[13]

This was not calculated to please. Nor could it stop the demands. And ultimately the Japanese had little choice but to reach separate agreements. With Canada, they agreed to decrease sales by 6%, with Belgium, 7%, and Germany accepted a modest increase of 10%. Elsewhere, it was simply decided to exercise caution in order to avoid another flare-up. The final result, however, was that the Japanese automakers were faced with one restriction or another on fully 70% of their markets.

An Uneasy Peace

Although the restrictions were not as bad as feared, the

agreement with the United States was immediately attacked by the automakers who, while accepting it, did not hesitate to criticize their own government for "politicizing" the automobile trade issue, which was essentially an economic issue, and reaching a decision in undue haste against their wishes. To this, Eiji Toyoda added that the American consumers would bear heavier financial burdens and the Japanese economy would suffer a serious blow. Ishihara claimed that the restraint would seriously hurt the automobile industry, all related industries, and the economy as a whole. And he warned that the automakers might eventually demand compensation for any damage.[14]

They did not seem to grasp the logic of MITI's Naohiro Amaya, who insisted that "regrettably there was no other option but to take such steps as an exception to avoid worse consequences."[15] For, if a decision had been held up much longer, it was just possible that American legislation would have been adopted and led to a major decrease in exports under a system that was stricter and firmer. By taking the first step, the Japanese government had not only removed a quarrel that was certainly not helping its overall relations and antagonizing its biggest trading partners. In addition, by making an offer rather than having one imposed on it, it was possible to make the cutback quite moderate. A 7.7% reduction in sales to the United States, and less elsewhere, was quite bearable and could be absorbed with little difficulty.

By stalling as long as they did, the Japanese automakers had plenty of time to ship large quantities of cars and trucks to the overseas markets, far more than usual and often more than could actually be sold. So the base level, calendar or fiscal 1980, was artificially inflated to begin with. And this production had resulted not from any supplementary investment on their part but simply running their production lines longer than usual. While Americans and Europeans were being laid off, Japanese makers forced their employees to put in 30 and more hours overtime a month and occasionally skip vacations and holidays. All they had to do now was return to a more normal pace.

Furthermore, it was not even certain that these limitations would actually decrease overall sales. The Japanese industry had pushed so hard for the major targets that it somewhat neglected the secondary markets. By generating more exports to the Middle East, Asia, and Latin America, much of the gap could be filled. The real problems ended up being elsewhere, namely on the domestic market which remained sluggish, and then worldwide as the recession deepened. When American and European automobile sales plummetted in 1981, it became evident that the Japanese automakers would be wise to exercise the same restraint in 1982 rather than unleash a further wave of exports.

Still, the essential setback was basically to restrict expansion rather than cut sharply into existing sales. But this was already enough to awaken the Japanese to the fact that at long last it was time to slow expansion of capacity at home. Toyota, which had recently constructed a major plant at Tawara, decided not to have the second assembly line built. And the automakers planned to concentrate their future investment on equipment to increase productivity, largely by reducing labor and introducing mechanization or robotization, so as to maintain their competitive edge.

So, what the Japanese lost was quite modest. And, it was not as if they did not gain something in return. These gains would accrue on the side of profitability. For, the cutthroat competition had resulted in increased sales which were hardly reflected by increased profits. After all, in order to sell a bit more, the Japanese makers had had to pare the margins to the bone and engage in costly marketing efforts and advertising to drum up more sales. They also had to incur higher costs due to considerable overtime pay. Meanwhile, the only price rises, usually quite modest, were to compensate for an appreciation of the yen. At the end of their best year ever, the Japanese makers on the whole showed slight increases in earnings that actually masked a decline in the profit margin.

Finally having a relatively stable market, in which each company knew how much it could sell in certain areas on the basis of a fair distribution (related largely to past sales performance), they were able to go about selling normally. Knowing they had definite advantages over their competitors, the Japanese could raise prices steadily until they approached the going rate. Although less dependent on profits for further investment, the money was nonetheless welcome at a time when they had to gird for the future.

If the Japanese losses were marginal at most, it is equally clear that the American and European gains were also quite minimal. After all, the cutback in Japanese exports was rather small and they had plenty of stock on hand. The restraints, such as they were, had been based on unusually high export levels. So any major increase of sales depended essentially on a substantial growth in the domestic market. When this did not materialize, due to high interest rates and a deepening recession, sales often slumped. And the only thing the American and European makers really won was a much-needed breathing space.

The future of Japan's foreign competitors therefore depended principally on what they did with the time they had gained. Within a few years at most, it was essential to rehabilitate industries and companies that had been weakened during decades not only by insufficient investment but loss of work will and harmful practices. Nor could they count on very much government assistance. As the Chrysler case had shown, the American government was not willing to bail out companies so readily. Even British Leyland was given three years to shape up or disappear.

The crucial point became whether the various companies could muster enough funds to invest in new machinery and plant. Only this could give a strong boost to productivity and bring costs down in the long run. It would also help somewhat with problems of quality and efficiency. However, to get these funds, it was almost a prerequisite that the companies be successful in earning profits and amassing large enough sums to cover many of the investments while encouraging the stockholders and banks to provide a handsome supplement.

In this respect, the Japanese onslaught had been most telling. Although Toyota and the others did not earn much on their automobiles, they were more than compensated for this by driving down the profits of their competitors and often turning them into losses. The American firms made an unprecedented loss of $4.3 billion for the year. British Leyland did miserably again, thanks to a peevish labor force. The Italians and French had a bad year. And even German companies like Opel, Ford, and Volkswagen were hurt. Those which made profits were few and far between.

This implied a powerful brake on any efforts at rehabilitation. The most serious threat to Japan came from the United States. The American Big Three had planned to invest $80 billion over a period of seven years to regain competitiveness. Meanwhile, and perhaps more important, they were switching to smaller models which were equally fuel-efficient. These cars did come out during 1981, but the pace was slower than planned and they did not sell quite as much as hoped. Moreover, an overall rationalization that would bring prices down would take much longer. This situation was not changed by the rather flimsy government plans which simply released the makers from some antipollution and consumer protection regulations that would have added to cost, while ignoring the basic problems of investment and productivity.

If nothing were done to alter the situation drastically, it was most likely that the Japanese makers would still have an edge on quality, efficiency and price when the "small car war" resumed. That is, unless one considers certain other changes

The trends toward small car sales were obvious.
Yet, Detroit ignored them.

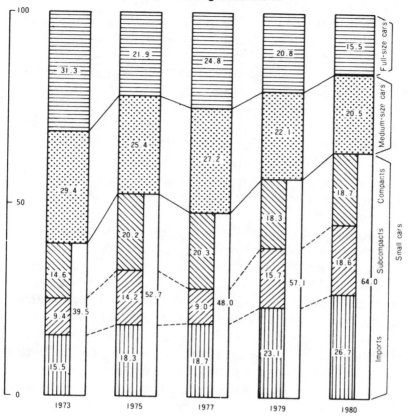

Source: Ward's Automotive Reports

Source: *Ward's Automotive Reports*

Credit: *White Paper on International Trade*, 1981, MITI.

that had at first gone unnoticed but could have a momentous impact not only on the automobile industry but the world economy.

During the heated exchanges over the trade conflict, not much attention had been paid to the other side of Fraser's demands, namely that "if the Japanese want to sell cars in America, they'll have to make them in America." Here, too, there was tremendous reluctance among the Japanese to act. There were some very good reasons for this. Setting up an automobile plant in the United States, or anywhere else, was a very costly proposition since it had to be large enough to run at a decent scale from the start. It was an awkward step for most of them since they had not engaged in full-scale manufacturing abroad before. And they did not really like what they saw. There was concern about finding capable suppliers. There were also nagging doubts about the "quality of labor" one could expect in America and Europe, this referring more to work will and discipline than concrete matters like ability or even wages.[16]

Thus, the first reaction was to make very vague promises and then introduce what were bound to be lengthy studies, in the hope that the problem would blow over in the meanwhile. Toyota, which was the most reluctant, eventually slipped out of its planned tie-up with Ford. But it realized that something had to be done to placate the Americans and accepted a looser relationship with General Motors. Nissan, which had also been hesitant, finally opted to open a truck plant in the United States (mainly to get around the higher tariff). Only Honda took a positive stance, deciding to produce automobiles near its existing motorcyle facility in Ohio, and this even before the trade friction arose. In Great Britain, Honda was also engaged in joint production of its cars through British Leyland. But the much touted Nissan plant fell through, although it got a foot in the European Community through smaller ventures with Alfa Romeo and Motor Iberica. Even while evading a major commitment in the West, Toyota was very eager to start production in Taiwan.

This meant that in another few years, the Japanese would already be producing fair numbers of their own automobiles and trucks on some of the markets that had experienced the greatest trade friction. On a smattering of other markets, they were already engaged in assembly of knocked-down kits. And, in an increasing number of cases, they would also be selling their vehicles abroad under the name of local manufacturers. The earliest to do this was Mitsubishi Motors, which sold its cars through Chrysler, a system it managed to squeeze out of. In return, it would help Chrysler to recover. Both Isuzu and Suzuki Motors would be producing small cars for GM. And Toyo Kogyo would supply its Mazdas to Ford. If the "world car" concept became a reality, Japanese manufacturers would doubtlessly be making parts and assembling vehicles within various groups.

If these various plans did work out, some of the trade conflicts would be relaxed and in a few cases even cease to exist, since trade flows would have been replaced by local production. Moreover, the Japanese would have a vested interest in maintaining good relations in the host countries and even protecting the sales of their overseas subsidiaries. But this would not solve the problem of foreign sales in Japan, which was bound to become sharper. Only one major step had been made in that direction when Nissan agreed to produce the Volkswagen Santana in its own plants, although at a rather puny level of 60,000 a year.

Meanwhile, to remind them that the best way of avoiding trade friction was to produce automobiles abroad, the American House of Representatives approved a "domestic content" bill in December 1982. It provided that foreign makers selling more than specified numbers of automobiles would have to use varying degrees of local parts and labor, from 10% of total content for sales of 100,000 cars to 90% for 900,000 cars. Without being mentioned, this was obviously directed against the Japanese primarily, and they reacted in kind. The bill was condemned by the automakers who warned that it would only discourage them from investing. Prime Minister Nakasone stated that the bill's passage was "extremely regrettable" and Foreign Minister Shintaro Abe added that it "bears a strong protectionist color" and could have "unfathomable adverse effects" on trade.[17] But that would not stop localization measures from being adopted in any number of places if Japanese exports became threatening.

NOTE

1. See Jon Woronoff, *Inside Japan, Inc.*, pp. 131–42.
2. *Japan Times*, September 4, 1980.
3. *Japan Times*, February 14, 1980.
4. *Japan Times*, March 9, 1980.
5. *Japan Times*, March 20, 1980 & April 18, 1981.
6. *New York Times*, November 11, 1980 and *Wall Street Journal*, February 9, 1981.
7. *Los Angeles Times*, October 19, 1980
8. *Japan Times*, February 20, 1980.
9. *Japan Times*, June 27, March 11 & March 9, 1980.
10. *Asahi Shimbun* and *Japan Times*, April 3, 1981.
11. *Japan Times*, March 20 & April 19, 1981.
12. For a blow-by-blow description of the negotiations, see Naohiro Amaya's article in *Bungei Shunju*, July 1981, pp. 318–38.
13. *Japan Times*, May 2, 1981.
14. *Japan Times*, April 29, and *Asahi Shimbun* and *Japan Times*, May 2, 1981.
15. *Japan Times*, May 2, 1981.
16. See *Asian Business*, September 1980 & January 1981.
17. *Japan Times*, December 17, 1982.

6
The "Model" Partner

Helping The Third World

The Japanese are second to none when it comes to the praise that is lavished on free trade. But they outdo themselves when it comes to pledging support of the developing countries. It is openly admitted that these backward economies need more than just a crack at foreign markets, they require special assistance and guidance. As the first non-Western country to rise to the ranks of highly advanced nations, Japan looks upon itself somewhat as a model and partner. Its representatives are overflowing with good will when they appear at international forums like the United Nations and OECD or when top officials make their periodic trips to the Third World. An authoritative, and unusually cogent, expression of this enlightened role was provided by the latest MITI White Paper on International Trade.

"It is necessary for Japan, in cooperation with other industrial nations, to carry out comprehensive economic cooperation addressed to the priorities of the recipient countries. This will include measures for the recycling of petrodollars, expanded technical assistance, the solution to their food and energy problems, and the training of technical and managerial personnel. Further, to deepen mutual understanding with other countries, contacts and exchanges with them on official as well as on private levels should be encouraged, and cooperation should be extended to them in the development of their human resources by inviting students and trainees to Japan. It is also necessary for the Japanese people to develop a truly international perspective on, and attitude toward, their economic, social and cultural affairs. It is only with such a perspective and attitude that Japan can achieve an economic structure harmonious with other countries and contribute to the welfare of other peoples and to world peace."[1]

One could hardly expect a finer statement of the basic principles. But the Japanese have gone much further on one particular, namely how the developing countries can rise in the world. Here, the Japanese swear that they will not fall into the same trap as less vigorous defenders of the cause by refusing to step aside for newcomers. The common good can best be promoted through a growing specialization of efforts among nations at different levels of development. The developing countries, especially those with abundant sources of cheap labor, will be entrusted with the more labor-intensive industries. They will obtain little added value but at least keep their teeming populations occupied and have an opportunity to upgrade their skills. Those which possess raw materials will increasingly process them on the spot before shipping them abroad where more advanced countries, like Japan, will do the refined processing and turn them into sophisticated products.

This extremely popular theory, which has become the government's official policy, was also reiterated by MITI. The primary role for Japan reads as follows. "It should endeavor to help the world economy achieve stable growth by developing creative original technology, by opening up new frontiers of industry and by creating highly adaptable industrial and trade structures on the basis of advanced technology and high productivity. The integrated industrial and trade structure of Japan will pave the way for active industrial and technological cooperation with other countries and will contribute to the establishment of a durable international division of labor, the development of interdependence, and efficient trade relations with the countries of the world."[2]

Thus, Japan is to become a leader. In order to make way for the less developed countries, it promises to keep moving upward as regards the quality and nature of its own products. It will seek higher technology and more capital-intensive sectors which can benefit from its solid industrial foundation and a knowledge-oriented society. Much of the spadework here has been done by MITI's division and council on industrial structure and the liberal industrialists of Keizai Doyukai. Some of the new growth sectors have actually been singled out in MITI's *Vision for the 1980s* and Keizai Doyukai's proposal of eight "frontier" industries. Notable among them are electronics, telecommunications, computers, nuclear energy, aerospace and genetic engineering.[3]

A perusal of these various sectors of the future will show that, as in the past, most of them are presently dominated by leading Western nations. So, for Japan to move up smartly, the West must make way, as it has been doing for some time already. At this late date, however, there seem to be few if any sectors to which the more advanced countries can switch. Japan's plans never indicate which products they should manufacture when their present ones are taken over by its industrialists. Perhaps that is an oversight. Maybe the Japanese, like the rest of us, simply do not know. At any rate, lack of enough high technology, high value-added sectors is likely to be a problem for some.

Nevertheless, Japan would seem to be pretty firmly committed to helping the developing countries rise by providing capital and technology, by offering aid and investment, and especially by opening its markets wider for their products. Efforts have already been made along these lines and there are some palpable results.

There is no doubt that Japan is buying more raw materials and especially oil from developing countries, and this is given among its supposed contributions to their development. But it could hardly be regarded as a disinterested gesture. What is much more promising is that Japan has finally begun leaving a greater degree of the processing of raw materials to the suppliers. The 1979 White Paper on International Trade shows that for textiles, the imports of raw cotton or flax are giving way to imports of yarn or fabrics. Much more zinc, lead, nickel and especially aluminum is entering now as ingots and alloys rather than ore. Judging by projects already under way, almost all the aluminum will ultimately arrive as ingots and many of the petrochemical products will be produced near the well.[4]

Meanwhile, there has been a lively increase in manufactured products from some developing countries, mainly the nearby Asian ones which have entered the category of semi-developed countries, such as Korea, Taiwan, Hong Kong and Singapore. Indeed, they managed to export about ¥3.5 trillion of such goods in 1978 which is not far from 4% of the total. The bulk of that consisted of light industrial articles, frequently textiles and garments. There were also items like simple electronics, watches or cameras. But some heavy industry products have also appeared as Korea and Taiwan became Japan's major suppliers of steel.

Investment has shown yet more progress as amounts invested in developing countries rose to over $25 billion by 1981 representing about 55% of Japan's total overseas investment. However, a lot of this did not contribute to imports. Many of the projects consisted of offices abroad to promote Japanese sales to the developing countries or facilities to produce some of the goods locally. The rest were factories set up in the export processing zones to benefit from cheap labor. These goods, although they could well have gone to Japan, were instead sent to other industrialized countries and the zones were just offshore production sites to get around quotas directed at Japan.

To make it easier for developing countries to export to

Japan a preferential tariff system was introduced in 1971. This was not a spontaneous gesture by Japan but rather a result of demands by the developing countries in the United Nations and GATT combined with pressure by the Western countries for Japan to grant concessions similar to theirs. In the end, Japan went along with the Generalized System of Preferences. But it did not go very far. Indeed, its first tariff preferences were rather modest and the quota ceiling so low that most of them were filled within a few months. Gradually, however, the number of countries included expanded and tariffs fell by 10% to 100% for a broad range of products.

By 1980, about ¥1.1 trillion worth of goods entered under the preference scheme, with the largest shares coming from Korea, Taiwan, the People's Republic of China and Philippines. On the other hand, since tariff levels had sunk considerably during the past decade, the actual margins were rather slim. Moreover, under the system as revised and extended in 1981, some of the more sensitive items like silk and cotton yarn were dropped from the list to protect domestic industries. Also, to give a chance to less developed countries, those which had been most successful and were promoted to the category of semi-developed countries were accorded smaller benefits.

This doubtlessly represented progress. But the degree was certainly not as great as hoped. By 1978, all forms of "aid," including government grants, export credits, direct investment, and manufactured imports, only added up to 1.6% of Japan's gross national product. If the much vaunted "new economic order" were to be attained in this century, it would be necessary to hasten the pace. Yet, Japan's official *Vision for the 1980s*, issued by MITI's Industrial Structure Council, only set a target of 3% by the end of the decade. This was not even a doubling in twelve years.[5]

With regard to trade in manufactured products, one can marvel at the speed with which the NICs did get into Japan's market. This was not at all bad for countries which had just taken up manufacturing some decades before. At the same time, there is reason to wonder whether they should not be selling much more in Japan. After all, they had already invaded major markets in the United States and Europe and driven Japan's own exports out. Taiwanese and Korean television sets, not only black-and-white but color, as well as radios, tape recorders, and other electronics goods, were of sufficient quality and cheaper price. Their textiles and garments, as well as those from Hong Kong, had already won a reputation that placed them in a positive light while maintaining price competitiveness. And Hong Kong was turning out more digital watches than Japan or Switzerland, much cheaper. Yet, there was just a trickle of such products into Japan while elsewhere it was a flood.[6]

This should prove that their quality was adequate, if not as high as Japanese goods, and that the price advantage would normally get them a lively market. With a wage level between a quarter and a tenth that of Japan, it was obvious that they could be competitive for labor-intensive products. So there must have been some resistance to penetration somewhere. The most logical place to look was, as for the industrialized countries, the invisible or cultural barriers. If it was hard for major companies from advanced countries to get a foot in the market, how much harder must it be for developing countries?

They could not afford to send salesmen to Japan repeatedly, to open a local office, or to incur the expenses of their own marketing channels. Producing in small quantities in most cases, they could hardly find a wholesaler even willing to deal with them. Most therefore went through the trading companies or their joint venture partners. But they were amazed to find their goods marked up phenomenally before they reached the consumers or diverted to other markets than Japan. Most trading companies bought cheap Asian goods to sell in America and Europe, not Japan. And many Japanese companies did not even sell products made by their own subsidiaries on the home market.

The NICs were dismayed by the amazing impenetrability of the Japanese market despite their advantages and successes elsewhere. They were even more upset to find that their trade balance with Japan, which had always been negative, was running a bigger deficit almost every year. It did not take long to realize that their situation was a variation on an earlier theme: they were buying from Japan so it could pay its oil bill and selling to America and Europe to pay their own. Only the resource exporters managed to run a surplus with Japan. And the truly underdeveloped countries, which had neither raw materials nor manufactured goods to sell, simply ran a deficit with no hope of redemption.

Lacking the clout of the Western nation, which were large and mature economies and Japan's major trading partners or allies, there was not much they could do. Nor did the idea of going without trade appeal to them since Japan was the closest, and best, source of capital goods, intermediate goods, technology and investment. Still, the complaints became more frequent, more strident and more formal. And some countries resorted to the only measures they could, no matter how painful to themselves. Taiwan purposely began redirecting its trade away from Japan and toward the countries it exported to, making as many purchases as it could in America and Europe both to balance trade and obtain larger export quotas. Apparently exasperated by the endless imbalances, in February 1982 it actually prohibited the import of some 1,500 articles from Japan. Korea might eventually have to follow suit. And lesser countries would be forced to restrain trade whether they wished to or not due to payments difficulties.

Other steps of a quite different nature, but also with a strong impact on trade, were being taken to promote economic development. Realizing that progress would come through their own efforts and not foreign generosity, many developing countries formulated more dynamic policies and strategies. In nearly all cases, this included raising protective walls around their infant industries and providing tax, credit and other incentives to potential growth sectors. Once they had developed to the stage where they could export, export subsidies or other measures were adopted to get them started. This did not always work. But, more often than expected, it did.

Protection A La Japonaise

Judging by their highly publicized statements, no one could be more against protectionism than Japanese government officials, bureaucrats and businessmen. Japanese industry can stand on its own two feet and compete with the rest of the world. This made a virtue of an apparent reality, namely the fact that many Japanese products became so competitive during the 1970s that they did not need special support and had more to fear of protection encountered abroad. But it conveniently ignored the fact that earlier Japan had been among the most protective nations. However, that seemed to be a thing of the past and this was shown by Japan's initiative in calling for what is known as the Tokyo Round of GATT negotiations.

It now looks as if that mood may have been a passing one. For, almost at the same time, the oil crisis and worldwide recession plunged the economy of most countries into a period of unprecedented difficulties. Japan came out of this most rapidly among the industrialized countries, largely by boosting exports of manufactured goods. But this does not mean that it was not considerably debilitated. That is shown most clearly by its growth rate which fell from about 10% a year to only 3%. Some of its weaker companies did not survive and bankruptcies have continued at a historical high to date. Unemployment was unusually great. Meanwhile, for the first time, Japan noticed that it was not alone on the path to development and was displeased to find products from some relatively backward countries driving its own off third markets and then competing domestically.

With this, the attitude to protectionism has changed subtly. Without meaning to be offensive, it can be summed up for Japan (like everywhere else) as strongly opposed to any protectionism abroad while tempted by the idea of introducing it at home . . . of course, only in dire necessity and then temporarily. This has resulted in a phenomenon, still largely unnoticed by many astigmatic Japan-watchers, of a neo-protectionism not dissimilar in some ways from what occurs in the West. Other measures are typically Japanese, stemming from its different economic structure and policies. The phenomenon should perhaps be called protectionism à la japonaise.

The reason so few Japan "experts" have noticed this is that they are still enamored of the theory invented by the correspondents of The Economist that the Japanese had classified their industries into categories, some of which they would strongly promote while others would, according to Herman Kahn, be "sabotaged" since they were "obsolete" or "not for Japanese."[7] Among the so-called "throw-away" industries in which Japan was uncompetitive are coal, non-ferrous metals, paper pulp, agricultural products, etc. A second category of "early-stage industrialization" in which Japan no longer wished to compete includes cotton textiles, sewing machines, bicycles, pottery, and so on.[8]

The most striking thing about this list is that, although it was compiled nearly twenty years ago, all of these industries still exist and some are doing reasonably well, like sewing machines and bicycles. The others are also around, albeit sometimes reduced in scale and perhaps ailing. And it is interesting to note that, far from anyone trying to throw them away, they are on the whole being aided or protected one way or another. In a pinch, Japan has not accepted the logic of its own principles of going upmarket and leaving the lower ranges to others. As soon as any sector got into difficulty, especially if it possessed substantial assets, had good bureaucratic or political connections, or could rally a large number of owners and workers in danger of bankruptcy or unemployment, an effort was made to rescue it or at least salvage the healthier parts.

The industries in trouble are usually suffering from one or more of three ailments. The first is that they have expanded too rapidly and are burdened with excess capacity. This is not uncommon in Japan given the fierce competition revolving around size and market share. Others face more fundamental problems since the industrial structure has changed altering the prices of certain factors. While they made sense just after the war, when Japan's labor was very cheap, it is impossible to sustain labor-intensive branches at a time when Japan's wages are among the highest in the world. If they were not very amenable to mechanization and too small to raise the funds, these sectors would rapidly cease being competitive. A few sectors were worse off, for they had never been inherently competitive and were based on massive imports of raw materials whose prices have since risen substantially.

When the oil crisis struck and its companies were in difficulty, the Japanese government did not regard this as a golden opportunity to weed out the weak ones. Instead, like most others, it adopted a package of special measures to help them out. Subsidies were provided to specific companies and industries not only to survive but to continue exporting. Companies were encouraged to keep their workers for better days through special subventions which wisely also included the alternative of retraining. Loans were facilitated to smaller enterprises while the major companies drew more heavily on their banks. The whole budget was inflated to stimulate the economy and public works became a major feature.

Companies or sectors caught with excess capacity, either

because the market had suddenly shrunk or because they unwisely expanded too rapidly, were aided through special anti-recession cartels. Most of them were formally established by MITI, as a temporary suspension of the antitrust laws, and were heartily welcomed by the producers (although some felt they could do better on their own). The primary aim of these cartels was a reduction in capacity, sometimes by as much as fifty percent. However, to maintain economies of scale, the reduction sometimes included a division of labor, whereby certain companies would cease all production of some lines and others of different lines. To avoid ruinous competition abroad, floor prices were occasionally set for exports. Once this operation was completed, free competition was restored and the companies were expected to get by on their own. In tough cases, though, the cartel might have to be renewed.

Cartels have been established officially for dozens of specific sectors, aluminum, copper, naphtha, caustic soda, chemicals, steel products and shipbuilding, among others. In addition, there were informal arrangements among companies in branches somewhat less afflicted. Most of them were viewed as a "success." Nevertheless, even if the sector was revived, there were always certain drawbacks. No matter how much this is denied, there was bound to be some restraint of trade since it was hardly likely that companies would accept to curtail their own production simply to allow more imports from foreign competitors. How such imports were blocked will be indicated later. Another disadvantage arises for the domestic economy. The decrease in production is usually accompanied by some increase in price, whether authorized by the government or arising out of collusion among the cartel members. This naturally results in higher prices for Japanese manufacturers using the product as an input and eventually for the consumers purchasing manufactured goods.

There was also some trouble with another type of cartel, this time imposed on Japan by partners demanding "volun-

An ailing industry goes under wraps. This textile machinery
won't be needed for the moment... or perhaps ever.

Credit: Foreign Press Center-Japan

tary restraint." The export cartels did achieve their primary task of cutting back on sales and accomplishing orderly
marketing. However, the standard method of distributing
quotas to producers on the basis of past export performance
implies a bonus for those which pursued their offensives most
aggressively and created the problem. Only one method of
reducing production seems to be relatively beneficial to all and
also approaches the notion of discarding backward sectors to
some extent. This involves efforts to help small, labor-
intensive companies migrate to developing countries where
labor is cheap, an operation they accomplish on their own to
survive and is sometimes subsidized by MITI.

Even if the action of a cartel or a restructuring of the
industry will help it get by somewhat longer, it is worthwhile
looking at some cases to see just how deep the weakness goes.

Products requiring considerable labor, ceramics, toys, garments and even certain textiles, will never fully recover since wages have been rising steadily and there is also a growing labor shortage as young prople refuse to work in backward sectors. Those using certain raw materials are even worse off, such as pulp and paper, petrochemicals and aluminum. In the latter two, costs are 20% and more above the level in the United States, Canada, and other sourcing countries. The reason is obvious. Raw materials and energy constitute 70-80% of total production costs and both have to be imported, at great expense, to Japan. For these reasons, the Japanese companies began losing their foreign markets and were then faced with a massive invasion of the domestic market as well.

Although it had always been admitted that Japan would be swamped by cheap light industry articles and especially textiles and garments, the reaction was most definitely not to accept the sad facts of life and withdraw gracefully. Like everywhere else, the manufacturers fought desperately to protect the home market. Early in the 1970s, the silk growers obtained quotas on the import of raw silk and this spread quickly to silk products. The spinners then demanded that textile imports be restricted and makers of simple garments urged that imports henceforth be monitored. For raw silk, Japan actually imposed bilateral agreements on China and Korea, and for silk fabrics, on Korea and Taiwan. For the other articles, no outright limitations were adopted. Yet, by the 1980s, the whole textile industry was agitating for protection and calling for orderly marketing while Japan even toyed with the idea of hiding behind the notorious Multi-Fiber Arrangement.

The reaction was not very different with regard to aluminum imports. There was immediate talk of unfair prices and dumping although America and Canada had a patent comparative advantage. The industry had evidently thought of stemming the tide more informally, through secret arrangements with the traders to curtail imports, but this apparently failed. For, in a rather unprecedented statement, the president of the aluminum refiners' association angrily chastised the trading companies for seeking quick profits and worsening the industry's plight.[9] The refiners then proposed that the government impose restrictions or adopt a trigger price mechanism. For cheap petrochemicals, there was a replay. Japanese makers complained of America's unfair cost advantage, which is nothing compared to what Saudi Arabia will eventually have. And Japanese chemical company executives suggested an orderly marketing agreement to restrict American petrochemical exports to Japan and Southeast Asia.[10]

An even more intriguing case has been the initiation of steel exports by Korea and Taiwan. There is no doubt that both countries are fully competitive since their steelworks are among the most modern and productive in the world, Korea's huge mill at Pohang actually being designed and equipped by the Japanese. They also have cheaper labor. And their products have gradually infiltrated the Japanese market with the two NICs accounting for the bulk of imports. However, even though imports only represented 2% of total consumption, the Japanese steelmakers were getting nervous and took measures to keep them strictly under control. China Steel and Pohang Iron & Steel were reminded that cooperation was far wiser than confrontation and it would be best not to export more than could be comfortably absorbed. Thus, the amounts of exports were set on a quarterly basis not by the exporters but their Japanese competitors in the most refined "orderly exporting" operation ever.[11]

More generally, Japan has gone to considerable lengths to avoid being faced with excessive imports from the two countries whose encroachment it feared most, Korea and Taiwan. Since the relations are often very close due to investments, joint ventures, and foreign aid, government and industrial leaders know one another well. They all have a vested interest in smooth cooperation in the future and the Japanese, in addition, act from a position of strength as major suppliers of capital and technology. Missions are sent periodically and special committees exist in many sectors to defuse problems before they arise. Just what transpires is rarely recorded. However, it was noted that at a meeting of chemical fiber executives, for example, the Japanese side urged their counterparts to make their capacity expansion plans cautiously in the light of worldwide overcapacity. The Koreans and Taiwanese dutifully promised to be cautious.[12]

Still, even if individual companies should wish to disregard such well meaning advice, it would not be easy. This applies to the advanced and developing countries, but more particularly the latter. Nearly all the trade is concentrated in a few dozen trading companies, and the top ten handle nearly two-thirds of total imports. It only takes some gentle guidance from the government or subtle hints from related firms for the imports of a specific product to expand or contract or a rambunctious exporter to find it no longer has entry to the market. In cases where Japanese trading companies or manufacturers are partners in overseas ventures, obviously their control over what is sold where is much greater. Since it is impossible to trace how decisions to import, or not to import, are taken, there is limited evidence of such a selective process.[13] However, what else could permit Japan to regulate imports as efficiently as it does or cause sales of certain products to rise and fall tremendously in too short a time for this to result from changes in competitiveness?

Of course, Japan is not always so furtive. Perfectly evident, and blatantly protective, measures are still used freely when it comes to helping the farm lobby. Few of the old quotas were scrapped and some were periodically tightened or relaxed depending on the harvest and food requirements. Import cartels were authorized to control Thai maize, Australian raw sugar, and Taiwanese onions. When compound butter imports rose too sharply in 1981, although it had been liberalized a decade earlier, the Ministry of Agriculture asked Europe and New Zealand to restrict exports and, just in case, told local users and importers to cut back.[14] During a brief "eel war" with Taiwan, the Japanese eel producers prevailed on the government to stop imports and ultimately impose quotas which the Taiwanese producers could scarcely reject.

Slowly but surely, the Japanese scene has begun resembling events in America or Europe. There are periodic complaints of import surges causing injury to local manufacturers, when not bringing about their ruination. The easiest explanations for such incursions are unfair prices and dumping. And the reaction is to call for restrictions or restraint so as to obtain more orderly marketing. Although Japan hesitated to impose, or even raise the question of, restraint on the United States, it was less reluctant to insist on discipline in relations with weaker neighbors. Indeed, it has already enforced a number of gentlemen's agreements just like those foisted on it, except that this time they were more discreet and bound Oriental gentlemen.

The Free Rider

The developing countries frequently claim that what they want is trade, not aid. Nevertheless, it is obvious that some of them face such serious difficulties that they could not possibly create a viable economy, or perhaps even survive, without a steady transfusion of external resources. Japan, as a highly successful developed country is expected to provide some of this flow. Indeed, this is a challenge which its leaders have accepted with particular pleasure since it is a neutral task which should bring only friends and would allow it to consolidate relations worldwide. Japan was also proud to be helping others and able to let them benefit from its vast experience.

From year to year, Japan's contribution has been growing until, by the late 1970s, it was pumping more money into the Third World than any other country than the United States. By far the largest portion was foreign investment, which amounted to nearly $25 billion by 1981. However, although investment can give a tremendous impulse to economic development, this is not what is usually regarded as aid. It is more in the line of mutual interest, since these funds are used to establish enterprises that will increase Japan's exports or, in other cases, carry out assembly or production of goods for which the businessmen are ultimately paid. Another purpose is to procure raw materials and energy. None of these investments would ever have been made without some hope of gain.

That is why the Organization for Economic Cooperation and Development has drawn up stricter definitions for its members with regard to "official development assistance" or ODA. This consists basically of grants and loans, the former non-reimbursable and therefore genuinely altruistic, the latter to be paid back with interest (albeit at a low rate) and thus a somewhat less generous gesture. With regard to ODA, Japan has also been moving up smartly, offering over $3 billion in 1981. This placed it fourth after the United States, France and Germany. However, when one regards the "quality," a grant component of 40% against an average of 76%, the achievement becomes considerably less impressive.

While Japan has constantly laid great stress on its total contribution, the other OECD countries repeatedly pointed out that in relative terms it is not doing so well. After all, with the second biggest population and the second largest gross national product of the seventeen Development Assistance Committee members, there is no reason it should not rank high in absolute terms. Looking at per capita contributions or the ratio of aid to GNP, there is nothing to boast of. For two decades, Japan has been at the bottom of the list, with ODA ranging from a low of .14% to a modest .32% of GNP. This latter figure is still less than the average of .37%, and far short of the goal of .70%, making Japan only 13th among the DAC members.

Another drawback to Japan's performance has thus been that, more often than not, any accomplishments were not spontaneous but a result of growing pressure applied by the developing countries themselves and equally firm pressure from its friends in the OECD, who wanted Japan to share the burden. As the economy became progressively stronger, the Japanese government found it harder to hold back and twice, in much remarked gestures, pledged to double ODA. The first doubling, or a bit more, came from 1978 to 1980. The second is scheduled from 1980 to 1985. However, it should be noted that the second doubling operation is much more modest. It will take place over five years and not three and the base is not the 1980 level but the 1978–80 average, which is much lower.[15]

This limitation was not stressed by the Japanese government. And it certainly did not announce that all of its contributions have been made somewhat on the cheap. The figures commonly used for ODA calculations are American dollars and, since the yen has appreciated sharply over the past decade, it was possible to raise the dollar figures substantially by making more modest increases in yen payments. Inflation has also played a role in making the progress look greater than it is. To judge by the amounts actually earmarked for aid, it would seem that the government is still counting on these factors to magnify the figures and there have been persistent rumors that the ratio of ODA to GNP will not even exceed the present level by 1985.

Whereas the Japanese government will make efforts to increase economic cooperation, from which its citizens benefit in various ways, there is less concern and sometimes resistance when it comes to humanitarian aid. In the event of major earthquakes, floods or other natural disasters, or aid to refugees, Japan has repeatedly offered less than much smaller countries. Indeed, sometimes the original offer was so embarrassingly low that the amount had to be raised for reasons of prestige. When pressed to do something for the Indochinese refugees, the government preferred granting more money to accepting even small numbers of human beings. Only after stalling an indecently long time did it agree to raise the ceiling for resettlement to 3,000, less than one percent of the total number of refugees received by the other countries.

In other sectors, Japan has also been dragging its feet. The most striking is defense. Due to a constitutional article renouncing war, and an alleged nuclear allergy, the nation has restricted itself to self-defense. Despite the fact that its self-defense force and budget have grown, and are impressive as compared to much smaller nations, it is clearly doing less than its allies and protector. Its budget, with an apparent ceiling of 1% of GNP, is consistently lower than NATO levels of 3% to 6%. Moreover, it clearly depends more for its national defense on American protection and the nuclear umbrella than its own efforts. This has led to periodic complaints of taking a "free ride."

There have also been complaints that Japan's economic development resulted largely from foreign technology licensed, borrowed or stolen, and that even now Japan is not doing its part. This has been tacitly admitted, and the *Vision for the 1980s* spoke of moving from a time when it "reaped" the harvest of imported technology to an era when it will "seed and grow" its original expertise. There is no doubt that the sums devoted to R & D have increased. But this has been mainly for commercial applications by companies and not fundamental research by universities or the government. Worse, Japan would seem to be reaping once again by using foreign space, nuclear energy, and genetic engineering technologies of others as once it used metallurgical, petrochemical or electronics.

Japan has manifestly benefited from the efforts of others. As a member of the Western Alliance, it has never been seriously worried about its defense situation and could put the strict minimum into defensive machinery which its top generals admit could not really hold off an enemy invasion more than a few hours. American control of the oceans and the Persian Gulf allowed it to ship its products abroad and draw its resources from the four corners of the earth. The advantages included, since it remained quietly on the sidelines, substantial trade with the Soviet Union, Eastern Europe and People's Republic of China. Its prosperity was even more directly based on the postwar trade system established by the United States, which has favored Japan immensely even while contributing little to maintain it.

The tremendous savings of the "free ride" were put to good use by the Japanese. They consisted of fabulous sums, indeed. Year after year, it paid from 1% to 5% of GNP less for military expenditures than other countries and perhaps another 2% was economized until quite recently by using the fundamental research of others and neglecting foreign aid. Much of these savings went into creating more productive machinery, increasing output and boosting exports. Considering that between 16% and 20% of gross national product were devoted to private investment in equipment, while personal consumption and social overhead were severely contained, a lack of those resources would have meant much slower economic growth. Meanwhile, its trading partners and allies, saddled with these substantial burdens, were being defeated by Japan in one economic contest after the other.

It is hard to tell just what Japan "owes" them, or what it "owes" the developing countries which are a major market and source of raw materials. But it does seem relatively clear that by prevailing standards Japan should be doing much more in one way or another. Given its high moral stand on defense, and a refusal to put up more money, there is not much prospect of an increased burden there. R & D expenditures are rising. But a greater effort could be made, at least for alternative energies which is Japan's greatest need. The one sector in which it should undoubtedly do more, and this is conceded by Japan, is aid to developing countries. In fact, it claims that it can do most for world peace and security by helping other countries to industrialize. Yet, it is so slow in reaching even the average aid levels of advanced countries that there is little hope of seeing it in the vanguard, where it belongs.

Moreover, the progress that was being made during the 1970s may not be continued very willingly. In order to come out of the oil crisis, Japan engaged in massive deficit financing and now has exceptionally high debts. To absorb them and keep its economy tough, it was decided that most items in the national budget will have to be kept stable or reduced. Even defense expenditures and aid contributions may only grow slowly, just a bit more than inflation. Demands for increased efforts here have met with resistance, the government talking of unavoidable financial constraints. True, certain constraints do exist. But they are the result of earlier overspending to Japan's own advantage and a somewhat contrived decision not to increase taxes although they are much lower than in any other advanced country. Still, the excuse sounds adequate to the Japanese and certainly suits their purposes.[16]

Other countries, however, will find it very lame. No nation in the world has enjoyed as long a period of continued growth and increasing affluence. Despite any lacks, Japan is clearly among the richest and most powerful. It is exceptionally free of the inflation, unemployment and general decay found in the rest of the advanced countries. With a per capita income over ten times that of most developing countries, a comparison hardly makes sense. When so many other countries are clearly in more difficult financial straits, with major social problems, and also less likelihood of a quick recovery, how can Japan plead that it is incapable of doing more? The time has come to throw off its "poor islands" mentality and admit in public what it knows in private, namely that it must adopt a more outward-looking policy.

Forming A Constituency

When compared to the actual efforts and results, many of the felicitous statements and high sounding principles put forth by Japanese politicians and businessmen tend to ring hollow. It frequently happens that the implementation is given less stress than the apparently more vital and uplifting task of formulating declarations and goals. Indeed, the implementation is quite modest when compared to what is being done in other countries that make less fuss about free trade or development assistance and have no lofty program to fulfill.

One cause of this should be dealt with right off. It is that all too often there is simply no one to take the principles and put them into practice. Thus, the fine ideas tend to float around, to be picked up and mouthed, to obtain increasing degrees of lip service, but to fade away when it is time to do something concrete.

The basic problem is that there is a huge gap between those in Japan who are entrusted with choosing principles and making declarations and those who actually engage in any form of implementation. This obviously creates a huge gap between what is said and what is done. A similar variance would lead to accusations of hypocrisy or bad faith elsewhere. In Japan, it is passed over as the normal difference between appearances (*tatemae*) and reality (*honné*) and probably stems more from institutional inadequacies and social inconsistencies than cold calculation.

For example, the high level businessmen who attend meetings of Keidanren or Keizai Doyukai or the dozens of bilateral trade and friendship committees are typical Japanese-style executives. This means that they have ceased playing an active role in the company's day-to-day operations. They enjoy tremendous prestige, they have important contacts and are still influential as regards overall policy or promotion of subordinates, but they do not take decisions that affect how their company does business locally or abroad. Those who take such decisions are lower level managers who must prove their ability and dedication in order to rise. This places them under immense pressure to succeed, succeed in the sense of strengthening their own company no matter what happens to others. So, what the semi-retired executives say or wish leaves little trace in the company's daily practice.

A somewhat different problem arises in the government. The most visible leaders and spokesmen are the politicians. But they are politicians in the Japanese mold, not American, or French, or African politicians who actively shape policy. Japanese politicians just formulate very broad principles and guidelines, but they have little say as to how they are implemented . . . or simply discarded and forgotten. Even ministers and prime ministers are frequently figureheads. It is the Japanese bureaucracy that drafts the bills, feeds speeches to ministers, and helps get the legislation through the Diet. Then, on the basis of laws or simply by using more informal means, it is again the bureaucreacy that implements policy.

When it comes to determining policy, the politicians are extremely interested in pleasing their voters, their specific local constituency, and hardly any think of the effect on foreign relations. Indeed, few show much concern with broader national interests. With little knowledge of the outside world, they hardly know what foreign countries might conceivably desire. On the other hand, they are painfully aware of what local groups want and are constantly solicited by them to fulfill specific requests. This is not fundamentally

Breaking the trade barriers. Margaret Thatcher
promoting British goods in Japan.

Credit: Foreign Press Center-Japan

different from other countries except that more than most
Japan has failed to accept any role in international relations or
show much concern for what happens abroad unless it is
directly affected.

In the bureaucracy, things depend much on the size and
prestige of the body concerned. Alas, the agencies entrusted
with maintaining smooth foreign relations or granting aid,
including the Foreign Ministry, are much smaller and far
lower in the pecking order than powerful bodies like MITI,
Finance or Agriculture. The Fair Trade Commission is a
midget compared to a mammoth MITI. They can inform the
politicians and public of problems and needs, but their voices
are listened to far less than the louder, more strident ones that
speak up for national interests. They also move fewer of their
former bureaucrats into key positions in companies or politi-

cal parties and thus are not really in the mainstream of Japan's amorphous decision-making machinery.[17]

The only thing that could make the government or business community show a keener interest in relations with the rest of the world, either to advance free trade or grant more foreign aid, would be a domestic constituency that would bring pressure to bear. Relatively little can be done by declarations or even laws. What is needed is a countervailing force that is strongly rooted in the people's own beliefs and interests. That, in Japan, is almost totally lacking. There are some grass roots bodies, a number of concerned academics, and a very few liberal politicians. But there is no active—or even passive—support in the population to help turn words into deeds.

Unlike many other countries, no dynamic or influential consumer movement has sprung up. People frequently grumble about high prices and occasionally meetings are held to combat some flagrant abuse. Yet, those concerned are neither numerous nor strong enough to effect much change. In one case, the price of color television was brought down after the manufacturers rigged it and there has been enough pressure to keep the rice price accessible. After a scandal over oil prices, the refiners and utilities companies have become more cautious about raising rates. But otherwise the cost of living is exceedingly high due to a lack of cheap imports and the many tricks that make prices rise before they reach the consumer.

So, the consumer campaigns have actually stopped short of attacking the essential causes of Japan's high cost structure. And, it is very doubtful that even if more people lobbied for cheaper imports much would be accomplished. For, most Japanese still regard themselves more as producers than consumers and therefore they try to improve their situation by increasing wages rather than lowering prices as well as boosting exports while holding the line on imports. Moreover, consumer issues are left largely to housewives. In the family division of labor, it is the women who shop and the men who earn money. Even nagging their husbands about the rising cost of living has little effect since women only get a modest hearing in society.

There is some change coming thanks to the emergence of more modern merchandising methods and especially the appearance of chain stores and supermarkets. They are big enough to import foreign products so as to offer attractive prices in their own establishments and increase their sales. Since some of them have grown into huge operations, bigger than anything in Europe and already in the American class, they can increasingly engage in importing on their own. But they are still too few, too recent, and also too low ranking in the social order. Merchants, just like women, are supposed to offer meek suggestions but not give orders or make undue demands.

One would expect more practical support for free trade from the businessmen in the sectors that praise free trade most heartily. Shipbuilding, automobiles, steel, electronics, and so on live very largely from exports. If there were any restrictions on trade they would be seriously hurt. This they know from experience since there are restrictions, and they have been hurt. Thus, they have formed a vocal lobby for freer trade. But they do not usually follow through in the sense of insisting that free trade also prevail inward to Japan. They will chide more backward industries on not making way for imports. But they have fought as hard, or harder, to keep imports out of their own sector.

Even the trading companies, despite their calling, are in a rather ambiguous position. They are much more aggressive in importing raw materials than bringing in manufactured goods. For, they are related to companies that need the former and, more significantly, to companies that are worried about the latter. Despite the tremendous profits that could be made by handling large amounts of cheaper manufactured goods, they tend not to carry anything that could annoy their partners back home and end up selling the cheaper Korean or Taiwanese products in the United States or Europe instead of nearby Japan.

The same dichotomy is often found even in the one institution that does show a more enlightened attitude, namely the press. Although, on the whole, it keeps a close watch on government and business in the interest of the people, it has not yet realized that it is in the interest of the Japanese, and the world as a whole, that imports find easier access. Instead, the press tends to support industry's claims that foreign companies have failed because they did not try hard enough while ignoring even patent cases of non-tariff barriers. It is therefore not in the least unusual to find a newspaper carrying in the very same issue both an article criticizing some foreign country for imposing restrictions on Japanese goods and another stating that due to a rise in imports action must be taken to help some Japanese industry.

This weak—and frequently ambiguous—support of free trade is obviously not sufficient to counteract the tremendous support for Japanese industry that makes it so hard to penetrate the market. In government, there are a number of bodies specifically entrusted with preventing any damage to local companies. On the financial side, there is the Ministry of Finance and state-run banks. In specialized fields, there is the influence of the Ministries of Health or Agriculture. And there is the extensive apparatus of MITI which involves not only nurturing industries but direct intervention to shore up ailing ones. Nor should it be forgotten that protectionism creates more work (paperwork and red tape) for bureaucrats while giving them greater prestige as defenders of Japanese interests.

In business circles, although Keidanren and Keizai Doyukai speak warmly of free trade, they have many other activities which are directly oriented toward helping member companies. The same applies to the Chamber of Commerce and Industry and especially the many trade associations which provide for incredibly close relations among the companies in most sectors in defense of their interests. Moreover, there is reason to wonder whether even the enlightened business leaders are as keen on free trade as they used to be. Former Keidanren President Toshiwo Doko was a firm believer in free enterprise. His successor, Yoshihiro Inayama, sometimes referred to as "Mr. Cartel" by the press, speaks more of cooperation and accomodation. "We should understand that the world economy does not function efficiently in these days unless the principle of free market competition is sometimes adjusted."[18]

In addition, it must be remembered that although the well meaning and relatively enlightened business leaders get most of the limelight, they hardly represent a majority of the business world. In fact, they are an infinite minority, those from very large companies with substantial market shares, and then only the ones in leading growth sectors. The others come from much smaller entities that are frequently in trouble. They also come from sectors with tight profit margins in distribution or services as well as manufacturing firms in an increasing number of stagnant and even depressed industries. They have no interest whatsoever in free trade and only crave enough protection to get by.

Finally, there is the strongest lobby that exists in Japan, the farm lobby. Since Japan still has relatively more farmers than most other advanced countries, this is a very large group of voters and they enjoy exceptional political clout since they inhabit the rural districts that elect disproportionately more Diet members. About a quarter of Japan's legislators are committed to protecting every crop that grows in the country by blocking imports or offering subsidies to local farmers. Despite the tremendous costs involved, and continued low productivity, there is little hope that the barriers will fall.[19]

With this background, one can understand what happens in Japan far better than through a learned exegesis of the unending flow of speeches and declarations extolling free trade. For, free trade is not a principle; it is a practice. And it is rarely conceded voluntarily by those who stand to lose. So, there must be a strong constituency to impose it either out of moral concern or self-interest. As long as no such constituency comes to the fore in Japan, there will be more talk than action.

That is why the situation contrasts so sharply with some other countries that are in the free trade camp. There, the fine talk is more frequently accompanied by action whether the governments and manufacturers want it or not. In many countries a vigorous consumer movement has gained ground and people would not be willing to accept dictation, either from government or distributors, as to what they should buy. Businessmen who export will openly counter businessmen who fear imports and they would all admit that progress only comes from reciprocity. Even labor, which gets hurt worst in a declining economy, still raises the banner of free trade although it droops occasionally.

This applies even to the least progressive, those with a long history of protectionism and many vestiges still today, such as France or Italy. Free trade is yet stronger in the very open economies of Scandinavia, Belgium or Netherlands, and in a traditional free trader like Britain or the new champion, Germany. It is also true, by and large, whether a conservative and pro-business government is in power or a socialist, labor-dominated one.

In the United States, where this often goes furthest, free trade is much more than an empty slogan despite any recent infringements. As we saw in the automobile conflict, it was not easy to mobilize the population to block Japanese imports. Even the trade unions, which were the driving force, did not like the action they had to take in principle and thus could ask for no more than temporary relief. The automakers were rather hesitant about restrictions and only acted much later, while General Motors refused to join the fold. The Federal

Trade Commission presented a report that went against them and their case was rejected by the International Trade Commission. Despite the many Congressmen backing action, others tried to prevent it. And, to the end, both the Carter and Reagan administrations sought a softer compromise.

This indecisiveness was a result of two things. First of all, there is no question but that many Americans are sincerely attached to free trade as a principle and willing to accept some pain—to "bite the bullet"—in order to defend it. The principle is espoused by countless politicians, academics, economists and journalists. Most businessmen and trade unionists admit the advantages. Federal Reserve Board Chairman Paul Volker, among others, criticized curbs as an example of "policies that provide protection to individuals or businesses from competition and the inevitable risks of economic life." And the Federal Trade Commission, theoretically the watchdog that might have protected business, was even more sweeping in its condemnation of protectionism, claiming that "the costs of protection invariably exceed the benefits."[20]

But another aspect is probably decisive. Those who back free trade have strong material interests to defend. They are no more noble than the companies which want to turn a profit or workers who hope to keep their jobs. The consumers, who provide the bulk of public support for imports, are eager to save money . . . nothing more. Some businessmen are earning a living by selling imports of foreign brand goods. Others are not willing to risk the loss of export opportunities if protectionism spreads. Opinion-makers in a country where one is expected to practice what one preaches (*tatemae* is not highly evaluated) cannot readily call for free trade in the 1970s and reject it in the 1980s. The American government has done so much to restore the economies of its trading partners, including Japan, that it tries to avoid unnecessary trouble. Successive administrations have striven to expand trade even if they sometimes had to take a step backward. Thus, no political leader feels free to go against this tradition.

It is this kind of coalition which keeps Washington from imposing restrictions or at least wards them off long enough for Japan to decide on restraint in its own interest. It is hard to tell just how strong it is and to what extent it can resist some present trends. But there is no doubt that it has made free trade more than just an empty slogan. This was seen most clearly by Doug Fraser, who had more of an uphill battle than he expected. Before it was over, he had to pay his opponents a rather back-handed compliment. "People talk a lot about free trade . . . they accuse people of my persuasion of being knee-jerk liberals. I can tell you there are knee-jerk free traders," he said. "As soon as you even talk about something . . . that would inject a fairness into trade then there's a knee-jerk from the free traders."[21]

With regard to foreign aid, although the United States has slipped somewhat, it is still the major source. Certain European countries, especially Scandinavian, France and Germany, follow behind in total but precede in per capita contributions, while Japan takes up the rear. This is not because the others are so prosperous. Indeed, most are facing much greater economic difficulties. Yet, they remain committed to lending a helping hand due partly to ideals which are rooted in Christianity or humanitarianism and carried over in certain aspects of the capitalism and socialism practiced there. Of course, there is also the pressure coming from the international organizations or the need to keep on good terms with certain allies or trading partners. But the predominant element would seem to be a strong tradition of charity among the people who organize lobbies to promote aid or form their own groups to collect and channel substantial amounts of voluntary donations. Little of this exists in Japan as yet, although there are some hopeful signs that it may arise. Meanwhile, people are far too concerned about what happens to their companies, their nation, and doubtlessly also themselves to worry about those in far greater distress.

It is this lack of a Japanese constituency for free trade or foreign aid which explains many of the problems that are encountered regularly. That is why liberalization was so slow to begin with. It explains why, once formal barriers were withdrawn, new impediments sprang up. It also makes one wonder how long the Japanese will wait before resorting to new protective measures, this time to shelter ailing industries. Or if they will really stop taking a free ride. So far every concession has been hard fought despite all the well meaning statements of Japan's leaders because these causes did not enjoy much backing from the people. Unless that changes, there is reason to fear that future steps will only come from further pressure, which is the least desirable—but most effective—method.

NOTES

1. *White Paper on International Trade*, MITI, 1981, p. 146.
2. Ibid, p. 145.
3. See *Vision of International Trade and Industrial Policy for the 1980s*, MITI, 1980, and *A Vision of the 21st Century—The Quest for Industrial Restructuring*, Keizai Doyukai, 1979.
4. *White Paper on International Trade*, MITI, 1979, p. 59
5. *Vision of International Trade and Industrial Policy for the 1980s.*
6. *1979 White Paper on International Trade*, p. 32.
7. Herman Kahn, *The Emerging Japanese Superstate*, p. 86.
8. Correspondents of The Economist, *Consider Japan.*
9. *Japan Times*, June 27, 1981.
10. *Business Week*, March 16, 1981.
11. Based on confidential interviews at the highest level.
12. *Japan Economic Journal*, March 10, 1981.
13. The Fair Trade Commission has uncovered many cases where traders regulate imports of given products, such as phenols, monosodium glutamate, and salmon roe. But this kind of manipulation is much more widespread. More generally, if manufactured imports can be increased at command, they can be decreased as well.
14. *Japan Economic Journal*, March 3, 1981.
15. See Woronoff, *Inside Japan, Inc.*, pp. 194-8.

16. Ibid., pp. 38–57.
17. See Chalmers Johnson, *MITI And The Japanese Miracle*.
18. *Japan Times*, July 11, 1980.
19. See Woronoff, *Japan's Wasted Workers*, pp. 151–7.
20. *Japan Times*, April 9, 1981.
21. *Japan Times*, April 17, 1981.

7
Where Will It End?

Tomorrow's Trade Conflicts

It really doesn't take an expert to predict that there will be more trade conflicts in the future. For over two decades, the same causes have had the same effects and there is no reason to expect that to change now. There has been a reasonably sustained growth in several rising economies and a protracted slump in the advanced countries which provide the biggest markets. Due to basic structural characteristics, exports are growing more rapidly in some countries then the ability to absorb them abroad. And, when the products are concentrated in specific sectors the impact becomes too great.

Those who count on the natural action of supply and demand to adjust exports and imports or who assume that free trade and free enterprise can accomodate all comers forget that the situation is far from what it should be in theory. Exports are expanded not only in response to market signals but as tools of national policy and then receive whatever incentives are deemed necessary. When export campaigns begin, sometimes just for reasons of convenience, they are restricted to a single market until that is saturated, only then moving on to the next, and the next. Due either to a bandwagon effect or the simple fact that so many manufacturers are on roughly the same level as their peers, this is paralleled by a tendency to push one export product until its possibilities have been exhausted, then the next, and the next.

The result is what Sir Terence Beckett, Director-General of the Confederation of British Industry, called the "laser beam approach." In one of the many speeches being made around the world on the increasingly popular topic of unfair competition from Japanese imports, he stated that the Japanese "adopt a laser beam approach, concentrating on particular targets and virtually obliterating those industries one by one." The image is amazingly apt, although perhaps somewhat overdone, since Japanese manufacturers do pick a product, then a market, and bring all their power to bear until they have succeeded. Since the total power is substantial, and the target selected artificially narrowed (and sometimes intentionally chosen because it can be destroyed), the effect usually is devastating.[1]

The energy coming from certain dynamic sectors in Japan, or the NICs, is incredible. It wells forth in pulses as huge shifts in resources bring about an astounding increase in output. These pulses are converted to trade surges with the sudden increase of imports in certain categories being much more intense than the growth of imports in the sector or the overall growth of imports in the country. We have already referred to cases of a doubling of specific imports from one year to the next even on a relatively large base. No industry can take such a battering for long. If the industry is already weakened, which is normally the case since the older ones are usually those first selected by new exporters, then its possibilities of resistance are even less. The alternative is either to let it collapse or to offer protection.

There is not much sense in saying a country should not resort to protectionism under such circumstances because it is obvious that it will no matter what one says. Moreover, it really doesn't have much of a choice. As a noted Japanese economist, Masamichi Hanabusa, pointed out: "This sudden surge in the imports of specific products not only makes adjustments by the affected industries difficult but also renders their future so precarious that the industries are unable to work out a sensible strategy for the future. When the economy of the importing country is depressed, such a situation, because of its implications on employment, engenders an attitude of outright rejection rather than that of constructive accomodation to the realities of international economic life on the part of the industries affected."[2]

The chances are therefore extremely good that in the future new sectors, or the same sectors in new countries, will come under such relentless pressure that the reaction will again be restrictions. This would be less worrisome if not for the fact that rather few sectors which once came under protectionism

There are some things that politicians just cannot ignore.
Nor should they try!

Credit: United Auto Workers

reemerged. Some of the less valid reasons for this, namely taking advantage of the protected status, will be dealt with later on. But, even if an industry made serious efforts and enjoyed broad support from the government, it would not be easy to recover. If the export offensive occurs at all, it is because there has been some loss of comparative advantage. Perhaps the machinery or technology is out-of-date or labor costs have risen too high. Foreign countries making a concerted effort to win, and hold on to markets, will see that the competitive edge they have grows. And, behind them, may be further countries which enter through the same breach.

Thus, the oldest conflict which involved textiles has not really ceased. American producers could not upgrade rapidly enough to meet the Japanese competition before they were faced with even cheaper articles from Hong Kong and Taiwan. The European shipbuilding industry has not attained the productivity of the Japanese yards and wages are much higher than in Korea or Brazil, so it has lost any competitive edge in both ways. Despite introducing sophisticated machinery, American shoe manufacturers—whose labor costs kept rising—were still undercut by the Italians, then the Koreans, then the Mexicans, and goodness knows who next. As each new wave strikes, even companies making serious efforts to improve would find it hard to keep ahead.

Meanwhile, protectionism has been spreading in another way as the former invaders find that they have lost their own competitive edge and are being pressed too hard by newcomers. The Japanese textile manufacturers would seem to have forgotten how bitterly they fought restrictions and their early hatred of the Multi-Fiber Arrangement. Although Japan is still a member of the MFA, they are more worried about imports than exports. Nor do the Japanese want to be overrun by Taiwanese footwear, or Korean steel, or Hong Kong digital watches. As long as each new exporter struggles to win markets, then to consolidate its position, and finally to keep others out, there will be no early end to protectionism.

GATT recently reported that the number of international trade disputes had reached a record level of thirteen in 1980. According to it, "protectionist pressures are high in many countries and international trade disputes have been numerous."[3] But that is only the tip of the iceberg since most of the recent measures have been taken informally between the countries directly concerned, outside of GATT and without reference, or in sharp opposition, to its rules. In addition to actual restrictions, the EC's surveillance system used to monitor Japanese exports of certain sensitive items is a form of pre-protectionism indicating where conflicts may arise and inhibiting trade as Japan tries to avoid harmful friction.

There are many candidates for the next trade conflict. Some are in electronics. Despite the huge American head start for computers and integrated circuits, the Japanese have been catching up on the home market and also abroad. Due to government subsidies and protection of the industry, then to the massive credit made available to boost output in order to attain economies of scale, the Japanese firms can produce far more chips and other components than they need as well as a growing range of computers. In some specific slots, their technology is also superior. But they are still more likely to expand by cutting costs and pushing hard for each additional percent of market share.

To avoid trade friction, what the Japanese want most is a product that no one else has. They came as close to that as they are likely to with the video tape recorder. Two of the primary systems were developed by Sony and Japan Victor, although Philips also has an alternative. Yet, the world has rarely seen commercial competition like that to impose one of the systems, at any cost, since it was assumed that whoever buys the product will stick to that type and also be an excellent market for software. Moreover, if one or the other gains a sufficient edge, it could drive the competing system out of existence. So far few disputes have arisen, although Austria tried to protect the Philips system on its market. But the unprecedented import surges still contributed to growing trade deficits abroad.

In their drive, which borders on an obsession, to stay ahead of all competitors by increasing productivity, the Japanese have developed an endless variety of automatic machinery and sophisticated machine tools. For many of them they were hardly the only producers since no advanced country could arise without such an industry. But they were increasingly ahead with regard to technology and price. The numerically-controlled machine tools in particular were desired abroad. For robots, the Japanese would seem to have a substantial head start. Yet, even if there are few local competitors to resist the inroads, a different attitude to labor-saving machinery is bound to exist in countries where there is massive unemployment.

There is already tremendous international competition for telecommunications equipment. Since much of it is sold to state-run or monopoly companies, the first round of the confrontation involved opening procurement to bidding by foreign firms. The Japanese only accepted under duress, and few observers expect NTT to release much of the market. If it does not, a second round could be more unpleasant. So far, there have been no complaints about Japanese exports of pharmaceuticals since the efforts only started recently. If the existing plans for expanding overseas sales go ahead, however, this could have a huge impact on existing currents. For aircraft, the Japanese have remained pretty much on the sidelines, partly because they could not decide whether to go it alone or join one of the major makers. If they ultimately choose the former, there could be serious friction on a rather tight market.

Most of these are cases where surges of Japanese imports could create problems. But there are also bound to be more conflicts revolving around real or imagined barriers to foreign products in Japan. One that has already begun arises out of America's efforts to increase sales of auto parts. The Commerce Department more than gently urged the Japanese automakers to buy $120 million in 1980, $300 million in 1981, and somewhat more in 1982. Whereas the first target was actually exceeded slightly, MITI seriously doubts a level of $300 million is feasible even though it only represents about 1% of Japan's domestic auto parts production of over ¥5 trillion a year. And the chances of further success are particularly dim since this sector is so strongly characterized by close relations between automakers and subcontractors. Aside from questions of quality or delivery deadline, the Japanese makers will resist any major increase in purchases abroad since they have a financial or other interest in these companies.

Agriculture is also bound to remain a major source of friction because it is increasingly the only sector in which some countries have any hope of boosting sales. If Japan will not buy more manufactured goods, what else can it buy other than raw materials and food? Thus, Bill Brock promptly served notice that the Reagan administration wants Japan to open its market further. High officials from Australia and New Zealand have made similar requests. Yet, far from reversing its earlier policy, the Japanese are apparently moving toward even higher barriers. For, that is the only way they can conceivably implement the plans for "self-sufficiency" and "security" being promoted by the Ministry of Agriculture with strong support from the farm lobby. This only differs in degree from comparable policies in Europe and even America. Agriculture could therefore become one of the most intractable, and politically sensitive, trade issues of the decade.

Despite the fact that many of the potential conflicts seem fated to erupt into real clashes, there is always the possibility that suitable action could defuse them. One very interesting case involves integrated circuits. Even though it came from behind, by 1980 Japan already exported more ICs to America than it imported. Yet, at that time, it had a tariff considerably higher than the United States and the rates were not to be equalized, at a low level, until 1987. By agreeing to accelerate this process, one hurdle was overcome. Meanwhile, the Japanese industry realized it was wiser to moderate exports and a relative balance was struck. Finally, by opening production facilities in America, and allowing American companies to do the same in Japan, the competition took another form that affected trade much less.

This brief survey, which only refers to some major industries, is enough to show that there is no shortage of areas in which conflicts can arise. As Japan moves upward, the conflicts will follow its progression. Even products it does not manufacture today may be exported in huge quantities tomorrow. In an effort to get into the Japanese market, one sector after the other can be singled out by its trading partners as particularly difficult and a suitable point to exert pressure. While the advanced countries are involved in more confrontations with one another, they will also be drawn into more collisions with newcomers, some of which still do not produce the articles they will insist be imported in a few years from now.

The individual disputes involving specific products or trading partners, of course, will become part of the broader problem of trade imbalances if there is not a radical change in the existing trade flows. At present, for example, there is absolutely no factor that indicates a disappearance, or even lessening, of the trade imbalance between Japan and the United States or Europe. . . unless it is protectionism. If there is no change in the trends over the coming decade, then according to Lionel Olmer, American Undersecretary of Commerce, the trade deficit with Japan should rise close to $50 billion by 1990.[4]

Even if one distrusts statistics and assumes gross error, a trade deficit of $25 billion or merely $10 billion is still worrisome. The size is already alarming enough. But the very idea of a continuing, major deficit, year after year, implies a constant drain on the United States. Given the present situation and trends, there would doubtlessly be even greater stress in Europe. When one considers that the present trade deficits have been rejected as unacceptable, and almost a cause for retaliation, it is easy to imagine just how explosive the anger and resentment could become.

Lapse Into Protectionism

It is already frightening enough to be living in a world where trade conflicts can break out at any time and, in fact, are almost guaranteed to occur with predictable regularity. But that is nothing compared to the threat that any one of those conflicts, and certainly the major ones, could lead to a rapid spread of protectionism in general. It is hardly necessary to demonstrate that the world economy has not been in worse shape since the Great Depression. Economic growth has slowed tremendously, prices are skyrocketing and inflation is often out of hand, unemployment is worsening and countries are seriously tempted to get out of their own problems at the cost of their neighbors.

It is perhaps only the memory of the depression and the fact that giving in to the temptation of protectionism made it so much worse that holds people back. Meanwhile, we have been tottering on the brink. On the occasion of every new crisis, as solutions are sought, the world's leaders renew their pledge not to repeat the disaster. In 1977, when voluntary restraint on television exports was imposed on Japan, President Carter stated: "Because of the seriousness of the unemployment situation, we are prone to fall prey to the temptation toward protectionism, but the leaders have confirmed that that is not the right direction."[5] When President Reagan imposed similar restraint regarding automobile exports, it was to avoid more distasteful formal restrictions.

More recently, the Ottawa Summit adopted a declaration that reflected the prevailing views by dealing with trade from three slightly different angles. First came the "strong commitment to maintaining liberal trade policies and to the effective operation of an open multilateral trading system." Then a noble promise to "resist protectionist pressures, since we recognize that any protectionist measure, whether in the form of overt or hidden trade restrictions or in the form of subsidies to prop up declining industries, not only undermines the dynamism of our economies but also, over time, aggravates inflation and unemployment." Then, since the principle and benefits seemed inadequate to obtain compliance, the leaders agreed to "keep under close review the role played by our countries in the smooth functioning of the multilateral trading system. . . while allowing for the safeguard measures provided for in the GATT."[6]

Thus, the appeals for free trade and against protectionism could barely mask the fact that so far more of the action taken has not really been a step back from the brink so much as an attempt to get around it without falling in. That this may not always be possible is shown by the attitude of those most deeply involved in the conflicts, those with substantial vested interests. One of the most active is American labor. Increasingly aggrieved by "cutthroat and often illegal foreign competition," former AFL-CIO President, the late George Meany, went so far as to urge President Carter to abandon America's free trade policy: "The answer is fair trade—do unto others as they do unto us—barrier for barrier, closed door for closed door." His successor Lane Kirkland more calmly warned the Senate that "a policy of government abdication of responsibility in the name of free trade can make the losses from trade much higher than the gains for most

Americans," and outlined basic points a "fair" trade policy should contain.[7]

The Japanese side has been no less blunt in pushing its views. Despite more than a residue of protectionist sentiment in the United States, the Japanese textile industry challenged a testy President Nixon for three years and then complained of a *shokku* when he responded. Nissan's boss Ishihara almost dared the Americans to act. "Even if the law were established, it would mean that the United States had pulled the trigger to destroy the free trade system, so the American government would most probably be very careful about its implementation." And Eiji Toyoda took on the Japanese government. "The minute MITI opens its mouth it always says 'voluntary restraint.' But MITI doesn't make automobiles, does it?"[8]

By now, even among those who are entrusted with solving the conflicts, protectionism has become both an alternative that is verbally rejected and a negotiating point in practice. France's Francois Missoffe warned that there could be no cooperation with Europe "unless the Japanese play by the same rules," otherwise "the Japanese way of behavior would inevitably encourage protectionism."[9] German Economics Minister Otto Lambsdorff insisted that, "The Japanese should give us access to their market and they should try to moderate their position. They must take care not to provoke political reactions in our country which would force our government to actions we do not want to take." And British Foreign Secretary Lord Carrington said in Tokyo, referring to Japanese exports in sensitive sectors, that "no elected government in Europe can watch this process gallop ahead unchecked." If it continued, "we would find ourselves caught up in a destructive cycle of protectionism."[10]

So, even while condemning it, the idea of protectionism is constantly being mooted. In such an atmosphere, with exporters defying vital trading partners and politicians repeatedly taking up the cause of some threatened industry, more than enough sparks are kindled. One of them, as Count Lambsdorff feared with regard to the automobile crisis, could touch off a "chain reaction all over the world." No one questioned him when he warned, "It would spread like fire once it gets started. Nobody is going to prevent it once it gets started." That the situation had already deteriorated quite drastically had to be admitted by none other than the Secretary-General of GATT, Arthur Dunkel, who noted ". . . we are told from the highest level that protectionism is no longer a possibility but a probability."[11]

But it would seem that such verbal fireworks and the threat of ultimate disaster are invoked mainly to impress the general public. The world's leaders have grown more sophisticated and experienced, they have been playing with less virulent strains of protectionism for decades already and think they can contain it. Of course, they may be wrong. Just as for concessions, safeguards and retaliation are reciprocal. No one ever knows when one minor gesture will provoke another, and another. Nor can one forget that the Smoot-Hawley Tariff of 1929 only began as a small housekeeping bill and became a massive cudgel with record tariffs on 1,250 items which struck a death blow against free trade. Similar legislation, and some has been suggested, could also plunge the world into a destructive cycle of decreasing trade, falling production, and deepening misery.

Since most of the measures were clearly directed against Japan, even when phrased in relatively general or neutral terms, the Japanese were increasingly worried. There was talk of imposing a requirement of up to 90% domestic content in all automobiles sold in the United States, a far harsher rule in practice than the voluntary restraint or even quotas. Some Congressmen also spoke of imposing a "tax" of sorts on Japan's gross national product to compensate America for defense expenditures incurred on Japan's behalf. But the most disturbing proposals revolved around the concept of "reciprocity," and they alarmed not only Japan but just about every trading nation and many Americans. Fortunately, for the moment at least, this did not mean a strict reciprocity in trade, either through a precise balancing of flows in both directions or, even worse, equal amounts of sales by both partners in specific sectors.

Rather, it seemed to involve a reciprocity of behavior. If some country, without mentioning names, adopted very restrictive practices and had numerous barriers, then the United States would be justified in being every bit as restrictive. Senator Danforth, the main proponent of the concept, stressed while in Tokyo that "the issue is not the size of the trade deficit; the issue is to make sure that both sides play by the same rules." He then explained that the onus for action lies with Japan, "because if Japan had no barriers to American imports, we would have no barriers to Japanese imports." But Special Trade Representative Brock insisted that the Reagan administration was opposed to "negative reciprocity" and urged instead more positive measures by Japan, such as to open its market wider or to transfer more sophisticated technologies to the United States as had been done for it. And Commerce Secretary Baldrige announced, with regard to possible restrictive legislation, "If the Japanese really are trying to open up their market, I would be opposed to any such legislation." However, he added, "if they don't, I would support it."[12]

If, for one reason or another, Washington or other capitals did switch from relatively free trade to stricter reciprocity, it is not hard to imagine what might happen as each country responded in kind. Still, this is no place to paint a doomsday scenario which each reader can well figure out for himself. What must be dealt with here are the more probable scenarios arising from a continuance of the existing trends, leading to a partial, if growing, restriction or "management" of trade and the adoption of yet more neoprotectionistic measures in many nations. This is likely not only because of the impending conflicts and inevitable trade imbalances but for a further reason as well. Although everyone realizes that any widespread regression from free trade would be generally harmful, partial steps could actually benefit some and they might just get away with it. Even if there were losses, they would be very unevenly spread and some would obviously lose much less than others.

So far, for some inexplicable reason, much of the dislike of protectionism has been expressed in the importing countries, mainly by the consumers. As everyone knows, and Robert McNamara among others stated, "The truth is that protectionism is inefficient, counter-productive and ultimately self-defeating." There are plenty of studies showing how much is lost by imposing restrictions. The ITC found it would cost Americans more in higher automobile prices and gas purchases to keep Japanese autos out than to let them in. Consumers for World Trade estimated that the total cost of protection for all American industries, including agriculture, amounted to a monumental $15 billion a year. The EC Commission admitted that simply the time and effort wasted on customs barriers added as much as 10% to the price of goods traded. Since the Japanese government is not interested in such calculations, the Americans calculated for them that agricultural protection cost the Japanese consumers about $5 billion in 1972, a figure that must have more than doubled by now.[13]

These are staggering figures and should make the protecting countries stop and think. Perhaps they do. But the problem is that those who foot the bill, namely the consumers in general, are less vitally concerned and may have less political clout than those who lose directly, namely businessmen and workers. In addition, while highlighting the losses to the public they tend to forget that this must be balanced against losses to the producers, such as waste of plant and machinery, loss of wages and need to provide unemployment benefits or welfare. Once the equation is complete, both sides will balance out more closely and, on occasion, protectionism may be cheaper.

Moreover, what happens to an importing country that closes its borders often appears less perilous because it involves a slow sinking of the whole economy rather than any spectacular manifestations. Indeed, this may well be less noticeable than the collapse of specific industries due to imports. By rejecting cheaper imports, it is possible to keep much of the economy intact. However, costs will rise for the consumers who will then agitate for higher wages, pushing costs up again, and justifying the next round of wage demands. When the imports are basic materials, such as steel, use of more expensive local steel would drive up the costs of all products incorporating it. A refusal to import better machinery would not only increase costs, it could directly undermine productivity and lessen competitiveness. Finally, although a country can defend its own markets, it would gradually lose any foreign markets to more dynamic competitors and thus forfeit possible economies of scale. Failure to export would then incite new moves to prevent imports and bring the process one round further.

Exporters, on the other hand, have paid relatively little attention to the general process and have concentrated their efforts on fighting each individual battle for markets. It is clear that some of their defeats have been very painful. The only reason the slump in Japan's textile industry, and the stagnation of other Asian exporters, could be overcome was that other sectors absorbed some of the resources. The decision to limit exports of automobiles, machine tools, or steel has basically implied restraints on growth for Japan. But, in the future, it could bite deeper and actually result in a decrease in production. This must give the Japanese planners and manufacturers sleepless nights when one considers that already most major export products face some sort of ceiling and the complaints of importing countries have only grown louder.

Efforts to contain damaging surges of imports could easily spread to insistence on a balanced growth in trade through increased efforts by Japan to import or, failing this, a decision to balance trade downward by blocking Japanese products. Such a return to bilateral methods is not purely imaginary. Most of its leading trading partners have already made a point of deploring their deficits with Japan and the European Community is monitoring the trade statistics very carefully. The United States, by concentrating on specific items like auto parts or integrated circuits, is even thinking in terms of balancing trade on a product-basis rather than more generally. And Taiwan has actually shifted some of its purchases to Western countries to lessen its surpluses with them as well as its deficit with Japan. If, to wipe out their own deficits, the United States or European countries were to do the same, Japan and others could find themselves in a serious crunch.

Can people like this save the world trade system? Leaders of the top industrialized nations at the Tokyo Summit.

The basic reason is that an export-oriented economy is heavily dependent on trade while those based on import-substitution or with no particular bias are relatively independent. This has been the price of rapid growth, a price that could once be ignored or accepted in the bargain but which may eventually become prohibitive. Even now, after three decades of development, most of Japan's growth comes from exports and part of the growth in the domestic sector is also due to plant and machinery investment only justified by exports. The NICs are in pretty much the same situation. If for any reason, say trade restrictions, some of the export growth became impossible, these economies could only expand at a rather modest rate. If it were necessary to reduce export growth substantially, the economy would become relatively stagnant. And a major reduction in present levels of trade would be catastrophic.

The effect of trade restrictions on most export-oriented countries would be even more telling due to various distortions that have arisen in their economies. The sectors which have been developed most are not necessarily those which arose naturally from inherent advantages or met domestic needs and could therefore count on a solid home market no matter what. Rather, they were chosen as a function of external needs, to meet a demand for certain products in other countries. Export success arose out of a strong mobilization of resources while capacity was intentionally built up to gain ever greater competitiveness. This has made these sectors highly dependent on continued exports. If this were to fall off, not only would there be a decrease in sales but the industry itself would become less efficient and almost pointless if restricted to the domestic market.

The fact that each country has specialized excessively in a limited number of products makes it that much more vulnerable. One can well imagine what would happen to Japan if, for example, its automobile industry—half of whose production

is for export and which represents a fifth of total exports—
came under more severe restrictions than in the past. And it
has hardly spread the risks very much by depending on its top
five export products for about 60% of its foreign trade. Korea,
depending on light industrial manufactures for over half its
exports, and textiles alone for 30%, is even more fragile.
Taiwan, with textiles accounting for 25% of exports and
electrical machinery and apparatus for another 16%, is no
better off. The same applies to the other export-oriented
countries whose growth was dynamic but risky.

A further element of risk has been to concentrate exports
too much on a small number of markets. This is already bad
enough without these primary markets being the very ones
that are now stagnant or increasingly protected. To make
things worse, due both to differences in size and dependence
on trade, the amount of leverage the exporters have in shaping
mutual relations is rather slight. For example, although some
23% of Japan's exports go to the United States, this only
represents some 13% of American imports. Similarly, about
13% of Japan's exports go to the European Community while
the EC's imports from Japan only represent 2% of the total. A
smaller, more export-intensive nation like Korea finds itself
exporting 32% of its goods to the United States while America
only imports 2% of its goods from Korea. It should be
perfectly evident from this which countries depend more or
less on which others.

The Japanese repeatedly insist that they cannot survive
without imports of raw materials, foodstuffs, and fuel. They
live, as they never tire of saying, in a terribly import-
dependent nation. For some reason they are inclined to
neglect that they are no less dependent on exports. . . and
perhaps more so. A trade boycott or simply higher tariffs on
certain goods would be as devastating as an oil boycott or
higher raw material prices. For, they cannot import without
the money they earn from exports. Seen from this angle, they

might be wise to revise some of their older, rather lopsided views and pay more attention to the needs of their export partners. They already know it is essential to keep on good terms with the oil sheiks and raw material producers. But they tend to forget that they must also maintain decent relations with their customers unless they raise a hue and cry about torrential exports and ailing industries.

What protectionism would imply for these countries is roughly the reverse of what happens to importers which close their markets. . . except that for the exporters that have gone too far it could be more abrupt and cataclysmic. Not able to export, they would have to cut back on production, suffering a serious loss of sales and profits. But that is not the end of it. This fall in production would make much of the capacity redundant and destroy the economies of scale which justified exports to begin with. Their products would thus become less competitive even on the markets left open to them and, judging by past experience, the companies would probably engage in ruthless and destructive competition to sell what they could. Meanwhile, it would still be necessary to import some of the products they did not make locally because too many resources had been directed toward the export-oriented sectors. In most cases, local production would be less efficient and prices higher. The rising cost of living, plus growing unemployment in export industries, would lead to rapidly deteriorating living standards.

Although both scenarios look equally negative, it is worthwhile remembering that, while export-oriented economies are terribly dependent on markets, the reverse is not always true. The United States or the European Community as a whole still produce most of the goods they need, even if they are a bit more costly, and could safely forego most manufactured imports. The same is even true of many less successful developing countries, or the Soviet bloc, which followed an import-substitution policy. All of them are relatively self-sufficient and could get along with less trade, albeit at a lower level of well-being. For them, exports are still just a supplement and not the very foundation of the economy. They are therefore more balanced and broader based making them more resistant to external shocks.

For such reasons, the countries which are likely to take protectionist measures may feel that they can afford this more than those the measures are directed against. Everyone can still agree with Prime Minister Nakasone when he calls on the world's leaders to resist protectionist policies that could result in a collapse similar to the Great Depression. As he said, "resorting to protectionism must be avoided at all costs if we want to avoid the serious tragedy we all experienced in the 1930s."[14] But they will still wonder why he and his countrymen have not realized that their economy, and others like it, will be injured more rapidly and more seriously by an intensification of the trade friction and should therefore make every possible effort to prevent conflicts from arising. Without the conflicts, most of these worrisome measures would never be adopted to begin with.

Export Overkill

As Japan, followed by the NICs, aggressively pursue their export policies, they seem to fear only one consequence, namely protectionism. This is the only thing that can block them completely and the mere threat is enough to moderate the tempo. There are already more barriers than they like and efforts are constantly being made to remove or get around them. But little thought is given to what lies on the other side. The only concern is to sell more goods and carve out a bit more market share no matter what. How this affects the economy of the importing country is immaterial.

This attitude may have had some validity in the early days, when the exporters had small and fragile economies and the major importers vast untapped markets, tremendous wealth and powerful economies of their own. But a broader view would seem necessary now that the newcomers already possess a substantial share of world trade and their export industries have become well nigh invincible. The impact is clearly strong enough even to stagger the American economy. And one can imagine what the consequences of a determined export offensive would be on smaller European countries and especially the weaker developing countries. The need to show greater concern for others, as we shall see, derives not only from charitable or diplomatic considerations but also some basic tenets of enlightened self-interest.

It does not take an economic genius to see that although the United Nations is still launching "development decades" most of the world's economies at the present time are stagnant or declining. This is an unwelcome and also a puzzling phenomenon since there would seem to be more than enough potential for further growth. Nevertheless, aside from the oil or raw material producing countries and the export-oriented economies, little progress is being made and those who fall behind naturally tend to blame their failure on those who do better.

Much of this is unfair. The slowing down of the advanced economies is partly a result of their maturation. There are fewer new growth fields and new technologies become harder to develop and more costly to introduce. Other competitors spring up abroad which are bound to claim some of the market even if they are just average and a greater share if they are particularly dynamic. Meanwhile, the work will and discipline which brought about the earlier success may sink as people want more leisure, or better living standards, and their children almost forget that wealth has to be created before it is consumed. In some unfortunate cases quarrels between capital and labor, or within the nation's leadership, as to how to use or divide the wealth can undermine the basic productive mechanism. Surely, if the Western economies have been weakened, it is largely their own fault and, even in the absence of higher oil prices or cheaper imports, they would have entered a decline. Inability to decide on, or implement, rational economic policies, often paralleled by a refusal to allow individual initiative to flourish, explain the failure of most Third World countries to develop.

However, when natural processes or regrettable failures are tampered with or exploited, the results are likely to be much worse. Economic maturation, as mentioned, is a normal but not necessarily harmful cycle. Any industry will eventually reach the point where expansion is slowed down or stopped by limits to the market. There is just so much of anything you can sell. At the same time, the original competitive edge may have weakened. Factories grow old and obsolete, newer, more efficient technologies are invented which hasten this, and the general wage level may have risen. If the same industry arises abroad, where the comparative advantage is greater, the older firms will be forced back gradually. However, in the meanwhile other opportunities may have emerged for the entrepreneurs and workers in new sectors and thus the loss is less serious or can even be a boon if these growth sectors are more promising or profitable.

On the other hand when an industry collapses due to excessive pounding by imports, the situation is quite different since the process is accelerated unduly. The smoothest manner of falling back is obviously for factories to cease expanding or slowly withdraw from the field as their equipment becomes amortized or obsolete. Meanwhile, the labor force would shrink largely through attrition. Even over a reasonably short period, it is possible to convert factories, retrain workers, and invest in different machinery to make something else. But it is impossible to do anything other than close down perfectly good factories and abruptly dismiss workers when massive import surges occur. Developing countries, which do not have much industrial capacity or knowhow to begin with would find themselves frozen out as one sector after another is preempted by imports.

The effect is compounded by the fact that the advance of many exporting countries has not been a smooth and gradual process but a result of very sharp export offensives. If exports are relatively broad and based largely on complementarity, then even substantial amounts can be absorbed with little or no damage to the receiving country. If, on the other hand, they are highly concentrated on narrow sectors and gain rapidly in intensity, basically the "laser beam" approach, even if the amount involved is a minute share of total imports, the impact can be deadly. A given branch will be faced with such tremendous competition, so suddenly, that even relatively efficient producers may succumb. Moreover, since it is hard to tell where the next onslaught will be, it is risky to move into any related branch and face the same thing all over again.

Worse, since some of the export campaigns have been excessive and almost irrational attempts to gain market share, the saddest consequence is probably that perfectly viable companies will be driven out as well as the less efficient operations. When foreign producers are strongly subsidized at home, or enjoy incentives for boosting exports, or are willing to forego normal profits and live off bank loans for a while, they can assume a temporary and artificial superiority that has nothing to do with their inherent competitiveness. Obviously, they must have some comparative advantage to enter a field and, once sales have been expanded and new machinery introduced, they may be able to continue selling at these low rates. But it is just as likely that with similar government or bank support, and by introducing new methods or machinery, some of the local producers could have been saved or would, under normal conditions, never have gone under to begin with. However, once having disappeared, their return is most unlikely.

That is why the advanced countries have reacted so angrily to trade disruptions and why developing countries have insisted on at least some minimal production locally. But it is evident that the concern of the affected industries and some government circles is not always widely shared. The consumers have remained insistent that imports be freely permitted to enable them to sustain a lifestyle that would otherwise be impossible. Cheap imports are desired even if this means the collapse of further companies, which may have some justification, and even if they are only cheap for a while, which has none. For, the consumers ingenuously forget that foreign exporters are not charitable organizations whose primary purpose is to reduce the cost of living. Once they have achieved the desired market share, they would tend to boost their own prices. Meanwhile, the Federal Trade Commission, America's theoretical trade watchdog, has apparently forgotten the basics of economics when it "proves" that losses by the consumers systematically exceed gains by the producers and labor and even deplores the existence of anti-dumping laws.[15]

No matter how logical some of the pro-consumer arguments may be, they are fundamentally undermined as soon as one forgets that the basis of every economy is production and not consumption. Unless a country produces wealth, it is doomed to decline and decay and encouraging consumption only hastens the pace. That is the most depressing aspect of the whole economic situation and why often no one wins from trade conflicts. Although it may not have been terribly visible at first, after two decades of economic warfare it is painfully clear that some countries are weakening and may have to opt out. Contrary to what people may think, and despite the complaints of the exporting countries, few of the advanced nations have ever really won a trade conflict. Almost every solution was a compromise, not even to limit or reduce imports in most cases but merely to slow down growth. The portion of the industry that collapsed under the onslaught was written off and then the remainder was gradually driven back.

This is no place to lament the disappearance of inefficient companies, no matter how strongly one may regret those which lost out to unfair competition. But it is about time that we consider the cumulative effect of losing too many battles in a trade war. It is fair to contend that the textile and garment industries, by and large, are labor-intensive and should be left to less developed countries. The same applies to shoes, and toys, and watches, and some electronics articles. If the Japanese can develop more efficient methods, there is no reason they should not also export steel, and ships, and automobiles. However, that does not dispense us from wondering about what happens to a country whose economy has been hurt in all these sectors, and more, without having the time, ability or sheer luck to adjust and move into new sectors.

We must also consider the relations between sectors. A weakening of the shipbuilding industry, for example, implies not just damage to that one sector. Shipbuilding is a major consumer of steel and, if fewer ships are built, less steel will be needed. If steel mills work under capacity and earn less, they cannot maintain their own competitiveness and steel imports will rise depressing local production further. More expensive local or imported steel will result in more expensive automobiles, making them lose their own price advantage. (Even if the automakers buy "cheaper" Japanese steel, this is usually more costly than what the Japanese pay back home.) From automobiles, the effect will ripple to parts production, tires, auto radios, and from there to rubber, aluminum, electronics and related industries. Not only are older sectors hurt. An ailing and high cost economy is hardly a suitable launching pad for the sophisticated industries of the future.

Similar relations exist, although to a lesser extent, for light industries like footwear or garments. But it is more useful to stress the employment factor here. When large numbers of workers are suddenly released by one sector, and no new sectors can absorb them (either because they have no room or the workers do not have the necessary skills), the cost is not limited to unemployment benefits and welfare expenses. It is not even quantified by taking the amount of wages they could be earning. Unemployment is a burden on society, and one which is paid directly and indirectly by employers through assorted fringe benefits and taxes. This raises the production costs and makes yet other industries less price competitive than in countries operating at full employment. Meanwhile, unemployed workers buy less and consumption decreases, shrinking the market and again hurting producers.

The repeated economic failures gradually begin to have other implications as well. The decay of the economy is paralleled, and reinforced, by unpleasant social phenomena. It is hard to have nearly a tenth of the labor force, and even larger shares of youth and minority groups, unemployed and with little hope of finding a job, without imposing serious hardship and creating great strains in society. It is hard to maintain a peaceful and disciplined population when hopes are shattered and it becomes impossible to maintain one's former lifestyle. A narrowing tax base eventually results in fewer schools and hospitals, less highways and housing, and also a weakening of the defense capability. Finally, it saps the nation's morale and undermines its ability to face and overcome challenges as opposed to avoiding them and taking the easy way out. Of primary concern here is the decision as to whether to reconstruct the economy or shelter it from external influences.

This argumentation will doubtlessly sound far-fetched to consumer advocates or the average citizen in countries which are so "advanced" that people have forgotten how an economy functions. But it makes perfectly good sense to the Japanese and others who are still building their economy by creating sector after sector and using the interrelations to increase the dynamics. What is happening in the "decadent West" is simply the same thing in reverse. As one sector falls, it weakens all the rest. They also know that one must consider intangible factors like economies of scale and even work morale between an expanding and a waning economy.

That is why Japan and the NICs fight so hard for each sale. But, in their almost primitive urge for more exports and larger market share, they have overlooked the most important factor. The crucial point is not to sell more this year but also to keep selling over the years to come. After all, a larger market share becomes meaningless in a shrinking market. With regard to this element, the future prospects are perhaps even more dismal than with regard to threats of protectionism.

Of the three basic world markets for industrial products, only one is growing substantially, namely the oil producers and other raw material suppliers. Growth is negligible, and sometimes negative, in the advanced industrial economies and in the developing countries as well. Overall growth being small, the growth of imports is also sluggish, although for some particularly prized products the rate is still considerable. This message must have gotten home by now after the growth of world trade dropped from a modest 6% in 1979 to an unprecedented low of 1% in 1980 and then, for the first time since 1958, total trade actually decreased somewhat in 1981. And this is only part of the story. For, with inflation and a devaluation of once strong currencies, even what is earned is worth less in real terms.

Markets for basic materials are hurt because industrial production is no longer as lively. Japanese steel exports are not stagnating because of the trigger price mechanism alone, they are hurt more fundamentally by the fact that less steel is needed if automobile or shipbuilding production falls or if, due to a general recession, there is less public works. Despite all the clamor for cheap imports, even consumer goods sales are inhibited by the worsening situation of many consumers.

Some advanced countries are advancing more than others. Relative share of the OECD's aggregate gross domestic product.

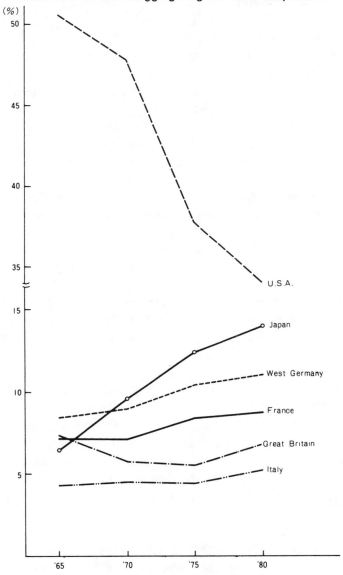

Credit: *White Paper on International Trade*, 1981, MITI.

In the "affluent" West, there are too many people living off a dole or welfare to purchase much while others are only going ahead because they can buy on credit, a privilege they may ultimately lose. As for the teeming masses of the Third World, they are just abstract statistics if they do not have the wherewithal to buy.

Somehow or other, a basic truth has been forgotten: people can only buy if they have money; they can only make money if they have something to sell. The fact that some advanced nations still have enough reserves, does not mean that they too will not soon have to sell something in order to buy. And all the loans and pump priming in the world cannot carry the non-developing countries much further. But, what can they sell Japan or the NICs? With a declining industry, or none at all, they are less valuable suppliers of capital or consumer goods. All that remains are raw materials. And even raw materials become useless if there is only a dwindling market for exports of manufactured goods.

This was the last, most unexpected twist of the process. The only remaining markets that could absorb more imports were the few countries endowed with abundant sources of raw materials, especially oil. Yet, as the demand for manufactured goods stagnated and some of the industrialized countries slipped deeper into the recession, they could no longer afford more oil and had less need for the basic inputs of an industrial economy. With this, commodity and oil prices slumped and the producers were in trouble. Even OPEC was thrown into disarray and some Arab countries cut back on their ambitious projects while Mexico stumbled into near bankruptcy.

It would therefore seem that the export campaigns have been *too* effective. The goal was to knock out the competitors in order to increase exports, it was not intended to cripple the economies as such. Yet, that is what happened. The loss of crucial industries and the increase in unemployment has turned what would normally have been maturing or slowly growing economies into ailing or depressed ones. By now, in many cases, the slower growth has resulted in an actual decrease in consumption which means the overall market has not only ceased growing, it is shrinking. Even if such countries impose no restrictions whatsoever on trade, they will be absorbing less imports and there is absolutely no way the exporters can get around this ultimate barrier.

If any lesson can be drawn, then it is that the best trading partner is one that retains its vitality and always has something to offer in return for what it gets. The best market is not one where market share is growing but where the market keeps growing so that sales increase. It is far better to have a smaller share of a viable and dynamic economy than a bigger piece of one that is declining. But, will the exporting countries pause long enough to draw such conclusions?

Impoverished Traders

When anything becomes an unquestioned routine or an obsession, like importing, processing, and exporting, not only is it hard to think of what happens to the competitors, one tends to lose track of what is happening to one's own country or the rationale for economic activities. The Japanese economy is a smashing success because of the drive of its entrepreneurs, discreetly aided by the bureaucrats, and the loyalty and discipline of the work force. However, if they get carried away, the results can be quite different from what is intended.

Such dangers apply more particularly to some of the newer economies which attained prominence not through a spontaneous process of growth but on the basis of willpower and abstract decisions. This includes not only Japan but others that adopted the same model, like Korea, Taiwan, and partly Brazil. And, going somewhat further, it applies to the centrally-planned economies of the Soviet Union, the East

Bloc and the People's Republic of China. Although the growth of the former was more attuned to market signals than the latter, all of them first set their goals and then took the necessary measures to attain them, sometimes with little concern for economic rationality or what the benefits would be.

The Japanese oligarchs in Meiji days a century ago, and then the architects of the renowned postwar "economic miracle," wished to fashion primarily a strong economy, and secondarily a prosperous and perhaps happy society. The path to this was the creation of heavy and chemical industries, the sinews of a modern economy, although light industry would have been faster and easier. In order to import the equipment and raw materials, they naturally placed stress on exports. Today, signs of their success abound and the Japanese economy is praised at home and abroad as one of the most powerful and productive in the world.

Yet, even admitting that, it is still necessary to consider the drawbacks to such a policy. One has obviously been to create certain sectors whether or not they possessed an inherent comparative advantage. This was done by allocating resources deliberately, usually by providing exceptionally cheap credit, offering further subsidies and incidentally ensuring artificially high prices through protection or collusion. Although the steel industry succeeded on this basis, aluminum did not and even shipbuilding became a heavy if temporary burden. The drawbacks are yet more visible in Korea, a smaller country that followed a more disproportioned policy.

Moreover, although often overlooked, promoting some industries automatically meant discouraging others, since it was impossible to channel sufficient resources to all. Cheaper credit for steel, or subsidies to shipbuilding, implied more expensive credit and higher taxes for sectors regarded as less crucial. In practice, the "key" sectors of the past and the future-oriented ones today, deprived the less glamorous sectors of essential resources. This included not only funds but also manpower, perhaps an even greater hindrance since most of them are labor-intensive. Cottage and light industry in general have thus been squeezed and become prematurely weak and obsolete. And manufacturing as a whole has constantly been diverting resources away from agriculture, distribution and services.

Building in an export bias has also had its attendant costs. Due either to direct government subsidies or funds more subtly derived from higher domestic prices, the exporting industries have augmented their production and sales. This would normally be to the good, except that in those companies where market share is regarded more highly than profits relatively little was repatriated to reward either the company or its employees. They naturally assumed that once a sufficient base had been established, prices could be raised and the long-term profits would be greater. Normally, this would probably have been the case. But there were some unforseeable events.

For one, Japan did not realize that Korea would catch up so quickly, nor Korea that it would have to compete so bitterly with Taiwan, and thus the fight to obtain and hold on to market share was longer and harder than planned. More serious was the growing recession that followed the oil crisis. In such depressed markets it was harder to boost prices. Meanwhile, faced with sluggish sales at home, the Japanese and others were more desperate than ever to sell as much as they could abroad at whatever price. According to a Daiwa Securities survey, in 1978 about two thirds of Japan's exports were sold under cost.[16] Even if things have improved somewhat, the situation is hardly promising since export prices have risen just marginally while import prices (including essential inputs) have risen substantially, seriously degrading the terms of trade.

Although less visibly than in the advanced or developing countries, the recession has had a disastrous impact on the rising economies. Paying too much attention to the possibilities of increasing scale and boosting productivity, and not enough attention to the potential difficulties of selling the greater output, manufacturers kept on building bigger and better installations. They failed to notice that they were outstripping the growth of markets and that the 1973 oil shock, at any rate, should have slowed expansion. Thus, they were caught with serious overcapacity which resulted either in destructive competition or cartels to reduce capacity. Whatever the outcome, the process was certainly a wasteful one.[17]

It was that much more wasteful because of the Japanese love for the latest gadgets and a desire to introduce the most recent technologies no matter what the cost. Any possible investment was justified by the need to keep ahead of the competition even if this put a serious strain on the company's finances. Thus, they repeatedly discarded methods and equipment that were regarded as quite acceptable elsewhere. Moreover, rather than introduce innovations piecemeal, there was a tendency to tear down the old and replace it with new facilities. Certainly, the Japanese can be proud of their high technology and growing productivity or the fact that the average age of a factory is about 7 years as opposed to 10 or 15 in other countries. But the price has been incredibly high.

Obviously, no economy can grow unless the people are willing to put off the rewards for some time. The Japanese, Koreans and some others, have shown that they had the courage to do so. They accepted incredible sacrifices and were willing to go through exceptional hardships to attain the goal of economic development. Tremendous amounts of savings were mobilized, massive investments made in equipment, and huge modern factories built. This was certainly to the good, for one day they would reward the people with cheaper domestic products and the initial costs would be more than paid back.

However, if the planners and managers concerned felt that

it was constantly necessary to expand, in order to sell more or to gain greater economies of scale, any rewards would have to be deferred. If, even after increases in capacity became impossible, it was deemed vital to maintain the highest possible level of productivity by introducing new machinery, the wait would be longer. If the investments were made not only to cover domestic needs but to conquer export markets, then the people would not really enjoy the fruits of their labor until more markets had been invaded and market share rose sufficiently. And, if unexpectedly the markets shrank and the competition was stiffer than thought, they would have to wait that much longer. That has been the fate of many people living in these dynamic economies.

It is often stressed that the Japanese are among the world's most prodigious savers and that an exceptionally large share of the nation's wealth is channelled into the economy. In earlier days, 20%, and even today, 16% of gross national expenditure is devoted to investment in machinery and equipment, about 5% higher than less hurried economies. In return, much less is left over for other uses. For example, only 10% can go into government capital formation for various infrastructure and 6% into housing, lower than abroad. During the past decades, production capital, such as factories and machinery, has been growing nearly twice as fast as spending on housing and household goods and more than twice as fast as investment in infrastructure such as railways, roads, schools, hospitals and so on.

No wonder then that Japan boasts such extraordinary factories but has a marked shortage of day-care centers and old age homes, and these are not very modern or attractive. There is plenty of office staff but it is impossible to hire enough teachers to bring the number of school children per class to an acceptable level. Automobiles are turned out at a prodigious rate, and bought, but there are not enough roads to drive or parking places to hold them. Dwellings are small, often remote, and lack conveniences such as piped water, flush toilets, let alone air conditioning or central heating, in many cases. And people still work very long hours and enjoy relatively little leisure. More serious for the future, they are insufficiently covered by unemployment benefits, social security or old age pensions.[18]

This explains the notorious quip about "a nation of workaholics living in rabbit hutches" that appeared in an EC report. In some ways, this is unjustified since there is no doubt that living standards have improved appreciably since the early postwar days, when poverty and unemployment were widespread. Things are better today. People do have their rice cookers, their TV sets, and often automobiles. But it is equally clear that the Japanese do not derive as much wealth from their highly productive economy as would be expected. Indeed, their standard of living is nowhere near as high as in countries with a comparable income level and sometimes even in supposedly poorer, more backward places.

The basic reason is that, nearly forty years after the war, the Japanese are still living in what can most aptly be described as a quasi-wartime economy. Too much of the funds are still being channelled directly into productive investment, yet more machinery and factories, and too little into social overhead and infrastructure. Too much attention is being paid to the needs of the managers, supervisors and workers fighting the economic war and too little concern is shown for the problems of less precious civilians, the young, the old, the family in general. Whereas once it was hard to choose the latter in the alternative of cannons vs butter, now Japan is stumped by the choice of factories vs butter.

The other reason is that any statistics on the income of the average Japanese are made meaningless by the high price structure. In theory, per capita income is already as high as most European countries and close to the American level. But what good does that do when just about everything is more expensive in Japan? Food is costly. Housing is costly. Education is costly. Even made-in-Japan consumer goods are almost as costly as abroad. This means that, as one learned professor explained, the Japanese are wealthy in book value only.

The explanations for the high costs are numerous. Part is due to the fact that many domestic products are protected, farm produce by outright barriers, other goods through private arrangements among the makers. Another part is due to the fact that even goods that can be imported cheaply miraculously become more expensive before reaching the consumer. In addition, the distribution and construction sectors are relatively inefficient, as indeed are services and government operations, which have not received enough resources to modernize. In short, the strong industry and virile

Top trade negotiators of Canada, United States, European Community and Japan smile for the public.

Credit: Foreign Press Center-Japan

export sectors are being paid for indirectly by the consumers and taxpayers.

On the personal level, especially of late, things have not been much better. This can be seen by looking at the figures for real income, real wages and consumption expenditure. During the 1960s and early 1970s, the real income of workers' households was increasing by 5.8% a year, not bad but still considerably less than the growth rate of over 10% since much of the wealth went into capital formation and not personal use. After the oil crisis, the workers were in more serious straits as real household earnings slipped and even became negative on occasion in the face of growing inflation. It could be assumed that a gradual improvement in the economy led by burgeoning exports would lead to better days.

Instead, 1980 turned out to be an absolutely incredible year that revealed how far the distortions had gone. As we saw, the year was highlighted by peak production and exports in the automobile industry and enviable progress in other export sectors. So good was the export performance that it aroused unprecedented complaints abroad. Despite some initial concern, gross national product grew by nearly 4%. Yet, in 1980, household income fell by 0.4%, real wages declined by 1.1%, and consumption expenditure dropped by 0.9%. And this was not a fluke, for the export-led growth of 1981 resulted in a similar slump in living standards. It is almost mind-boggling how a country could have gotten that much richer while its people actually became poorer. This is the sort of feat that should go into a Guiness Book of lamentable records.

That many people are tired of this system has already become amply clear. An improved quality of life has long been given a higher priority by the general public and this has actually moved the government to some action. A sounder environment and somewhat more leisure are among the results. But it will not be easy to convince the captains of industry or MITI bureaucrats, nor the politicians who live off business donations, that the basic purpose of any economy should be to provide a reasonable degree of affluence for the population as opposed to becoming yet stronger in its own right. Therefore, Japan and some others can be expected to operate terribly powerful economic machines that can crush their competitors without really benefiting their own people that much.

NOTE

1. *Japan Times*, June 12, 1981.
2. Masamichi Hanabusa, *Trade Problems between Japan and Western Europe*, p. 56.
3. *Japan Times*, April 24, 1981.
4. *Japan Times*, June 23, 1981.
5. *Asahi Evening News*, May 24, 1977.
6. *Japan Times*, July 23, 1981.
7. *Yomiuri*, December 10, 1977 and *AFL-CIO American Federationist*, September 1981.
8. *Asahi Shimbun*, April 15 & 17, 1981.
9. *Japan Times*, March 25, 1981.
10. *EC News*, May 11, 1981.
11. *Speaking of Japan*, May 1982, p. 3.
12. *Japan Times*, January 13, 15 & 28, 1982.
13. *South China Morning Post*, September 6, 1979, and *Task Force on United States-Japan Trade*, 1979.
14. *Japan Times*, January 18, 1983.
15. *Japan Times*, August 5, 1980.
16. *Japan Times*, September 14, 1979.
17. For starters, just imagine the waste of scrapping 35% of Japan's still relatively new shipbuilding capacity.
18. See Woronoff, *Japan: The Coming Economic Crisis*, pp. 250–83.

8
The Way Out

More Of The Same?

It is indeed heartening to see that two decades of trade disputes have not dampened the enthusiasm of the United States and Japan for free trade nor weakened their dislike of protectionism, any realities notwithstanding. . . . Shortly before Prime Minister Suzuki left for a summit conference in Washington, his government again resorted to "voluntary restraint" to settle the automobile conflict. Yet, a few days later, the joint communique could note that the two leaders "expressed their concern about the rising pressure toward protectionism in many countries and affirmed that Japan and the United States are determined to continue their efforts to maintain and strengthen free and open trade principles embodied in the GATT framework."[1]

Obviously, at a time when there is usually one step backward for two steps forward, it is necessary to return to GATT if the world does not want progress to cease entirely. There are still many tariff barriers and quantitative restrictions which hamper trade and should definitely be eliminated as quickly as possible. Three particular sectors merit special attention at present, since they are among the most significant. There is certainly no excuse for retaining the residual quantitative restrictions imposed on Japanese products alone, many of which are hardly exported any more, but which are an ugly affront to a leading trading nation. In return, Japan's good will is essential to solve the two problems that have remained so intractable over the years, namely freer trade in services and agricultural produce.

But this will not be enough. Most of the steps backward were taken not in GATT but by avoiding the official framework and working out informal agreements that ignored or circumvented the generally accepted rules. Although safeguards can be introduced under Article 19 if import surges disrupt trade or a domestic industry is faced with serious injury, this has rarely happened. Instead, after a barrage of political complaints, then a bit of arm-twisting, and finally a calmer assessment of what each party could expect, a mutual agreement was reached. It is presented as "voluntary" action just in case, to avoid trouble with GATT, other partners and antitrust laws. But the result is much the same.

This makes it necessary to review the safeguard clause itself, to define it more precisely and determine just when and how it should be invoked. There is also the question of whether it can be applied against individual countries, in most cases Japan and the NICs. Differences on this are still substantial and, when combined with the complications and delay in using the mechanism, make the chances of a satisfactory solution remote. Still, along with the remaining tariffs and quotas, the safeguards should be added to a new round of negotiations slated for 1983.

Aside from the likelihood that any decisions will be long in coming, there are reasons for doubt as to whether some of the biggest hurdles can be overcome at all. What is blocking entry to Japan more than anything else, including the non-tariff barriers, are the cultural impediments. Their presence is denied by Japan and they could not be talked out of existence anyway. For, as we saw, strong social proclivities are reinforced by more palpable constraints like lifetime employment or crossownership and debt relations. Voluntary restraint and invisible restrictions on Japanese exports don't exist either.

Japan could ignore them. But it knows such action would be very risky.

That is why an increasingly dense network of relations and machinery has grown up outside of GATT between the countries directly concerned. Greatest progress has been made between the United States and Japan, starting with an informal Trade Study Group located in Tokyo and consisting of businessmen, embassy personnel, and officials. Working on a more formal, government-to-government basis, there is the Trade Facilitation Committee. On a broader, and sometimes merely amicable level, there are various assemblies of businessmen, former government officials, and other dignitaries, such as the United States-Japan Businessmen's Conference or the more imposing "Wise Men's Group."[2] Gradually, similar bodies are being formed with European and other countries and mention has been made of a French and a German "Wise Men's Group" with Japan.

Naohiro Amaya, who helped settle the automobile conflict, often referred to himself as a "fireman." Much could doubtlessly be gained if he and his counterparts tried to prevent fires or put them out right away rather than waiting until they become dangerous. One step in the right direction was the recent establishment of a trade "ombudsman" and a complaint bureau of sorts in Japan. Certainly any effort to solve grievances simply and quickly is desirable. And there is no reason such procedures should not exist abroad as well, for Japanese and other businessmen who encounter difficulties. Meanwhile, as trade problems become more frequent and protracted, some countries have decided to centralize their efforts, the most notable example being the creation of an Office of the Special Trade Representative in Washington. Japan briefly had a Minister for External Economic Affairs but more often turned to trouble-shooters like Nobuhiko Ushiba and Saburo Okita.

Obviously, in an increasingly interdependent world, there

must be some way of bringing opposing interests together and seeking common policies. One forum has been the annual "economic summits" among top leaders of seven major industrial democracies. Whether they like it or not, one trade dispute or another is usually on the agenda. In January 1982, for the first time, a trilateral meeting of trade negotiators was held. Yet, much of this is too infrequent and sporadic to effectively deal with serious conflicts and somewhat more elaborate and permanent machinery seems needed. Its purpose should not be to duplicate GATT's operations but rather to handle matters which, for one reason or another, require a political solution.

The existence of such bodies, however, is no guarantee that solutions will be found. . . or even sought. GATT did not

Trade negotiators in the Land of Smiles. Special Trade Representative Strauss, Minister of External Economic Affairs Ushiba, and Ambassador Mansfield.

prevent the rise of neo-protectionism nor could the close bilateral relations forestall the textile, and television, and automobile conflicts, or many more. But, to their credit, they did keep things from getting worse. The Trade Facilitation Committee cleared up a few complaints, negotiations opened NTT a bit, and restraint or restrictions were better than continuing the trade war. Japan's love of face and status made it accept liberalization as a membership fee to GATT, IMF and OECD and led it to settle any pending issues just in time for the next summit conference.

But much more could be accomplished if any groups or institutions were oriented more toward deeds than words. One problem has been that the Japanese are usually represented by older, semi-retired executives with little direct influence even over their own companies. The political leaders are insufficiently influential, or too involved, to act independently. They also tend to be somewhat less than outgoing. Admitting that, one Japanese businessmen's group replaced its 75 year old chairman with someone who was merely 73. They also promised to stop reading prepared speeches and enter into direct debate. Still, the Japanese businessmen, or officials, or academics, will get nowhere until they cease being vague, ambiguous and abstract. These are fine Japanese virtues which regrettably only confuse foreigners. In return, the foreigners might try being somewhat less blunt, simplistic or aggressive.

Differences in form are, of course, less worrisome than differences in substance. In most broader forums so far, the Americans and Europeans have both criticized the Japanese and conceded their own mistakes. Some actually took great pleasure in baring their chest and admitting every failure they, or more likely their predecessors, had made. As an act of courtesy, and because the "experts" warned them that Japanese are very delicate and sensitive creatures, they usually went easy on the criticism. When they did not, as when

Francois Missoffe, a former French ambassador and reputed "friend of Japan," told them some unpleasant truths, the Japanese were shocked. In return, the Japanese criticized little, but insinuated much, in trying to convince the Westerners that it is mainly their own fault. Very few were willing to risk the ire of their compatriots by avowing the failings of their own side or appealing for greater generosity.[3]

Under such conditions, it is hard to speak of an exchange of opinions. The Japanese will agree that the others made mistakes, but brush over their own; the Westerners have trouble bringing the discussion to bear on what the Japanese can do to help. A series of monologues does not add up to a dialogue no matter how much whiskey or *saké* flows after the meeting or how good personal friends the members may become. These divergent approaches also turn the debates toward neutral issues or questions of indirect or remote importance. This can readily be seen from the conclusions or "decisions" of most meetings. There are appeals for cooperation, mutual respect and good will, reference to a few concrete steps, then the presentation of a major challenge confronting all, followed by the firm resolve to meet again next year.

Thus, in order to solve or prevent trade conflicts, one might simply urge "more of the same." However, on second thought, this should not really apply to two aspects. One is the tremendous delay in tackling problems due especially to hesitation among the Japanese. This is partially attributable to the very time consuming decision-making process that calls for a broad consensus and some compensation for every party.[4] It is compounded by the eternal divisions within the Japanese government and business circles, and between the two when the time comes to reach a specific compromise. But cultural traits are doubtlessly reinforced by the fact that any delay appears to benefit Japan by allowing its exports to continue a bit longer. This "gain" may be more than nullified by greater frustration and growing anger in the partner country, or damage to mutual relations, but it is rarely seen that way. So, most conflicts are only solved at the eleventh hour.[5]

Even more mischief has been caused by the astonishing lack of understanding of why trade conflicts occur and how they can be settled. This has led to almost as many non-solutions as solutions and diverted attention from the true problems. The Americans, rather than deal with petty or ugly quarrels, get carried away by their idealism and look for a common goal which can unite the parties in a greater cause and perhaps resolve the present issues in passing or at least diminish their significance. Without the money for another Marshall Plan, they resort to joint projects to develop alternative energies, or space technology, or put a Japanese on the moon. If the Japanese will only bear with them, once they have created a new society, or a great society, or reindustrialized, the Americans can go back to business as usual. Only the Europeans, vile materialists that they are, still quibble over a percent of exports here or a billion dollars there, and upset the harmony.

But this doesn't stop the Japanese, who are bubbling over with new plans and projects and seem to care more about entering the 21st century in style than solving a few pressing problems during the remaining decades of this century. In so doing, they have come up with several red herrings that not only confuse the debate but make it pointless. One has been the stress on productivity, a subject dear to their heart since they have done so well and others fared so poorly. If only the United States and Europe would learn from Japan, and boost productivity, they could defend their markets and export. It sounds good. And productivity is obviously a key to successful growth. But this overlooks the fact that even today productivity in certain sectors is much higher abroad than in Japan and yet foreign companies cannot sell their goods on a difficult market.[6] Moreover, it is not productivity but price that makes goods competitive, and this depends just as much on costs of raw materials, wage levels, currency rates, and so on.

Insisting that trade problems can be overcome by boosting growth all around is no longer offering a solution but running away from the problem. Of course, it is not surprising that countries with higher growth should regard this as a valid proposition. Thus, Toshio Komoto, Director General of Japan's Economic Planning Agency can proclaim that "in order to eliminate trade friction, it is first and foremost necessary for the world economy as a whole to recover." Then the individual issues will be resolved automatically.[7] The fatal flaw here is that certain basic changes have cut into growth as such. Raw materials are more costly, harder to obtain, and painfully finite. Many markets are already saturated. And it is out of the question for most advanced or developing countries to expand as rapidly as Japan just as Japan finds it impossible to grow as quickly now as it did a decade ago. Expansion of national economies, and also of international trade, is bound to be slower in the future and nothing is accomplished by denying it.

Not even the exaggerated hopes vested in the future-oriented sectors can alter this conclusion. A look at the various plans and visions of the enlightened businessmen and liberal thinkers will show just how few alternatives have actually been worked out concretely. The "sunrise" industries, as they are so prettily called, are terribly limited and most are quite nebulous. No one has gotten as far as launching them, nor even amassing the tremendous capital needed, and only some token products like space satellites, nuclear reactors, or VTRs are on the market. Nor is the list of "sunrise" industries likely to grow at anything nearing the pace of their counterpart, the "sunset" industries, which are encountering increasing difficulties.

Judging by other proposed solutions, the supposed experts and advisors are frequently blind and deaf, but not mute. They have not ceased proposing one of the most damaging "solutions" ever, to have Japan stimulate its economy so as to pull the other economies out of the recession just like a locomotive. This was strongly suggested in 1978, and actually imposed on the Japanese government as a worthy goal. The idea still has not lost its charm. Unfortunately, it forgets that most of Japan's growth, especially during a slump, comes from exports. So, accelerating the motor results in more exports than ever and Japan only derails the other economies rather than helping them along. What is needed is not *more* growth in Japan but *balanced* growth!

The favorite "solution" among the Japanese experts and advisors is also a non-solution, that is, to restore some balance to trade by making special purchases in those places which complain the loudest. The more impressive import promotion missions have reportedly racked up billions in sales during a quick tour of the country. Alas, many of these deals had already been negotiated much earlier and the announcement was simply put off for a more auspicious occasion, so there was no real addition to trade. Other notable measures involved high cost items like aircraft and nuclear power plants or stepped up purchases of raw materials like oil, uranium or coal, which would then be stockpiled. It should be obvious that all this accomplishes is to buy more today and less tomorrow, to improve the trade balance in the short run without making any basic readjustment in the longer-term imbalance.

But the one element which could have a major effect in a relatively short time is consistently snubbed, the proper alignment of exchange rates. There is no doubt that Japan has repeatedly improved its trade balance by undervaluing the yen and makings its exports cheaper. It really should not be allowed to do so, in the interest of balanced trade flows with its

It doesn't take long to get out of the red. Japan's external trade snaps back.

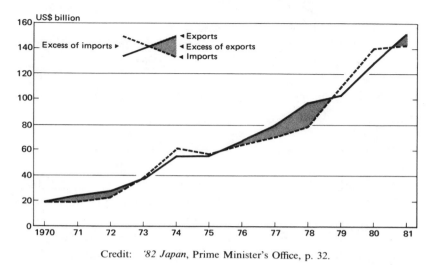

Credit: '82 Japan, Prime Minister's Office, p. 32.

partners, and in its own interest as well. However, this can hardly be avoided when other countries are so obsessed with inflation that they forget that monetary restraint and high interest rates have an effect on trade as well, enhancing the value of a currency which really is not worth that much in international terms. They should thus not be surprised when their own domestic policies discourage exports and encourage imports from others following a more normal policy or actively stimulating the economy.

If the powers that be really want broader, more challenging issues, then they might finally tackle the ones this book is devoted to, namely those which are at the root of the trade conflicts. The never-ending trade war will never end unless the fundamental problems are solved. Action might be undertaken at two levels. First is the highly practical, if rather monotonous and bothersome chore of uncovering the trade barriers, tariff, non-tariff, cultural and "voluntary," and eliminating them, one after the other. This can be done within

GATT or any other suitable multilateral framework. The second is of a somewhat higher order, but no less practical, and entails a reshaping of the national economies so that they can participate more actively and fruitfully in international exchanges. These two efforts do not in any way conflict with one another but rather combine to remove the immediate impediments while strengthening the underlying economic foundations of trade.

Policing Protectionism

So far, most efforts have been concentrated on removing the so-called barriers to trade, tariffs, quotas, NTBs, and so on. No matter how harmful they may be, it would appear naive to assume that they represent the whole problem. In fact, at present, they are probably less than half. While they prevent imports, and thus distort trade, other measures can distort trade no less effectively by artificially promoting import substitutes or exports. Thus, measures such as tax benefits, subsidies, and other incentives, should also be carefully reviewed and perhaps eliminated. Even then, the underlying assumption is that basically the trade patterns are reasonable and sound and it is simply necessary to keep them from being unfairly influenced. Is that a safe assumption?

What if the basic trade flows themselves do not emerge naturally and are not the most beneficial for all concerned? This is more than just a suspicion. Theoretically, free trade is part and parcel of the broader system of free enterprise and *laissez-faire*. It is assumed that domestically those industries will rise which have the best comparative advantage and, if the competitive edge is sufficient, the goods can be exported elsewhere in the world. Unfortunately, as we have seen, frequently nowadays products are simply chosen by governments as worthy of promotion and export sectors are artificially created by shifting resources there or actually subsidizing exports. This occurs regularly in developing countries and centrally-planned economies with little thought to comparative advantage.

Competitors which continue to play by the formal rules of the game will obviously be hurt. It is not surprising that they will then call for assistance and/or protection from their own government, and perhaps obtain it. Even the relatively liberal trade system established by GATT contains provisions for certain eventualities. Some refer to various forms of "unfair" competition, as when governments offer subsidies, rebates, etc. or exporters engage in dumping. Others are related to hardship should there be sudden and massive surges or serious damage to the sector or economy.

But insufficient thought has been given to two cases which are fundamental, and rather extensive, deviations from the accepted rules. The first involves what is known as "infant industries." Since developing countries are admittedly weaker, to compensate, they are allowed to protect certain sectors which they try to nurture and cultivate. The infant industry argument has been worked out and refined by economists, and politicians, for centuries already and there have never been more apologists for one sacred cause or another than today. The fact that one week they appear before GATT to demand free trade, and the next at UNCTAD to demand protection and preferences, no longer surprises anyone. And the world is already full of tariffs and quotas to protect, and subsidies and incentives to promote, a bevy of such infants.

More recently, no less persuasive arguments (at least in the view of their sponsors) have been developed for industries at the far end of the maturation process, the ailing and depressed ones. In order to protect them from premature aging and a sudden demise, many countries have adopted special measures. This is less often outright tariffs and quotas than the more fashionable restraint and orderly marketing procedures.

Meanwhile, other types of measures are adopted to make them more resistant at home or competitive abroad. This includes direct and indirect subsidies, government contracts, tax and depreciation benefits, special rehabilitation loans and sometimes absorption by the government as nationalized companies. By now, most countries offer loans, guarantees, and insurance to exporters and the varying rate of interest on these quite substantial credits has become a crucial selling point. Where governments leave off, larger conglomerates or multinationals take over in assisting sales of key items.

The arsenals of measures, both for infant and ailing industries, are broad and growing and often the result is to pit supported industries from developing and developed countries against one another. This kind of competition clearly flaunts the basic trade rules and makes one wonder whether free trade should not also have a greater degree of fairness about it. It is obvious that an infant industry can survive and even prosper as long as it benefits from all sorts of advantages that other industries do not. It can also export much more than otherwise as long as its products are subsidized. This is hardly proof of any comparative advantage. Although not enjoying as much moral support as "infant" industries, the more decrepit oldsters of the advanced countries now get by nicely as "senior citizens." Certainly, as long as they have massive and cheap loans as well as some secure domestic market, they can operate even if retirement would be wiser. Once in the government service, they may actually thrive and sell their goods long after any true competitive edge is gone.

Fortunately, over recent years, both the "infants" and the "senior citizens" have discredited themselves enough for most countries to reject some of the more facile arguments and realize that those who suffer are not only the competitors but the sponsors. A glance at the hundred and more developing countries will show that pitifully few of them have come up with any successful industries let alone a viable economy.

Rather, there has been a disturbing tendency for these overly protected and pampered "infants" not to grow up. Indeed, why should they? Companies are given subsidies which rise rather than fall the more trouble they encounter. Meanwhile, they are protected from imports at a high level and can easily raise their prices accordingly. The result has been some failures but many more lazy and fat ventures that are a burden on the economy.

This has led to a distaste for import-substitution and a fascination with export-oriented strategies since they, at least, seem to work. There is no doubt that Japan, Korea, Taiwan and others have constructed a very viable economy on their dynamic export sectors. Protection and promotion were among the contributing factors. Yet, there is every reason to believe that they were not the primary causes. More essential was the role of the private sector which organized workers, introduced new technologies, scouted for markets, and so on. In addition, favoring growth sectors had its drawbacks, as noted, since promoting key sectors implies discouraging others and is a drain on the economy as a whole.

The drawbacks for Japan have already been described at length. Korea, which outdid its neighbor in export-promotion eventually realized that its economy suffered even more from misallocations of resources and distortions. This became painfully clear in Park Chung Hee's later years and a new policy of liberalization and free enterprise was introduced under Chun Doo Hwan. If one is looking for a model, then Hong Kong would seem a much better candidate, since its export industries are as dynamic as any in the NICs, while they are also more balanced and based on genuine comparative advantage. Its growth rate, which has been among the highest in the world for decades, is all the more impressive coming from a tiny patch of land completely devoid of natural resources and terribly crowded. Yet, it succeeded on the basis of nearly pure *laissez-faire* domestically and free trade internationally.[8]

Thus, "infant industry" protection should be reviewed very carefully by the countries applying it, especially if the companies concerned never shape up. Even if they do, it is worthwhile measuring the burden placed on others. Meanwhile, there is no harm in outside countries looking at the situation a bit more sharply. Although it is fair to ask for a chance to get started, this chance sometimes drags on for too long and the special protection and promotion are maintained even after the industry is successful. No matter how good the reasons, and how altruistic the motives, beyond a certain point the industry should be on its own. If not when it can produce efficiently enough to defend the home market, then certainly when it becomes so competitive it can conquer foreign markets.

As for nurturing infant industries, there are more failures than successes in nursing ailing industries. The decision as to which sector or company to aid is more often political than economic, more often emotional than rational, and a country may find itself shoring up ventures that stand no real chance. If they are too labor-intensive or the machinery is too old, only a radical change will do the trick. But there must be a will for change and this can be undermined by the protection itself. If companies feel that now they can get by and squeeze the existing plant for what it's worth while paying out profits or workers assume there is no need to accept discipline or modest wages since they are on the government payroll, or otherwise secured, there will be little improvement. Thus, years and sometimes decades later, many textile, steel and television companies are still clamoring for support, although some have revitalized.

Therefore, if advanced countries are going to request a suspension of the general rules, or simply bend them unilaterally, they should also accept reasonable limits for such action. If a sector is ailing, then obviously it is too large and inefficient so, either through market forces or government intervention, the least competitive units should drop out or be absorbed by more dynamic ones. The financial or other support should thus not be exaggerated to the point where painful slashes in capacity or personnel are rejected. Whatever protective measures are adopted should also be moderated, high enough to provide some shelter but not so high as to remove competition as a factor encouraging companies to react and upgrade. Finally, there must be some end to the period of support and protection after which the company or industry has to stand on its own.

Both operations, the promotion of new industries in rising economies and the protection of old industries in declining economies are fundamental breaches in the free trade system and represent the bulk of the existing neo-protectionism. Neither side is in a very good position to accuse the other of not playing fair. It might therefore be better if all countries tried to agree on some basic ground rules for each exception. This would make them considerably less arbitrary and might actually enhance the value of each technique by making abuses less frequent and flagrant. It will not be easy to find a compromise. But one is more likely to arise by looking for it rather than making believe that the phenomena do not exist or are not as widespread and powerful.

Changing Course

Since trade is a direct emanation of the underlying economic structure, the most decisive measures will arise from broader policies. In the case of Japan, ever since the economy got moving after the war, it has progressed in much the same manner without due attention to changing circumstances. Whatever the conditions, businessmen have been ploughing more money into industry, expanding where possible, upgrading as they went. They sought new markets on which to sell new products. And they neglected most other things that could distract them from this primeval, almost sacred, task of building a strong nation.

They would seem not to have noticed, or at least not adequately reacted to, the fact that the situation has changed radically over recent years. The growing demand for raw materials has led to growing prices as well, especially for oil, and thus the inputs for Japan's productive machinery are more costly. On the other end, prices of exports have also risen making it harder to sell such large quantities to begin with. And the terrific competition amongst Japanese companies and between them and foreign companies (both from advanced countries and the NICs) has meant that Japan is getting less out of this process than planned. Worse, in some cases its aggressive efforts to sell have led not to more sales but artificial constraints.

If the Japanese businessmen and bureaucrats would only pause a moment, they might find that the time has come to alter the process and perhaps go into reverse. No matter how unorthodox this may sound, an argument can be made for weakening or just discarding the import-process-export syndrome. If it is so difficult to export in large quantities, rather than push harder for every last sale, it would be better not to produce the extra articles. In this case, it would be possible to save on processing costs and especially the high prices of raw materials and fuel. The actual savings on what is not purchased would probably be supplemented by a gradual fall in the price level, as happened even for oil, when demand slackens. With a decreasing need for raw material imports Japan could finally break the nasty habit of exporting at all costs.

Once importing and exporting become more normal functions, processing could also be seen in a new light. First of all, it would be more purposeful if geared to the potential market rather than the urge for economies of scale. The Japanese have repeatedly constructed factories only to find that they could not use the full capacity even in good times and had to cut back or close down many of the facilities if competition was excessive or a recession decreased the levels of consumption. It would certainly have been less wasteful never to have built the excess capacity to start with. And, as regards the growing efficiency of its factories, there does not seem to be much sense in insisting on ever greater productivity when it already has a tremendous advance over its competitors. A smaller margin is still quite adequate to outsell them and anything extra is not only superfluous but terribly expensive.

How then could the Japanese get by with less production and, more specifically, less export production? Although this may appear yet more heretical, it could be done by replacing the goal of market share, at least in external trade, with the goal of profit. Market share has its advantages. But, beyond a certain point, the gains from boosting economies of scale are minor and, in freer economies, it is not so easy to tie down the distribution network or impose higher prices later on. Moreover, constant export campaigns and bitter price wars only antagonize local manufacturers and worry the politicians. Whether justified or not, such action is likely to end with charges of dumping and imposition of restraint or restrictions which halt the growth of market share anyway.

If the Japanese exporters were to charge somewhat higher prices to begin with, it would be hard to accuse them of dumping. These higher prices would naturally also result in somewhat reduced sales which would take a bit of the pressure off local manufacturers. Depending on exactly which price levels were set the Japanese could export larger or smaller quantities, thus balancing the goals of market share and profit. However, since they are presently burdened by such high raw material costs and face so much resistance on foreign markets, it would seem more intelligent to strive for profits. The fact that most Japanese goods already sell more on quality than price actually makes it absurd to emphasize cheapness, as had to be done a decade or two ago, and moderately higher prices would probably decrease total sales slightly while boosting total profits.

This lesson seems to have been learned by the older, more mature sectors, such as textiles, television and steel. Admittedly, the learning process was hastened by trade barriers. Still, whatever the cause, they have been able to raise prices and move into higher value added products once it was no longer possible to press for larger quantities. This also permitted them to stabilize production and avoid excessive competition. But these advantages are ignored by VTR or automobile makers which have since launched aggressive campaigns that coincidentally keep their margins tight. Obviously, it is not only the manufacturers who suffer by making smaller profits but also the workers who earn lower wages, the stockholders who receive smaller dividends, and the government which derives less tax revenue.

On the other side of the ledger, the Japanese economy would be helped in many ways by increasing imports. If some of the tariff barriers were lowered and quotas expanded, especially for foodstuffs, goods would become much cheaper and have a substantial effect in reducing inflation. If, in addition, foreign manufactured imports were not discriminated against by higher markups or being kept out of some channels, the price level would drop further. This latter measure would be far more important simply by offering the consumers, individuals and companies, a wider choice of suppliers and interesting alternatives. Whenever imported goods are cheaper, the actual saving to the purchaser is multiplied many times over by forcing the domestic manufacturers to align their prices downward. Naturally, none of this will come about unless the government practices free trade a bit more actively, or is forced to do so by the consumers.

All of these reforms would decrease Japan's dependence on

manufactured exports and raw material imports enabling it to obtain a more natural balance. But it is yet more important to break with the decades of excessive interest in the external sector as a whole which led to exceptional neglect of domestic needs. This is necessary for the Japanese people to finally obtain more in return for past sacrifices. It will also be necessary in order to replace external demand as the main stimulus for growth. How badly this is needed is amply shown by the fact that exports still provide three times more of Japan's growth than whatever is accomplished domestically.

By now even the government realizes that the population is tired of working hard without seeing more tangible benefits. Since the early 1970s, when the first "down with growth" reactions became manifest, leading politicians have espoused one scheme after the other to improve the quality of life. First, it was decided to clean up Japan or at least keep it from getting dirtier, by stricter anti-pollution legislation. Then there was talk of remodelling the archipelago to spread the benefits of modern civilization, such as they were, more widely. Lately, there has been a spate of plans for garden cities, regional plazas and technopolises and other symbols of finer living. Also, in response to foreign pressure, it was conceded that the economy had to be readjusted to obtain more growth from the domestic sector. Alas, little of the implementation for all this has materialized.

Thus, the Japanese population and foreign critics are pressing for more rapid action. The lack of infrastructure has become a bottleneck in urbanization plans and housing, the most ardently desired commodity, has become prohibitively expensive for growing segments. If Japan wants to keep ahead, it is no longer a question of more schools but much better schools than it has today. Yet, even concrete needs like more roads, sewers or playgrounds become petty when compared to the needs of a swiftly approaching future. In another few decades, Japan will have the largest proportion of aged people in the world (and the smallest proportion of working age people). Although such a dramatic shift in the population must be prepared for, there are inadequate numbers of decent hospitals or old age homes. More seriously, the funds for health insurance and social security will never be sufficient unless they accumulate more rapidly. Nor are there enough funds for eventualities like greater unemployment or a major earthquake, both quite possible.

The time has obviously come to restructure the whole economy taking into account the accumulated needs of the past and present as well as many needs everyone already knows will arise in the coming decades. Still, given the past record of the Japanese government, there is reason to doubt it will rise to the occasion. In order to build the necessary infrastructure and hire the personnel to develop the domestic economy, a larger share will have to come from the national and local government budgets. But the refusal to pay higher taxes by the businessmen and private citizens has made this impossible for the moment. Indeed, in collusion with the bureaucrats, they have created a highly artificial financial crisis which is blocking public works and welfare expenditures. That Japan can make the effort, when its people have the wisdom and courage to face up to the problems, is obvious since tax and social security levels are much lower than in any other advanced nation. And this effort could be greatly facilitated by earning more off exports so as to pay the higher taxes needed.

Whether they like the potential changes or not, and it is clear that government and business circles are less enchanted by the prospect of a new domestic economic order than the people, Japan must change. Now that the economy is expanding slowly and markets are more costly to conquer, market share becomes a less valid goal. Meanwhile, with a recession and higher interest rates, companies have no choice but to think more about profits simply in order to avoid the reverse, losses and conceivable bankruptcy. With their earnings growing more slowly, and inflation eating into that, the workers and unions are likely to demand higher wages or at least more holidays. A whole younger generation is less eager to work and more addicted to consumer goods and leisure. Meanwhile, the first contingents of the elderly who must be looked after are already there. As for the continued use of exports to prop up the economy, Japan finally realizes that it must proceed cautiously or simply have them cut off.

The same realization is coming to a number of similar economies as well. Korea, which actually went further in the direction of planning and export-led growth, already discovered under the Park regime that it is possible to produce no end of exports and still not meet domestic needs while subsidizing export sectors too strongly could result in severe

Cosponsoring a trade show in Japan. JETRO's
Hisashi Murata and HKTDC's Len Dunning.

distortions and selling exports too cheaply could impoverish the country. President Chun's economic advisors have been busily rectifying the growth strategies by making them less constraining and providing more room for the free play of market factors. There has also been a liberalization of trade, investment and banking, far less than in Japan today but much greater than in Japan at the same stage of development. Taiwan, whose businessmen are more commercially minded and profit-oriented, never went quite as far. And Hong Kong and Singapore, whose growth and export record are just as good—and lately even better—attained their successes by maintaining free enterprise at home and free trade abroad. In so doing, they avoided the drawbacks of the Japanese model.

Japan's Special Effort

There is no doubt that certain basic readjustments in the Japanese economy, when they come, will also help restore a balance in world trade that is sadly lacking. But it is equally clear that there will be serious difficulties if nothing is done before that. Since Japan's export prowess is so great, and it is so hard to sell to Japan, Leslie Fielding, head of the EC delegation in Tokyo mentioned more than facetiously that the Japanese might accept a handicap as in golf.[9] Although its businessmen are avid golf players, there is little chance they would approve the idea. Yet, even they realize that something must be done to even the odds.

Moreover, without asking their views, Japan's trade partners have already started imposing a series of handicaps in the shape of formal restrictions or informal voluntary restraint. This basically makes an increasing number of markets for a growing range of products "off bounds" to the Japanese (and others). By now, the majority of Japanese exports are actually covered by one curb or another (while the NICs only suffer to a lesser extent). Periodically, if the domestic industry recovers enough, the ban is withdrawn. But "orderly" trade is clearly the order of the day.

Better late than never, the businessmen concerned have grasped that it is probably wiser to exercise restraint of a truly voluntary—if hardly spontaneous—nature by holding back on exports before a crisis arises. It is obviously smarter to win market share slowly and gently without creating unnecessary resentment or nasty reactions that frequently take back part of what had been won. For this reason, Keidanren has been lecturing its members on the need to consider local sentiments and avoid creating friction. Various ministries have been doing the same. In the case of integrated circuits, the message got through. Still, it would be hasty to conclude that there will not be many more conflicts when manufacturers fail to coordinate actions and get into unseemly competitive races or if increased exports are the only way of avoiding serious overcapacity, and perhaps bankruptcy, at home.

This is a sort of handicap with regard to exports. When it comes to imports, other measures have been taken to offer foreign companies advantages which may compensate for any handicaps they have or claim to have. It is quite normal for foreign countries to send trade missions to Japan. But the missions have never been more numerous, nor have they been as well received by the Japanese. The government makes every effort to publicize the arrival, slews of agents and buyers turn out to inspect the merchandise, and sometimes sales are concluded on the spot. The most spectacular event so far occurred when the Japanese fitted out their own exhibit ship as the "Boatique America" which steamed into half-a-dozen Japanese ports to display American goods to the populace. This was certainly a worthy successor to the famed "black ships" and a most unexpected one.

Reversing the usual procedure, the Japanese have also been sending "import promotion missions" to foreign countries to see what might be of interest. The very first visited the United

States just after the Nixon shock and many more followed as trade imbalances grew in the late 1970s. Led by prestigious businessmen from major companies, these groups looked into potential products or made actual purchases in America, Europe and Asia. More discreetly, Japanese companies have expanded their own merchandising activities. More purchases are being made by trading companies, department stores and chain stores. In a kindly, if not entirely disinterested gesture, Sony offered to market foreign goods through its own channels back home.

A most astonishing change has come over the Japan External Trade Organization. Widely regarded as a Trojan horse which helped Japanese exporters enter foreign markets, it has now begun teaching foreign companies how to enter Japan. JETRO gets thousands of sales enquiries which it channels to potential buyers. It receives foreign businessmen in Japan and puts them in contact with local counterparts. Periodically, exhibits are held in its premises, partly or entirely at its expense, to display foreign products. It is now busily translating pertinent regulations, issuing publications on marketing of many products and distributing literature on "how to do business in Japan." It is a bit early to change "external" to "internal" and call it JITRO, but the conversion is striking.

The private sector has also taken a number of notable initiatives to get things moving. It has participated actively in import and investment missions sent abroad. And, in Tokyo, it helped establish the Manufactured Imports Promotion Organization, along with MITI and other bodies, in 1978. Among other activities, it organizes numerous exhibitions in the World Import Mart. This ten-story building devoted largely to import promotion houses not only various exhibition halls and conference rooms but also the trade offices of several foreign countries, and a special ASEAN Center, as well as product show cases and a shopping area run by

Mitsukoshi where foreign goods are sold directly to Japanese consumers. So radical has been the change that when MIPRO recently opened an office in Washington D.C. people simply could not believe that the Japanese were looking for potential imports.

These promising beginnings were given a further boost when Prime Minister Suzuki realized that there was still a lack of credibility in some quarters and, more seriously, that imports still could not keep up with exports. In a highly unprecedented move, he instructed MITI, Agriculture and other ministries and agencies to seek measures for increasing manufactured imports "not only to avoid greater criticism of Japan but to prevent protectionism from rearing its head."[10] His successor, Yasuhiro Nakasone, was even more energetic in urging that annoying non-tariff barriers and testing regulations be discarded. Meanwhile, a necessary shift was made away from excessive concentration on American interests and toward meeting the problems of European countries whose deficits were worse and whose criticism was more pointed. This step was duly noted, and welcomed, by the EC Commission as a "contribution to a greater openness in the Japanese market."

However, whereas the more experienced and solidly financed companies in the West might get by with only a bit more help, businessmen from the developing countries often did not have the slightest idea of where to start. For years already, JETRO has had a special exhibition hall for products from the Third World. On occasion, it also sends missions on the spot to seek possible export articles and advise on how best to enter the Japanese market. But such efforts were recently intensified for the ASEAN countries when a special promotion center for trade, investment and tourism was set up jointly with them and largely financed and staffed by MITI and JETRO. This is now paralleled by a joint ASEAN-Japan Development Corporation established with over a hundred

The ship that launched a thousand sales. Japanese shoppers
return with goodies from "Boatique America."

Credit: JETRO

private companies to channel more Japanese investment into
the region.

This clearly shows a new awareness of the need to balance
trade by importing more manufactured goods from the West
and whatever can be offered from the developing countries.
Indeed, the process has reached the point where one could
speak of very explicit "administrative guidance" from the
government and a degree of compliance, genuine or contrived,
from the business community. Still, for these measures to
succeed, it will be necessary for foreign manufacturers and
exporters to take a more constructive approach to Japan even
though it will still be a tougher market than most others and
will still demand a stronger initial push no matter how
attractive the potential results may be. Meanwhile, the Japanese businessmen will be launching their own export cam-

paigns, with considerably more determination and fervor than before, and the outcome is likely to remain more exports than imports for many years to come.

What little can be expected on the trade front may well be supplemented, and perhaps exceeded, by Japanese investment activities. It could hardly be claimed that the Japanese have taken to investing abroad with quite the same glee as exporting since they prefer controlling every aspect of the manufacturing process and then just shipping the products. The first investments, in fact, were merely for representative offices to promote sales, then a bit for after-sales service, and finally to handle the marketing. However, various incentives eventually made them attempt local production. The incentives were as often positive, cheap loans or tax rebates, as negative, namely fear of being kept out by anticipated tariffs and quotas.

Whatever the reasons, local production is gradually replacing imports, at least partially. For, first the country must import some capital goods which cannot be procured locally. Often the production is, in fact, nothing more than simple assembly of knock-down kits with little added value. But eventually there is a genuine transfer and less has to be imported. In the case of processing of local raw materials, products of higher value added are ultimately exported. This does much to strengthen the balance of trade of the country concerned. Although it weakens Japan's position, there are gains in the form of profits and dividends, continued sales of intermediate products, and royalties for technology. Should this not be enough in all cases, the companies concerned may still feel that it is better than to have lost a market.

Normally, investment is considered on its own merits. But, within the ongoing trade confrontation, it has assumed a very special importance since it is the only trade-off that seems acceptable to all parties. Japan does not encourage foreign imports or investment, fearing some imagined interference or domination. Although not particularly liking overseas investment, the advantages are enough to constantly incite new projects. Countries which are weary of too many Japanese trade offensives are far more willing to allow Japanese investment. This creates jobs while bringing in more capital and technology. So, whether it is eagerly sought after or just tolerated, Japanese investment has increasingly become an alternative to trade. The only catch is that the Japanese often fail to invest until *after* trade restrictions are imposed.

One last area in which an extra effort can be expected is to increase Japan's contribution to economic assistance. As indicated, with the second biggest economy in the OECD group, there is no reason why it should not be doing more. It benefited from aid in the past and could at least repay this with aid to others. Since these others are also trading partners and sometimes crucial sources of raw materials, there are more than just moral reasons for helping out. Similarly, Japan should engage in more basic research to replenish the world's store of knowledge. And, if it is so inclined it might at least look after its own defense even if it is unwilling to pull its weight in the Western alliance.

After surveying all these matters, it is only with trepidation that one proceeds further. If Japan were to make the efforts called for in trade, investment, and aid, it would still only be making modest gestures and catching up with others no richer or more powerful than itself or granting as good conditions to others as it receives from them. There is nothing truly exceptional about this. Yet, any progress is fought every inch of the way and each concession has to be seized even when Japan gets as much, or more, in exchange. How then can anyone seriously ask Japan to take the lead?

But, this is what is repeatedly done and must be done again in the future. Once the world trade system was restored by the United States which also helped revive the economies of its wartime allies and enemies, including Japan. During much of the postwar period, the United States has accepted the biggest burden in maintaining peace and security and promoting economic development. Of course, it has made some terrible blunders and tended to be overbearing. But it was also willing to make sacrifices for what its people and leaders saw as higher goals. Presently its role as a leader is disputed and, more seriously, the might and wealth a leader needs to obtain unquestioning allegience are no longer in its possession.

In a multipolar world, it is essential to find new leaders who can share the burden. One of them must be Japan since it presently has the necessary wealth, if not the power, to forget minor or immediate concerns and shape a better world. Appeals have been made repeatedly. But the only echo is modesty and lip service. Japan mouths the words and refuses to act. Worse, it shows no spark of imagination or shred of idealism in forgetting its own concerns long enough to think of others. Hopefully, this will change. Even if it does not act out of noble motives, it should at least consider the base. No nation has benefited more from the world trade system, no country would fare worse if it collapsed, and no country would have greater trouble surviving in a period of chaos than Japan.

Back To The Basics

It finally looks as if, whether the Japanese like it or not, their economy will be slowing down, although probably less rapidly and not quite to the same extent as many others. With a bit less exports, and a bit more imports, Japan could fit into the world trading community somewhat more harmoniously. Of course, this will take time. And some more economies may collapse in the meanwhile. The whole process would be faster and smoother if more "advanced" countries managed to pull their own economies out of the doldrums and more "developing" countries would actually start to develop. This, too, could bring about greater harmony. Part of the problem of Japan's

mission that the economy must come first and new methods should be tried.

Encouraging as this may be, no one knows if any of the attempts will succeed or indeed how many of the promises are precursors of action and how many are empty rhetoric or whistling in the dark. Most people still refuse to admit just how much must be done. It is almost as hard to turn an economy around as to get it started in the first place. And the resistance will be tremendous from those with vested interests. By now, in comfortable welfare states, that includes nearly everyone to some extent. Yet, before they can see the first noticeable signs of recovery they will have to make unprecedented sacrifices and pull their belts in more than they thought would be necessary.

Putting the economy first does not mean voting for a popular leader or marching through Paris with a rose in your lapel. It does not mean cutting taxes, or shortening the work week, or creating jobs for the unemployed any which way. It means reducing consumption ruthlessly by the people and by government so that more funds flow into savings and from there into productive investment. Neither of these problems has been tackled seriously. Left to their own, people will keep on consuming as in the past and entrepreneurs will not accept the higher risks and lower returns that prevail nowadays. Pure *laissez-faire* will not work yet.

For the liberal economies to function as they once did, it is necessary to revise the existing incentives or introduce new ones. No one, individual or company, will invest readily unless the returns are great enough to cover interest costs, depreciation, taxes, and still leave a good premium in case of success (and also to cover the possibility of failure). No manager can run his company efficiently burdened down under superfluous regulations or those which force costs up above the competitors. No worker will sell his labor, or work diligently, if taxes deprive him of the fruit thereof while he sees others doing nearly as well on unemployment benefits. It will take a lot of changes to reward people again for investing or working and penalize those who consume even beyond what they earn or prefer taking things easy at the expense of society.

Nevertheless, none of this is impossible. Where excessive regulations have been a cause of weakness, some of them can be cut back or at least arranged more rationally. There is a point where legitimate concerns like safety or the environment have to be balanced against other concerns like the efficiency or survival of an industry. Where taxes, for welfare or defense, have been too high, they can also be reduced. When an economy loses its drive, any money laid aside today will be worth less tomorrow anyway. And no one can wage modern warfare without a modern economy as its foundation. Where overly generous wages (for labor or management) have been higher than justified by productivity, or too much higher than the competitors, it would be wiser to reduce them than lose the jobs altogether.

Even if that old fighting spirit can be aroused, it will take a tremendous amount of money and many years of effort to restore the productive machinery. Investment has been so low that much of the plant and machinery is truly archaic. It is time to scrap and build, not because that is the best way, but because some of the factories are so old that they are more than worthless, they are terribly expensive in terms of waste of raw materials and fuel, inefficiency in production, and inadequate quality. When a country has to renew its plant and machinery in a hurry, rather than gradually over the years, that is bound to be a heavy strain.

The best place to start is what most enlightened experts regard as the worst, namely the ailing sectors. It is much easier to revive an industry than create one from scratch and even "losers" deserve a fair shake. If they are being hurt by dumping or predatory pricing, the FTC or government should definitely intervene. No company can resist unfair com-

-289-

petition and the consumers will also be better off in the long run. However, any protection should be coupled with strict demands that the sector be rationalized. This includes reducing production, improving efficiency, and if necessary merging firms into larger, more viable units. There is no reason why the government should not offer preferential loans in return, once again, for special efforts by the company and its personnel. Once this is done, it may turn out that the sector, or parts of it at least, was more competitive than believed.

Of course, it is unwise to throw bad money in after the good. But is is clearly no smarter to let the tremendous amount of assets tied up in existing industries go down the drain if a reasonable effort could have saved the healthier units. As for the "winners," they might also benefit from some incentives so as to expand more rapidly. However, it should be remembered that it is not that easy to recognize winners until they have reached a stage where many can fend for themselves and also that, by providing too much support, more companies than desirable will enter the field, making it overcrowded and reducing everyone's chances. Thus, the best investment is not to help specific companies but the industry as a whole through research grants or by encorgaging joint projects.

But it would be terribly dangerous to keep clutching at the straw of moving rapidly upmarket into higher technology fields as the ultimate solution. There are simply not enough products in that range and the competition will be intense as many countries and companies set on the same sectors as soon as they appear promising. Moreover, all of these sectors are highly capital-intensive which implies a serious drain on limited financial resources. On the other hand, they make very little use of labor. Worse, some of the products are specifically designed to replace labor as for robotics and computers. So, concentrating here is not likely to bring the big returns expected, will take long before paying off, and will certainly not solve all the problems, especially not that of unemployment. Nor is there any reason to believe that these new sectors can be promoted without a strong industrial base which is itself afflicated in some older economies.

The policy outlined here may appear very unfamiliar and thus suspect. A closer look, however, will show that in many ways it resembles the policy followed by Japan in practice as opposed to the highly imaginary descriptions of what it does in theory. As one of the most regimented market economies, it is actually at a middle point where more liberal and more socialistic countries could both copy some measures that would pull them out of their rut. A bit more planning and intelligent government support would not hurt the former, a reliance on the private sector's business acumen and ability to decipher the market signals would help the latter. But this should remain a corrective since going all the way in "learning from Japan" has its own drawbacks.

Although rescuing an economy, either by the means suggested or any other that works, is feasible, none of the Western governments has developed a coherent program to do so. They are still counting predominently on the Keynesian magic of fiscal and monetary policies or make-work projects while forgetting so many other aspects. No matter how finely tuned, no economy can prosper when its foundations are rotten. A modern economy needs a better educational system than many of the "advanced" countries have at present, it requires a modicum of law and order, and especially a willingness to work together for commonly accepted goals. No company can succeed with managers who are primarily interested in their own career and employees who come late, leave early or goof-off during working hours. Something will have to be done here, too, without necessarily going as far as Japan in instilling loyalty and discipline and stifling initiative and imagination.

In this context, there is probably nothing more important than increasing the productivity of the weaker economies, in the West or the Third World. It is quite impossible to expand production, as well as consumption, significantly unless more can be accomplished by those engaged in the economy. Productivity is thus a way of offering the population a higher living standard in real terms, not through wage hikes that only result in more inflation at home and devaluation of the currency internationally. More crucially, with regard to trade, higher productivity is one of the keys either to defending domestic markets or producing goods cheaply enough to sell abroad. Although this goal has finally been accepted as a valid one, putting it into practice will involve radical changes in business practices, labor-management relations, and the personal behavior of all concerned. It will also cost a lot of money. And it may never get started unless there is some agreement on how to share the fruits of the operation (still

No, it isn't a mirage. General headquarters for import operations right in the heart of Tokyo.

Credit: JETRO

−292−

hypothetical, mind you), probably the toughest issue of them all.

Finally, since the ultimate concern here is trade, there will have to be a more realistic assessment of the function of trade in countries which have been running deficits. The United States, like the Soviet Union or China, is no less obsessed by the idea that it is so vast and rich that it can do without trade than Japan is by the idea that it cannot survive without yet more trade. There is no need to repeat the popular refrain of "this is an increasingly integrated world" or that "other countries can make some things better or cheaper than we do." Their dependence on trade is amply shown by the fact that they do run a deficit. Any country in that position is obviously buying more than it sells and badly in need of a somewhat greater concern for exports. Whether the solution is found by specially developing export products, or setting up trading companies, or allowing the exchange rate to fall is secondary once the less successful trading countries realize that trade can only become a two-way street through increased efforts on their part as well.

All this means that the reindustrialization of the advanced countries and the first hesitant steps toward development elsewhere are not for tomorrow. It will take at least a decade to introduce enough new machinery, to restore ailing sectors and to open up more future-oriented ones. It may take as long to introduce quality control widely and adopt the sort of behavior needed to boost productivity or run companies wisely. But it will not even be for the day-after-tomorrow unless the overall approach to economics becomes more constructive. Most of the steps so far have been largely verbal or intellectual. The challenge is recognized, but no new economy has actually risen to it. So, only the future will tell whether a positive trade equilibrium can be reached through more balanced economic expansion.

NOTES

1. *Japan Times*, May 15, 1981.
2. Its formal name was the Japan-United States Economic Relations Group.
3. MITI Vice-Minister Amaya allegedly won himself the none too honorable titles of "foreigner's concubine," "Reagan's mistress," and "national traitor" for his role in settling the automobile conflict. Few Japanese have the guts to suffer such social opprobrium.
4. See Ezra Vogel, *Modern Japanese Organization and Decision-Making.*
5. According to STR William Brock, "arriving at a decision to liberalize trade is an excruciating process for the Japanese—as well as for those negotiating with them." Acting STR Robert Hormats put it more graphically: "every concession is like pulling teeth."
6. For some comparative statistics, see *International Comparison of Labor Productivity*, Tokyo, Japan Productivity Center, 1981.
7. *Japan Times*, April 19, 1981.
8. See Jon Woronoff, *Hong Kong: Capitalist Paradise.*
9. *Japan Economic Journal*, December 9, 1980.
10. *Japan Economic Journal*, July 21, 1981.

9

One More Chance

Once having examined the trends in some detail, rather than skimming over them as usually happens, it becomes perfectly evident why the world trade situation is so troubled. In fact, given the sharply contrasting and often contradictory policies pursed in different trading nations, it would seem inconceivable that there should not be quite a few conflicts. After all, some newcomers to world markets have been increasing exports at an unprecedented pace, several times the rate at which the older traders are doing so. The older countries, which provide the major markets at present, have not been expanding their economies rapidly enough to absorb anywhere near the amount of new exports. In a fierce competitive struggle, someone is bound to get hurt: either the older countries if they import too much and let their industries be crushed or the newcomers if they find the markets closed or restricted.

The cause of the crisis is thus rooted in fundamental differences not only in the actual trade of goods but the industrial structure of the countries concerned. Some are intentionally export-oriented and shift resources to specific sectors not only in keeping with comparative advantage but to meet the high priority placed on exports while artificially encouraging them through special subsidies or company and bank support. On the other hand, there are many countries which have not only paid less attention to exports but have become hooked on imports, whose people blindly assume they can continue importing cheap goods without increasing their own exports commensurately to pay for them. This has resulted in basic imbalances among the world's economies which could not avoid generating a corresponding imbalance in world trade.

The crisis is not a passing or temporary one nor is it just sporadic, flaring up periodically when one industry or country or another gets into trouble. It is ongoing and endless. The bitter conflicts over textiles, television, steel or automobiles are not exceptions to the rule of otherwise smooth and tranquil trade flows but flash points where the irreconcilable differences burst into public notice. There are hundreds of other cases that are not noticed not because they are minor or unimportant but because they are simply less visible or affect less vital sectors or countries. The strongest current remains one of basic and gross imbalance which must rise to the surface on occasion.

It therefore doesn't take a prophet to predict that this decade will witness a painful aggravation of the already serious trade situation. Many more trade conflicts are on the way. Some are already clearly rising on the horizon and should arrive soon. Indeed, it almost looks as if they were waiting in line for the earlier conflicts to be "solved" so that the next, and then the next, can receive proper attention. It may take a while to get anything as impressive as the automobile conflict, but many lesser ones will add up to a big enough predicament as is.

As if it were not enough that more products will become subject to litigation, there will also be more countries involved in one way or another. Even if the Japanese economy slows down somewhat, or its exporters exercise greater caution, desperate efforts by further developing countries to enter trade will keep the older sectors agitated while Japan probes at new ones. As one market after the other is saturated or blocked, those once put off for later since they were regarded as smaller or tougher, will also come under attack. As this happens, Japan may well find itself on the other side of the fence while the NICs apply the pressure.

If, in an age of relatively fast economic growth and substantial trade expansion, it was possible to record as many trade conflicts as have occurred over the past two decades, it must be evident that things will be much worse in the future. Even the most optimistic projections show that economic growth will be minimal in many countries and overall trade expansion will slow down. But the crunch will be worse because the economies slowing down more are the older, advanced ones, the very ones that must be counted on to absorb the bulk of the additional products offered by the rapidly growing sectors of certain dynamic countries.

If the United States textile industry had to curb Japanese imports, then those from Hong Kong and Taiwan, how can it possibly absorb yet more from Columbia, and India, and China? If Europe's shipbuilding industry was scuttled by Japanese production alone, what will happen now that Brazil and Korea have also joined in? World steel capacity, despite reductions in some countries, is still probably adequate to meet any demand two times over. What will happen when the many countries hurridly building their own steel mills, or already exporting like Korea, insist on their share of the market?

Whatever friction existed in the past is bound to grow. For, whether we like it or not, the world has entered a period where trade has come perilously close to being a zero-sum game. Any country that develops domestic industries is likely to reduce its imports and any country that promotes exports is even more likely to injure the industries in the markets it exports to or reduce the share of other exporters. In this kind of a situation, where the chances of someone getting hurt every time someone makes a gain are pretty high, trade conflicts are bound to proliferate.

Due to the zeal and efficiency with which exporters expand capacity, the injury is magnified. And it takes on a sharper edge when they also upgrade. If everyone is after higher added value and introduces machinery as quickly as possible to attain it, the impact on employment is bound to be greater even than the trade effect. There is no denying that a machine can produce more, and better, and cheaper than a human being in most cases. During the 1960s, when there was often a labor shortage, it was quite justified to make the switch. Now, with business slack, each new machine will add to unemployment. But it will probably add more to unemployment abroad than at home, as Japan's robots drive American autoworkers or Swiss watchmakers out of a job.

Is it any surprise then that trade conflicts immediately take on political overtones? Those being hurt are no longer just the factory or shop owners but the whole staff. The former are worried about lower profits or bankruptcy, the latter about lower wages or being out of work. Ordinarily, these are economic problems. But they change in nature when there are few alternative investments and broad unemployment already. They also assume an added dimension if the blame can be pinned not on natural occurrences but aggressive trade offensives from abroad. In any country, company executives and trade unions have considerable clout. If they are organized, and especially if an industry is crucial or heavily concentrated in a given region, their leverage is enough to obtain some redress.

And, if trade conflicts so readily assume political overtones, how can anyone be surprised that political—rather than economic—measures are adopted to "solve" the problem. When one country repeatedly runs a major trade deficit with another, it will forget about the overall balance and worry about the partial imbalance. It will start protesting that it is being too generous and, in exchange, is prevented from selling its own products. It will complain of exporting unemployment or some vague form of exploitation. After trying to restore any balance by improving its own industry and exporting more it may discover that the reverse is much easier, namely to prevent imports, especially if they are creating difficulties.

All this is so obvious that it is hard to imagine why many leaders and authorities, who should know better, keep talking about misunderstandings. There are pitifully few misunderstandings in trade relations and innumerable conflicts of interest. It is the latter that one must deal with if there is to be any hope whatsoever of finding compromises and shaping an economic and trade order that can satisfy most of the participants most of the time.

But, where does one start? The basic tasks are so immense that they clearly exceed the petty efforts that have been made to date or even the wildest proposals of the supporters of free trade. Given the underlying economic imbalance, the only positive and lasting solution to the trade problem implies a substantial restructuring of many economies. There must be a toning down of the exaggerated, and sometimes almost blind, drive for exports by countries which do not seem to know how else to develop. There must also be a considerably greater effort to get the advanced countries moving again and the underdeveloped countries moving for the first time.

As pointed out, none of this will be easy. A restructuring of the export-oriented economies is just conceivable over the coming decade. Unfortunately, the reason to expect it is far less an awakening of the businessmen or government officials to the dangers of overdependence on exports than the fact that more and more of their export markets will be closed. Some of the advanced countries have embarked on policies for revamping and perhaps reindustrializing their economies. However, considering that they are adopting such different approaches, there is little reason to assume all will succeed. Even those that do will take many years to make up for the laziness and foolishness of the past. As for the developing countries,

Unemployment lines are not as productive as
assembly lines. Yet, they can be more costly.

the relatively mediocre results of two development decades do not leave much room for hope.

That is why one must reject out of hand the ideal solutions of the proponents of untrammeled free trade. Let them argue that the best way out would be for those who are hurt to move into other sectors which should expand to absorb them. Let them insist that if everyone would expand production and trade all the problems could be solved. That is the way things would work out in the best of all worlds but not the world of the 1980s. We are now faced with limits, some of them terribly close now that the finiteness of natural resources and markets has become so obvious. It will not be easy to expand output of the existing range of products and there is little likelihood of finding enough new ones so that all countries can specialize in something or other. And, no matter how many potential buyers there may be, solvent ones will be hard to come by.

In the same vein, setting the preservation of free trade as the primary goal is nonsensical. Free trade doesn't exist. It was never quite accomplished by the Bretton Woods mechanisms and, even while further advances were made for tariffs and quotas, losses were being scored in the form of restrictions, restraint and orderly marketing. No matter how hard we try to disguise them as "positive" or "voluntary" actions, they always result in less trade than before. Whereas once the efforts to expand trade were progressing more rapidly than the measures to curtail it, they seem to be almost on a par now and there are so few new horizons for GATT and so many signs of rising neo-protectionism that the movement may well be backward soon.

This means it would be wiser to set more modest goals, namely to keep the system as such intact and to halt and conceivably reverse the trend away from free trade. Although this is certainly less ambitious than most leaders would propose, as we shall see, it will be anything but simple.

The first of these intermediate goals might be "fair trade."

This should really not be seen as a step back from free trade since in most cases we have not really gotten that far. With regard to imports, it has repeatedly been seen that any gains obtained through tariff concessions or elimination of quotas could be frustrated by more devious measures to protect markets. Some of them are the usual non-tariff barriers, matters of safety, health or industrial standards or the practical application of customs regulations. They at least can be compared and aligned. But, when it comes to cultural barriers or differing business practices, certainly an attempt at greater fairness would help. The same approach can be adopted as regards exporting. It is certainly not very fair, although it may be devastatingly effective, to engage in dumping or predatory pricing. Such practices can be blocked. But the trade system would be far better off if they were never adopted to begin with.

The second intermediate goal might be "mutually beneficial trade." In theory, this is a step backward from free trade. In practice, however, it is a bit more demanding than the growing network of restraints, restrictions and orderly marketing agreements. It is obvious that no country will remain within a trading system that does not offer more gains than losses. To limit their losses, as in the previous cases to enhance their gains, some countries have bent the rules by adopting steps to avoid "injury" to domestic industry. This being the case, it would doubtlessly be in the interest of the exporting countries not to push sales so aggressively that the importers react by blocking trade. In return, the importers might make a some-what more determined effort to rationalize or curtail industries that have lost their competitiveness.

Finally, as with all previous efforts to expand trade, there should be balanced concessions, ones that may not be strictly reciprocal but at least offer something to all parties. There would obviously be little that a relatively open economy like the United States could give a much more closed one like

Japan in exchange for greater access to the market. But they can still help one another through Japan's special measures to promote imports and America's willingness to encourage investment. A far more important step would be to gradually cut back on the two biggest exceptions to free trade, namely the developing countries' "sacred" right to protect infant industries and the "inalienable" right of the advanced countries to defend their ailing industries. As we saw, in many cases these measures not only limit trade, they hurt the countries which take them. Both groups of countries might therefore find it in their interest to restrict these exceptions more than in the past.

All of these various tasks could be accomplished more successfully by bringing them into the framework of present and future trade bodies. Too many crucial decisions are based on vague and hazy concepts like "unfair prices," "surges," or "injury." More seriously, the determination is made by one party alone, namely the one that is hurt. And the informal methods worked out to avoid or solve conflicts are only bilateral in theory since the actual terms result more from power relations than economic rationale. There could be no better place to define the terms and lay down the rules than GATT. By having decisions taken or at least confirmed in multilateral bodies they would more likely be fair and provide mutual benefits. It may seem unpleasant to deal with breaches of accepted trade practices within a body created to prevent them, but this is better than allowing them to occur outside.

None of this implies that the ultimate goal of free trade should be discarded. It simply admits the existence of the trade situation as it is and not as it is supposed to be. There is little point to pressing ahead with the few minor tasks that remain and can be accomplished with a bit of effort while all around the basic foundations are collapsing. It is far better to stop long enough to seek a new consensus on what kind of a trade system is desirable and viable and to find new compromises among the participants. The outcome is not likely to be a flawless or ideal system. It may even fall short of the goals that have been reiterated time and again. But, rather than destroy a trade system that doesn't live up to everyone's expectations, it is wiser to patch it together until better times come or the atmosphere changes.

Like it or not, the present difficulties faced by the trading system are deeply rooted not only in the economic structures of the countries concerned, they are a manifestation of certain economic policies that are irreconcilable with smooth or free trade. Neo-protectionism is just a result of a neo-mercantilism of sorts. Too many countries are producing goods for reasons other than that they possess a comparative advantage. As a matter of fact, often they do not know or care. Economic development has become a crusade in which building modern factories and creating sophisticated industries is a coveted sign of success even if the products are poorly made and more expensive than imports. Exporting has become a challenge for the ambitious and a duty for the laggards. Governments rejoice over surpluses, or frown at deficits, and they revel in rising reserves of foreign exchange and SDRs as kings gloated over their hoards of gold and jewels.

No wonder trade has become something quite different from what it should be, merely an exchange of goods and services which one party happens to produce better or cheaper than another. When the exchanges are contrived and overly competitive, trade cannot help turning into just another form of warfare thereby losing many of its inherent advantages. Thus, the suggestion of a pause for fairness and a thought to mutual benefit is hardly a retreat. It is an essential prerequisite for rediscovering what trade means and trying to restore a more congenial atmosphere for it to evolve successfully.

Of course, there is little hope that even the slightest of the tasks mentioned will be pursued unless the trading nations realize how perilously close they have come to destroying the system that sustains them and decide to take another look and reconsider their positions rather than plunging ahead into further conflicts, mutual recrimination, protective measures and heartily justified retaliation. More exactly, little can be expected unless some crucial countries reverse their earlier policies and lead the rest of the trading community onto a safer and saner path.

But, who can this savior be? In the past, leadership was taken by the United States which basically established the postwar trade system and kept it afloat. It can hardly continue to do so alone at present. Some European countries have since shared the burden. Yet, the only country which can make the decisive difference is the one that has benefited most and contributed least, Japan. Only if Japan is willing to open its markets more, and accept that there must be limits to its exports, can a team be formed which might reinforce or reshape a presently flagging system.

At this point, having stated the goals, outlined the solutions, and assigned the roles, authors traditionally brace for an intoxicating leap into phantasy. The hour is late, the odds are against us, and it is time for all men of good will to unite in a crusade to restore free trade for the greater prosperity of mankind! Yet, why make one more appeal when thousands have gone unheard? Why expect men of good will to accept an arduous challenge when there are still easier ways out? How can countries be convinced to change their policies and show a bit more generosity when it is so hard to manage a modern economy nowadays?

I do not have the faith or imagination to assume that there will be another "miracle." The past decades, they say, have witnessed more economic growth and the creation of greater wealth than the world has ever seen before. That is doubtlessly true. But they have also witnessed more economic folly and shameful waste than anyone thought possible. The path to renewed economic development and freer trade, to a better life for all, is far from obscure if people make the effort to look. But it will never be followed until they act rationally and think of others as much as themselves. For such reasons, I merely hope that we will have the ability to avoid the worst.

Bibliography

American Chamber of Commerce in Japan, *Report on Trade/Investment Barriers, Membership Survey*, 1982.
———, *United States-Japan Trade*, Tokyo, 1980.
———, *United States Manufacturing Investment in Japan, White Paper*, Tokyo, 1980.
Barnds, William J., editor, *Japan and the United States, Challenges and Opportunities*, New York, New York University Press, 1979.
Blaker, Michael, editor, *The Politics of Trade: US and Japanese Policymaking for the GATT Negotiations*, New York, Columbia University Press, 1978.
Clapp, Priscilla, and Halperin, Morton H., editors, *United States-Japanese Relations, The 1970s*, Cambridge, Harvard University Press, 1974.
Destler, I. M., Clapp, Priscilla, Sato, Hideo, and Fukui, Haruhiro, *Managing an Alliance, The Politics of U.S.-Japan Relations*, Washington, D.C., Brookings Institution, 1976.
Destler, I. M., Fukui, Haruhiro, and Sato, Hideo, *The Textile Wrangle*, Ithaca, Cornell University Press, 1979.
Destler, I. M., and Sato, Hideo, *Coping with U.S.-Japanese Economic Conflicts*, Lexington, Mass., Lexington Books, 1982.
Dodwell Marketing Consultants, *Industrial Groupings in Japan*, Tokyo, 1981.
———, *Structure of the Japanese Motor Components Industry*, Tokyo, 1980.
Hadley, Eleanor M., *Japan's Export Competitiveness in Third World Markets*, Center for Strategic and International Studies, Washington, D.C., 1981.
Hanabusa, Masamichi, *Trade Problems between Japan and Western Europe*, London, Saxon House, 1979.
Henderson, Dan Fenno, *Foreign Enterprise in Japan*, Tokyo, Tuttle, 1973.

Hollerman, Leon, editor, *Japan and the United States: Economic and Political Adversaries*, Boulder, Westview Press, 1980.

Japan Center for International Exchange, *The Silent Power, Japan's Identity and World Role*, Tokyo, Simul Press, 1976.

Japan Society, *Comparative Industries: Japan and the United States in the 1980s*, New York, 1980.

Japan-United States Economic Relations Group, *Report of the Japan-United States Economic Relations Group*, Tokyo 1981.

Johnson, Chalmers, *MITI And The Japanese Miracle*, Stanford, Stanford University Press, 1982.

Kearney International, *Non-Tariff Barriers Affecting the Health Care Industry in Japan*, Tokyo, 1980.

Kojima, Kiyoshi, *Japan and a New World Economic Order*, Tokyo, Tuttle, 1977.

Little, Arthur D., *The Japanese Non-Tariff Barrier Issues: American Views and the Implications for Japan-U.S. Trade Relations*, National Institute for Research Advancement, Tokyo, 1979.

Ministry of International Trade and Industry, *White Papers on International Trade*, Tokyo, various.

Scalapino, Robert A., editor, *The Foreign Policy of Modern Japan*, Berkeley, University of California Press, 1977.

Subcommittee on Ways and Means, House of Representatives, *Task Force Reports on United States-Japan Trade*, Washington, D.C., Government Printing Office, 1979 & 1980.

Tsurumi, Yoshi, *The Japanese Are Coming*, Cambridge, Ballinger, 1976.

Weil, Frank A., and Glick, Norman D., *Japan—Is the Market Open?*, Law and Policy in International Business, Vol. 11, No. 3, 1979.

Wilkinson, Endymion, *Misunderstanding: Europe versus Japan*, Tokyo, Chuokoron, 1981.

Woronoff, Jon, *Hong Kong: Capitalist Paradise*, Heinemann Asia, Hong Kong, 1980.

———, *Inside Japan, Inc.*, Lotus Press, Tokyo, 1982.

———, *Japan: The Coming Economic Crisis*, Lotus Press, Tokyo, 1979.

———, *Japan's Wasted Workers*, Lotus Press, Tokyo, 1981.

INDEX

Abe, Shintaro, 183.
administrative guidance, 68, 282.
aeronautics industry, 187, 223.
agricultural products, 61, 93–6, 199–200, 224, 231; *see also* farm lobby.
aid (to developing countries), 200–3, 205, 215, 284; *see also* investment-overseas.
ailing industries, 267–71, 289–90, 303.
aluminium industry, 197–8, 248.
Amaya, Naohiro, 171, 173, 177, 258.
American Federation of Labor-Confederation of Industrial Organizations (AFL–CIO), 140, 227–8.
Arthur D. Little Report, 71–2.
ASEAN-Japan Development Corporation, 281–2.
Askew, Reubin, 167.
automobile industry, 131, 134, 148–84, 213, 235, 242, 256, 274; parts industry, 224.

Baldrige, Malcolm, 145, 173, 230.
barriers (to imports), *see* protection.
Beckett, Sir Terence, 219.
Brock, William, 145, 167, 173, 224, 230.
bureaucracy, 207–9.
Byrd, Robert, 119.

Carrington, Lord, 228.
cartels, anti-recession, 195; export, 195–6; import, 69, 94, 133, 199–200.
Carter, Jimmy, 119–20, 125, 128–9, 140, 144, 163, 167, 214, 226–7.
consumer movement, 209–10.
"cultural" barriers, 74–82, 190, 257, 261, 302.

Danforth-Bentsen Bill, 170.
Davignon, Etienne, 128.
defense, 203, 204, 284.
deficit financing, 205.
distribution system, *see* Japanese management-distribution system.

Doko, Toshiwo, 142, 171, 212.
"domestic content" bill, 183.
Donovan, Raymond, 173.
dumping charges, 48, 116–7, 123–8, 134.
Dunkel, Arthur, 229.

electronics industry, 187, 222, 235.
Europe, European Economic Community (EEC), 10, 51, 57, 130–6, 140, 142–5, 164, 174–6, 231, 278, 281, 287.

farm lobby, 94, 212.
Federal Trade Commission, 214–5, 241.
Fielding, Leslie, 278.
Flanigan, Peter, 112.
Fraser, Douglas A., 163, 166–7, 173, 181–2, 215.
Fukuda, Takeo, 119, 140–1, 144.

General Agreement on Tariffs and Trade (GATT), 20, 60–1, 91, 110, 115, 129–30, 145, 189, 192, 222, 229, 256–60, 267, 301, 303.
government measures and incentives, 24–5, 37; *see also* administrative guidance, ailing industries, infant industries.
government purchases, 91–3.

Hanabusa, Masamichi, 219–20.
Heinz, John, 125.
Hong Kong, 26, 49–50, 130, 134, 188, 190, 269, 277–8; *see also* newly industrialized countries.

import barriers, *see* protection.
Inayama, Yoshihiro, 126, 145, 171, 212.
income, household, *see* living standards.
infant industries, 267–70, 303.
integrated circuits (ICs), 225.
International Trade Commission (ITC), 117, 119, 128, 169, 214, 231.
investment, foreign investment in Japan, 61–2, 71, 99; overseas, 62, 105–6, 120, 188, 201, 283–4; *see also* local production.
Ishihara, Takashi, 172, 177, 228.

Japan External Trade Organization (JETRO), 45, 280–1.
Japan Tobacco Corporation, 92–3.
Japanese management system, 27–53, 41–3, 75–6; abroad, 101–6, distribution system, 29–30, 70–1; expansion mentality, 28, 272–3; lifetime employment, 27–8, 32–3, 138; market share mentality, 29–31, 34–6; personnel recruitment, 78–9.
Jenkins, Roy, 142–3.
joint ventures, 81–2, 90, 99–100.

About The Author

Before becoming a journalist and writer, *Jon Woronoff* ran a small company with offices in Hong Kong, New York, and Tokyo. He would have been blind not to notice the glaring differences in style. Some of this motivated his other books, including *Japan: The Coming Economic Crisis, Japan's Wasted Workers,* and *Inside Japan, Inc.,* and numerous articles that were carried in leading publications including *Asian Business, Asahi Evening News, Oriental Economist,* and *Japan Economic Journal.* In addition, he has written dozens of articles on the various trade conflicts and has lectured at several U.S. universities.